# Textile Futures

# Textile Futures

## Fashion, Design and Technology

Bradley Quinn

Oxford • New York

English edition
First published in 2010 by
**Berg**
Editorial offices:
First Floor, Angel Court, 81 St Clements Street, Oxford OX4 1AW, UK
175 Fifth Avenue, New York, NY 10010, USA

Berg is the imprint of Oxford International Publishers Ltd.

**Library of Congress Cataloging-in-Publication Data**

A catalogue record for this book is available from the Library of Congress.

**British Library Cataloguing-in-Publication Data**

A catalogue record for this book is available from the British Library.

ISBN 978 1 84520 807 3 (Cloth)
      978 1 84520 808 0 (Paper)

Typeset by Apex CoVantage, LLC, Madison, WI.
Printed in the UK by the MPG Books Group
www.bergpublishers.com

# Contents

# CONTENTS

# CONTENTS

# General Introduction

Aburning, all-consuming interest in textiles was sparked in April 2005, when Toshiko Mori, then chair of the Graduate School of Design at Harvard University, placed a wet paper bag in my hands. 'It's a book,' she said. 'A present for you.' It was pouring with rain outside, and I had just arrived at Harvard to kick off a workshop with a group of architecture students. I thanked Toshiko for the book, but given the scope of the project, doubted that I would have much time to read in the month ahead. 'This is worth making time for,' Toshiko said. 'And when you get back to New York you *have* to see the exhibition.'

By the time I finished briefing the students, the paper bag had dried out enough to open. Inside, I could see an exhibition catalogue with a bright yellow cover. The words 'Extreme Textiles' were cut deep into the surface, spelled out in a material so futuristic it didn't resemble a textile at all. The subject was exciting, thought-provoking and visually spectacular, and I understood why Toshiko had been so enthusiastic. Fresh directions for fashion, architecture and interior design dawned as I turned the pages, opening up whole new worlds for textile design. By the time I boarded the train back to New York, I was transfixed by the thought that tiny fibres could rebuild the world. I had gained a general understanding of fibre technology while researching my books *Techno Fashion* and *The Fashion of Architecture,* but I realized that if 'Extreme Textiles' was predictive, something far bigger was looming ahead.

The train from Boston arrived at Penn Station, and from there I made my way to the Cooper-Hewitt Museum. Once inside, I moved through sections titled 'Stronger', 'Faster', 'Lighter' and 'Smarter', where showcases revealed sleek fibres able to stop a bullet at close range, hoist a satellite into orbit and withstand temperatures hot enough to melt steel. Lengths of shiny sailcloth cut sharply through the space, showcasing striking tri-axial weaves and criss-crossing strands of carbon fibres. The web-like,

Developed by Philips Design, the 'Frison' body suit uses biometric sensing technology to detect changes in the surface of the skin and trigger an LED visual output as a result.

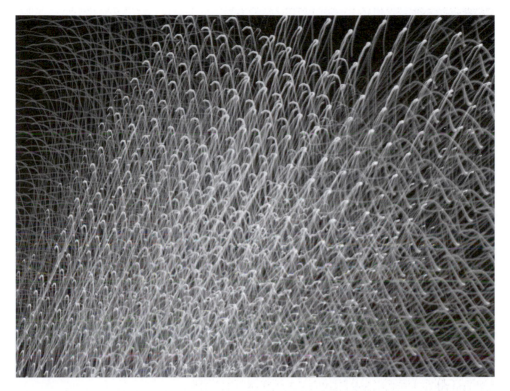

Electronic textiles rely heavily on fibre strength to create structures with specific architectures and properties. Strands of glass and polymer fibres are often used to transmit light and colour.

gossamer fabrics made to propel satellites took my appreciation of textiles to new heights, while car parts, industrial composites and ski helmets revealed that fibres are found in surprising places. Best of all were the medical implants—although normally sickened by the sight of blood (and terrified of needles), I gazed at these hand-stitched, embroidered body parts for a long time, and didn't feel ill at all.

By the time I left the exhibition, I could sense that my newfound passion would lead me to wider horizons. I was right. Margaret Helfand stepped forward to design the exhibition based on *The Fashion of Architecture,* which opened later the following year. As she and her team threaded steel cables throughout the galleries and wove them into display structures, I got to witness exchanges between textile techniques and cutting-edge architecture firsthand. Conversations with materials scientist Andrew Dent introduced me to some of the fibre forms and textile techniques revolutionizing product design. Chance meetings with 'Extreme Textiles' curator Matilda McQuaid and a lunch with Lars Spuybroek whetted my appetite for more knowledge within this exciting area.

Luckily, some of the magazines I contribute to shared my enthusiasm, and as they published my articles, invitations to speak publicly about textiles began trickling in. In 2006, a project undertaken with the United Nations High Commissioner for

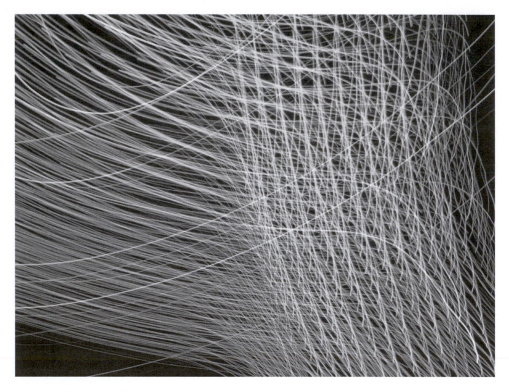

Technical fibres are designed to be electrically conductive, lightweight, flexible and strong. Their uses range from aerospace applications to computing devices, but they are gaining ground in fashion textiles too.

Refugees to write a report on the role of textiles and apparel in emergency relief enabled me to reflect on textiles' role within the emerging field of humanitarian design. Later the same year, Andrew Dent invited me to contribute to the book we called *UltraMaterials,* which challenged me to grasp the scientific and quantum mechanical principles underpinning fibre technology. In 2007, an invitation to contribute to *Contemporary Textiles* enabled me to explore recent textile practices in contemporary art. A proposal submitted to Laurence King Publishers resulted in *Textile Designers at the Cutting Edge,* a book that took me into the studios of leading professionals throughout the world.

 *Textile Futures* reflects the research conducted for these articles and publications but also takes account of the feedback I received at my workshops and speaking engagements. It became apparent that designers and researchers wanted to voice their views, so I included interviews in the book to enable them to communicate with readers in their own words. Other texts survey textiles' changing roles in fashion, interior design, art and architecture and chart recent developments in material science, technology and medicine. Although readers are likely to have a general awareness of technical textiles, the book does not intend to alienate any who may not.

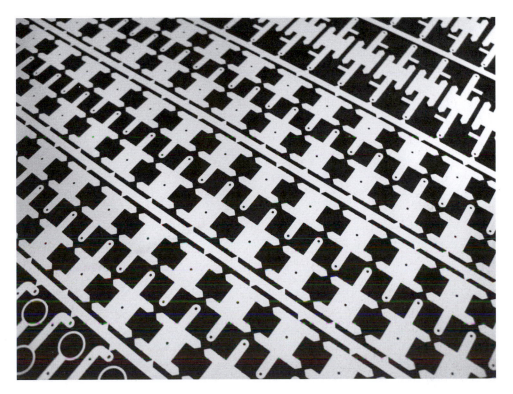

Metals such as silver, copper and nickel can be combined with technical fibres to create flexible, wearable substrates that conduct electrical signals.

Textiles are transcending their traditional functions, and *Textile Futures* centres around my conviction that they are morphing into uniquely tactile interfaces through which broader sensory stimulus can be perceived. Because fibres, fabrics and textile techniques are becoming seamlessly integrated with technology, textiles represent an interconnected collective that links many disciplines. Our world seems polarized around sensory extremes: hard and soft, protection and exposure, intransigence and tactility. As textiles embrace new types of fibres and fulfil new roles, they bridge these polarities better than any other material. Fibres are dramatically transforming the world around us, and as they do so, they also inspire radical new visions for the future.

# one

# Body Technology

Visionaries know that the cutting edge of technology is not sharp, but sensuous and soft. As fashion textiles embrace technology, they give it a sleekly sculptural silhouette that fits the body like a second skin. Textiles are transforming information technology into wearable interfaces that integrate software, communication devices, surveillance systems and haptic sensors into fibre form.[1] New textiles are changing how the body interacts with its surroundings and how designers and architects are fashioning the built environment. And as textiles move forward now more dramatically than ever before, they reveal their capacity to transform the human experience more than any material ever has.

At first, integrating textiles and technology seems riddled with problems. Fabrics are usually perceived as flammable, vulnerable to water, impermanent and weak, while technology is equated with resilience, electricity and hardware parts. Although heavy-duty hardware and delicate fibres may seem irreconcilably diverse, technological advances are making each of them lighter in weight and sleeker in appearance. Fibre technology is one of the most advanced areas of material science today, resulting in high tech filaments refined enough to craft the couture garments of Parisian fashion yet strong enough to hoist a satellite into space. Twenty-first-century fibres are strong enough to create rigid, architectural components yet still soft enough to cradle a baby's skin. And while some of them look more like space age materials than conventional fabrics, many recreate the look and performance of traditional textiles.

Despite the high tech allure of futuristic fabrics, the appeal of natural fibres promises to endure. New generation textiles may surpass them in performance, but the fibres that have dressed the human race for several millennia have a feel-good factor that is likely to persist. Natural fibres are almost as ancient as the earth itself, and inextricably linked to humanity's long history. Fibres are nourished by the earth and

7

Angel Chang collaborated with engineers and interactive designers to develop a vinyl raincoat hand embroidered with conductive wire and battery-powered LEDs.

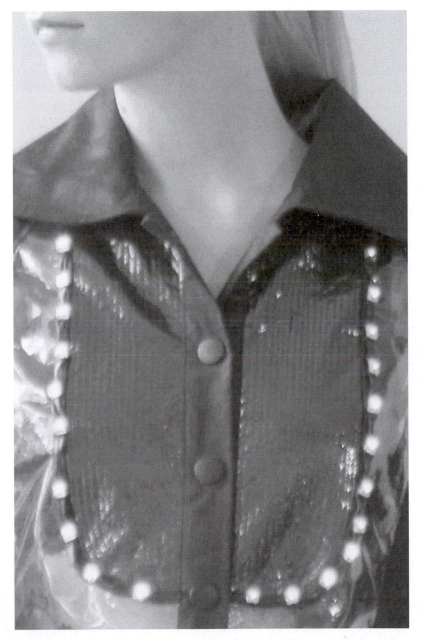

Chang used conductive X-Static silver fibres to make the raincoat illuminate, adding an unexpected element to the decorative trim.

nurtured by the sun, and their growth reflects the processes that sustain human life. Water, nutrients, sunshine and oxygen transform dry seeds into rich fields and sustain whole forests of fibres. Natural textiles bring nature's bounty to the artificial environments of man, where they provide reminders of our connections to the earth.

Because many of our earliest haptic experiences are fibre based, a single textile can evoke a lifetime of memories and sensations. Identifying a fibre with the fingertips provides unique physical and sensorial information about surfaces and textures. Touch is one of the earliest senses to develop, and its relationship to the development of other senses, especially vision, is generating new areas of research. As haptic technologies evolve, textile researchers are gaining a deeper understanding of why fibres hold eternal appeal.

Reverence for the natural has formed the basis for modern movements to slow down and rediscover low tech, Luddite approaches.[2] Advocates of such movements sometimes wear natural fibres and hemp-heavy fabrics to symbolize an alterative approach, or perhaps antidote, to modern technology. At a time when the textile is virtually indistinguishable from technology, making it a cipher for analogue forms is paradoxical. Technology pervades every aspect of the fibres' growth, harvest, production and manufacture, and the drive for efficiency continues to govern the wearer's experience also.

It is inspiring to discover that movements to slow down have impacted on textiles in unexpected ways, such as by encouraging people to be more aware of how they feel. As we begin to care more about feeling good, we seek the means to gain control over our emotions and boost our mood. Advanced textiles promise to do just that, by becoming somatic interfaces that can alter the wearer's emotional mood in a number of ways. Textiles promise to monitor mood and heighten awareness, administer medication, broadcast our feelings or dampen them, and transmit information about our well-being to the environments around us. Classifying textiles in terms of their emotional, sensory and empathic capabilities shows how far forward they have moved in a relatively short time frame. As the texts in this chapter reveal, textiles are moving beyond notions of embedded and electronic, and, subsequently, terms such as techno fashion, e-textiles and i-wear already seem out of date.

# Electronic Textiles

Wearable technologies promise to transform the fashioned body forever. As technologized textiles redefine garments as mobile, networked environments, they anchor the cerebral world of intelligence to the intimate environments of the modern human. The exchanges between them are facilitated by fabrics woven from fibres capable of conducting electrical impulses and transferring information. Known as electronic textiles, the new generation of fabrics are fibrous substrates into which microelectronic components and connectors have been seamlessly integrated. As technical hardware and tactile textures become one, the fabrics that result are free from the bulky external components that make earlier generations awkward to wear.

Like computing devices, electronic textiles can relay information via conductors, switches and sensors and exchange signals with remote systems via transistors and woven antennae. Threads coated with metals such as silver and nickel make excellent

German designer Moritz Waldemeyer embedded thousands of LED lights into jackets for each of the four performers in the rock band OK Go. The illuminating jackets were among the first technologized garments seen in menswear and nearly stole the show.

conductors, and ductile fibres made from materials such as carbon, polymers and finely drawn copper sit snugly on the body. Advances in wire-bonding technology have resulted in electrically isolated wires encapsulated in polyurethane to eliminate bodily contact or friction with other fibres. Minute silicon chips and sensors can be downscaled to fibre-size and interwoven with plastic-threaded chip carriers and tiny flexible circuit boards. Like most types of programmable hardware, the networks created by these parts can sustain a range of software applications and easily adapt to changes in the computational and sensing requirements of an application.

Although high street fashion and high tech devices may seem irreconcilably diverse, electronic textiles were developed in order to integrate garments and technology. They have the drape, flexibility, and resilience of most fashion fabrics, and like conventional textiles, they can be engineered for desired resistance, thickness, density, weightlessness, porosity, surface texture and flame resistance. Whether sewn and stitched, bonded together or simply draped around the body, electronic textiles can be worn for everyday use. As fashion designers and technologists create garments from electronic textiles, they reconceive clothing as a system of active materials that has the ability to change colour, form and texture over time. At the same time, collaborations like these forge a uniquely neutral space as the traditionally feminine-gendered practices of garment making meets the previously male-dominated worlds of technology and material science.

The process of integrating textiles and technology isn't just surface deep; it actually begins at a molecular level. Fresh developments in molecular templating processes led to a stronger bond between the conductive polymers and the electronic circuitry integrated into the fabric. A patented technique developed collaboratively by scientists at Australia's Commonwealth Scientific & Industrial Research Organisation and the University of Wollongong dramatically heightens the textiles' electroconductive properties by binding the inherently conductive polymers (ICPs) indissolubly to the fabric's fibres. By making electronic conduction more stable, the garment becomes more durable as a result, even capable of withstanding the hostile environment of the domestic washing machine.

The earliest garments made with electronic textiles were the Smart Shirts designed by researchers at the University of Virginia Department of Electrical and Computer Engineering and at Georgia Institute of Technology. The shirt developed by Sundaresan Jayaraman and patented by the Georgia Institute of Technology was funded by Defense Advanced Research Projects Agency (DARPA), the primary research and development arm of the US Military's Department of Defense. Jayaraman engineered a supple textile substrate from a mixture of natural fibres, gossamer wires and optical fibres. The garment revealed that virtually any type of fabric fibre could be bonded with a conductive fibre to create a sensor system. The system woven into their Smart Shirt was designed specifically to calibrate heart rate, respiration and body temperature and relay the data to a remote system in real time for analysis.

Similarly, a range of smart garments developed by Thomas Martin, an associate professor at the University of Virginia, bonded electrical wires, sensors and actuators to fibres and wove them into an electronic textile. Crafted into apparel similar to sportswear, Martin's garments were able to sense their own shapes and monitor the movements of the wearer.

The clothing developed by Jayaraman and Martin highlight the importance of configuring the sensor networks so that the garment can monitor itself at the same time that it monitors the wearer. For example, if the wearer decides to roll up the sleeves while sensors in the cuffs are monitoring the pulse, the sensors should inform the network to temporarily suspend their function. When the network senses areas of damage, strain or power shortages, they should reroute their surveillance to other parts of the garment so that monitoring can proceed without being short-circuited. Such capabilities are essential for electronic textiles worn in battle, medical diagnostics and chemical biosensing.

If smart garments were able to sense stimuli in the ambient environment, they would be able to see and smell on behalf of the wearer. A shirt for the blind, for example, could be woven with indicators that provide warnings about approaching objects. Workers in the chemical industry could wear overalls that smell leaching toxins and detect them before they cause harm to the wearers.

All electronic textiles rely heavily on fibre strength to create structures with specific architectures and properties. Classes of fibres are usually categorized according to filament length and the type of material they are made from. Glass, carbon and polymer fibres are widely used, and each has a distinct advantage. Glass is regarded as inexpensive and versatile, while carbon fibres are said to have the highest strength and durability. Polymer fibres tend to be chosen for technical fabrics with specific properties, or to produce fibres for high tech applications. Long fibres of any type provide more tensile strength, creating fabrics which are highly flexible, impact resistant and are less likely to fracture. Shorter fibres provide reinforcement and absorb impact, providing an easy and inexpensive way to improve strength and stiffness.

The, type, length and surface compatibility of fibres can be engineered to maximize a textile's performance, enabling it to achieve strength-to-weight values unparalleled elsewhere in the world of materials. Super-strong fabrics aren't created through fibre technology alone; their strength is augmented by the construction techniques used to craft them. Bundling fibres together has a strength in numbers effect that makes them more resilient, while braided fibres are even stronger.

The build–up of individual flexible filaments into a warp and a weft enables any abrasion or impact to be distributed among a large number of filaments, making in less likely to fracture a single fibre. This is the main reason that woven constructions are the best choice for electronic textiles. Although it is possible to get the same fit, texture, tactility and washability from other types of constructed textiles, they rarely have the comfort that woven fabric has. Weaving is an ancient technique that creates a simple and effective system today and continues to be at the forefront of materials innovation.

Biopolymer and polymer science are forging exchanges between biopolymer molecular structure, fibre behaviour and the colouration of polymers. Technologists from both fields are working to develop organic, plant-based polymers that can be utilized to replace oil-based nonwoven fabrics. Polymer fibres are generally lighter, smaller, softer, less expensive, safer and more colourful than other types of fibres, and clear polymers can create fibres with translucent properties. Polymer foams have the density, hardness, mouldability and printability that makes them perfect for fashion applications, and technologists are currently developing ways to adapt them for electronic textiles.

Although advances in polymer development have led to super-strong plastic filaments such as Spectra or Dyneema, carbon fibres still have the highest tensile strength; experiments have shown that a filament just one millimetre in diameter is strong enough to hoist a four-door car above the ground. Although carbon fibres are strong, they lack tenacity and impact absorption. Whereas a carbon fibre is likely to shatter when impacted, a polymer fibre yields easily and absorbs the impact. Polymer fibres such as polyethylene are stronger and, like Kevlar, aramid and Twaron fibres, are uniquely impact resistant. Carbon nanotube films are substantially more robust than the indium tin oxide films commonly used to make computer screens and mobile phone displays, which makes them ideal for the touch screens and flexible displays developed for electronic textiles.

Such innovations are made possible by technical fibres, such AmberStrand, which is electrically conductive, lightweight, flexible and strong. AmberStrand's base is the high-modulus Zylon fibre, a filament technically known as polyphenylene bisoxazole (PBO), which is a polymer/metal hybrid. Zylon is coated with metal through a proprietary process that produces strong, flexible stands that are bundled together to form yarn. The yarn contains conductive metals such as silver, copper and nickel, and is said to be less toxic to manufacture than copper beryllium alloy wire, another popular conductive material. AmberStrand is mostly used in aerospace applications and in computing devices but is gaining ground in electronic textiles too.[3]

Microfibres are responsible for making synthetic fibres chic again. They can create textiles that are lighter, softer, more elastic and more durable than those made from natural fibres. Microfibres are a popular choice for fabrics ranging from faux suedes and furs to high-performance textiles made for sportswear. Nanotech engineering succeeded in making it possible for individual fibres to repel liquids, and, as a result, stain resistance took a quantum leap. Previously, stain resistance resulted from coating the fabric's surface with materials such as Teflon, which disintegrated with wear. Nanotechnology alters individual fibres on a molecular level, making their ability to repel liquid an inherent part of a fibre's composition, and subsequently it can be maintained throughout the life-span of the fibre. Nanotextiles, as such fabrics are called, result from the production and manipulation of nanoscale fibres including those created through the synthesis of carbon nanotubes, electrospinning, polymer nanofibre processing and the extrusion of nanocomposite fibres.

Advances in fibre technology have made three-dimensional textiles possible. Typically produced on a Raschel machine, three-dimensional fabrics (sometimes known as spacer fabrics) transform textiles from two-dimensional surfaces into materials that have volume and depth. Developed for use in cushioning, these textiles are rapidly replacing foam, especially in the sneaker and sports gear markets. They eliminate the need for an additional decorative textile layered onto the surface of the foam, precluding the use of adhesive to bond the two together. Synthetics such as polyesters and nylons can be used as well as cottons and other natural fibres, and the density and cushioning properties can be varied throughout the textile. Because the thickness is customisable and variable from area to area, it makes it possible to cushion sensitive electronic components or reinforce critical subfabric interfaces.

Not all electronic textiles are based on fibre construction. The composite materials known as quantum tunnelling composites (or QTCs) consist of metals and nonconducting elastomeric binders that function as pressure sensors and become conductive when they come into contact.[4] The material's name refers to the quantum tunnelling process that results when the composite materials are compressed. Without pressure, the conductive elements are not close enough to conduct electricity. Applying pressure moves them into contact with each other, enabling the electrons to tunnel through the material.

One of the most notable garments featuring QTC is the No-Contact jacket designed by Adam Whitton and Yolita Nugent. The jacket was made to protect women from attackers by creating an outer surface that deploys an electrical charge when grabbed, gripped or constricted. 'Essentially, we created a sandwich of conductive fabric with a middle layer of QTC,' Whitton explained. 'The jacket's conductive fabric is Aracon from DuPont, which is an aramid fibre clad in silver. The conductive material is woven or sewn into pathways throughout the jacket that delivers the high voltage. The jacket has a layered system that includes a liner, electrically insulative layer, the conductive/electrified layer and then an outer shell which is waterproof.'[5]

# Illuminating Fabric

For most of their long history, fabric surfaces were made to communicate, and given their capacity to transfer information, it's no surprise that today's textiles continue to relay data in the digital age. As a wearable communication platform, an electronic textile functions as a dynamic surface around the body that interconnects people and places. Electronic fabrics are capable of absorbing mobile phone technology, and as they do so, they provide the perfect interfaces for Bluetooth technology and iPhone and Blackberry-type systems. Speakers and microphones are weaving their way into collars and cuffs, and flexible, battery-powered optical fibre screens are being woven into sleeves and jacket linings. Made from flexible plastic fibre-optic threads and illuminated by tiny LEDs (light-emitting diodes) fixed along the edge of the display screen, these fibre screens are controlled by microchip interfaces. The optic fibres will be configured into pixels as they designate sections that remain dark and areas that illuminate when the LEDs are activated. One of the early prototype screens developed by France Telecom displayed crude, but readable, symbols. As the prototypes evolved, research organizations such as International Fashion Machines developed more sophisticated versions that displayed text characters, advertising logos and a range of geometric ciphers.

Textiles woven from optical fibres harness their luminous quality to create illuminating textiles.[6] The Italian-made, nonreflective Luminex fabric, which is produced from fibre optics and coloured LEDs can be cut and handled like any other tailoring material. Luminex uses energy-efficient LEDs to transmit light at low voltages and can be powered by rechargeable batteries. Luminex can also incorporate microchips into the fabric to create a variety of radiant effects, Microchips could also transform Luminex into an interface capable of processing signals and responding to environmental stimuli. Technology like this also features in the Lumalive fabric developed by Philips, which has the potential to display as many as 16 million colours in a detachable, flexible panel sandwiched between layers of fabric. Lumalive textiles are composed of coloured LEDs that have been fully integrated into the fabric without compromising the softness of the cloth. Their surfaces can broadcast texts, graphics or multicoloured motifs.

When made from plastic, optical fibres are woven into the fabric's structure during the fabric production process using a three-dimensional technique. The technique employs spiralling movements that prevent any discontinuities at the armholes, hems or seams using a novel modification in the weaving process. This process eclipses the need for traditional cut-and-sew operations that produce fabric two-dimensionally. This process was a significant breakthrough in textile engineering as it enabled a fully finished fashion garment to be completed on a weaving machine.

Electroluminescent wires appear similar to optical fibres in their luminescence and have the same flexibility and versatility. Their durability and weatherproof characteristics make them ideal for outerwear applications. Like optical fibres, they do not generate heat and can easily be woven into a variety of textile forms. Electroluminescent wires have a very low current draw that makes it possible to power a thirty-metre-long length with just a single one-amp fuse. However, a driver (similar to a transformer) is necessary. The type of driver is chosen according to the volume of wire, the voltage and the degree of brightness desired. The colour tones are determined by the optic wavelengths rather than colour particles. Lower frequencies give the fabrics softer shades of primary colours or pastel hues, while higher frequencies make their colours appear deeper and more solid.

Fabrics made from optical fibres and electroluminescent wires show that, in addition to data, both light and power can be transmitted through a textile substrate. The batteries that power electronic textiles are now smaller and lighter, and seldom cumbersome for the wearer. Although equipping textiles with an integral energy source is a breakthrough for textile technology, concerns about the health risks associated with wearing batteries and other power sources in close proximity to the human body question the viability of these fabrics.

Marin Soljačić, a technologist based at the Massachusetts Institute of Technology, foresees a future when electronic textiles will not need an integral power source at all. Soljačić's vision for nonradiative energy transfer draws on an experiment conducted in 1831 by the physicist Michael Faraday, who discovered that an electric current flowing through one wire invariably induces a secondary current in a neighbouring wire. Faraday was unable to confine the electrical current to the two wires; the power was transmitted in all directions, meaning that the energy dissipated with distance.

Soljačić's experiments with nonradiative energy transfer have shown how near-field magnetic resonance between two strongly coupled induction coils can transfer sixty watts of electrical power with 40 per cent efficiency across a distance of two meters. Because the external fields of this transmission process are magnetic rather than radioactive, the health risks are believed to be less than the power transmission in systems that emit electrical fields. Soljačić's experiments were able to recharge an object the size of a laptop within a few meters of the power source. The intent of these experiments was to extend the range of nonradiative wireless power and create a system that could provide coverage throughout the office or home, meaning that electronic textiles and other devices could be recharged ambiently when positioned within range of a power source. Right now, electronic textiles are not equipped with hardware and a software system to route the power efficiently throughout the garment. A single electronic textile or smart garment may include a wide array of sensors—including accelerometers, gyroscopes and detectors that pinpoint location, as well as microphones, ultrasonic emitters and piezoelectric films that change voltage in response to shape change.

Low tech experiments with conductive fibres have revealed that solar power can be harnessed by fabric and interspersed throughout the fabric's structure. Designer Andrew Schneider created a solar-powered bikini made by overlaying narrow strips of photovoltaic film onto a swim suit and sewing them on with conductive thread. The swim suit produced a five-volt output, that, via the attached USB connector, could slowly recharge electronic gadgets like the iPod.

# Embedded Fibres

Equipped with cameras, microphones, speakers and sensors, embedded textiles once held the promise of the future. The first wearable computer prototypes of the early 1990s were actually body-mounted devices attached to jackets, waistcoats and vests. Their cables and connectors were anchored in place by fasteners and stitching or crudely fed through seams, and wireless antennae were attached to collars and cuffs. Gadgets such as the MP3 player were among the first to be embedded in textiles; fitted to denim jackets and water-repellent, metallic-coated nylon parkas, their wiring and hardware were encased between layers of fabric. Although such garments were often described as interactive, the wearer triggered various interfaces manually rather than activating them through a truly integrated system that interacted with the wearer and the textile itself.

The embedded interfaces of such intelligent garments proved to be awkward for the wearer and frustrating for the designers, and they subsequently sparked the demand for the new generation of fully integrated electronic textiles. Although the success of electronic fabrics will soon make embedded textiles a thing of the past, embedded fabrics continue to play an important role in the development of technical textiles. To describe an object as embedded implies that it can be removed or detached, resulting in a portal that other devices can be linked into. An electronic textile, for example, could also be embedded with portals to facilitate information exchanges within systems not yet capable of transferring data wirelessly. Embedded portals could also accept power transfers, audio-visual exchanges and debugging diagnostics.

Hussein Chalayan was one of the first fashion designers to engage with technological systems, and many of his collections have pioneered garments that feature wireless technology, electrical circuitry and embedded connectors. Some of Chalayan's most groundbreaking uses of materials and processes were presented in his spring/summer 2007 collection, titled 'One Hundred and Eleven', when he designed dresses powered by machine-driven levers that opened and closed to reconfigure the garment's shape and silhouette. The technology embedded in the garments enabled hemlines to rise autonomously, a bustier to open of its own accord, and a jacket to unfasten itself and pull away from the model's torso. These designs were made possible through collaboration with the team behind the special effects for *Harry Potter and the Prisoner of Azkaban,* who microchipped fabric panels so that they would move according to the sequences Chalayan programmed them to.

The mechanical dresses were ingeniously fitted with electronic components and engineered pulley systems. The garments' surfaces were painstakingly embroidered with thousands of Swarovski crystals, giving them the dual appeal of opulent elegance and high tech savvy. Although the technology was streamlined and embedded into corsets and pads worn beneath the garments, it was still cumbersome to the models wearing it. Further research is needed to reconfigure the shape-changing features of the embedded system into an electronic textile that can assume different shapes and morph back to its starting point again.

London-based wearable technology company CuteCircuit developed a textile Nerve, a sleeve-like Bluetooth accessory for mobile phones. When the device receives an incoming call, receivers embedded in the sleeves cause pleats to form.

Chalayan's collection marked a radical departure from a world where distinctions between body and technology, body and dress, natural and artificial, once seemed clear. This illustrates how, as Michel Foucault described, social and cultural discourses construct our bodies in a way that makes us as analogous to a machine as possible. The design of the dress is imbued with technologies that make interaction efficient, productive and empowered, akin to the machine-like principles of controlled automation. The presence of high tech systems in fashion fuses its body-conscious ideals with a belief in automation, speed and accuracy as the means to achieve it.

International Fashion Machines were one of the first companies to pioneer a new generation of fashion based on interactive technology, electronic textiles and embedded computer interfaces. In 1998, they designed the Firefly dress, a garment constructed from two layers of conductive metallic silk organza separated by a layer of tulle embedded with LEDs and conductive Velcro brushes. When the wearer moved, the Velcro conductors came into contact with the LEDs, completing the circuit and causing the LEDs to light up.

International Fashion Machines also created a jacket with an integrated synthesiser and embroidered keypad that functions as a musical instrument. The jacket is embedded with sensing electronics, speakers, a customised MIDI synthesiser and batteries.

CuteCircuit's Nerve device combines smart textiles and telecommunication technology to integrate garments with mobile phone technology.

By touching sensors embedded in the jacket and pressing keys embroidered in conductive thread, the wearer can create music. The keypad uses a capacitive sensing method to discern pressure and emits a small electrical charge when the individual keys are touched.

New York fashion designer Angel Chang was one of the first designers to bring embedded textiles to the catwalks of New York Fashion Week, creating garments that explored the potentials of smart fabrics. Through collaborations with engineers and interactive designers, Chang developed designs for the collection which included a metallic-finished knit hoodie with iPod controls and an Edwardian-inspired jacket which could connect to an iPod.

Chang's work revisits the interactive jackets pioneered by companies such as Eleksen, whose ElekTex fabric has been used by Zegna Sport and Marks & Spencer, and gives them a feminine update for the urban woman. Eleksen's touch-sensitive textiles have proven usability in outerwear as touch controls for iPods and cell phones.

Embedded technology can also effect colour changes in fabric or configure new techniques. CuteCircuit is a London-based wearable technology company with a mandate to make technology beautiful and comfortable to wear: hard shells, trailing wires and pockets full of batteries are banished from their design methodology. They have also developed a textile called Nerve, a sleeve-like Bluetooth accessory for mobile phones. When the Nerve receives an incoming call, receivers embedded in the sleeve's pleats change pattern. The sleeve can be programmed to morph into a range of different patterns, and linked to an incoming number, the motifs recognized in the sleeve announce who the caller is.

Moondial, a research organization based in Vienna, also embed electronic devices in high-performance textiles to combine the multifunctionality required by today's urbanites with durable, wearable clothing. One of Moondial's designs, the SlopeStyle jacket, is based on an athletic jacket concept and has the potential to function as a wearable display screen. The jacket is embedded with Wi-Fi, Bluetooth and organic LED (OLED) electronics. Pictures taken by a digital camera or a personal digital assistant (PDA) can be relayed directly to the jacket's software or downloaded wirelessly from the Internet and shown on a display panel embedded in the jacket.

# Subtle Surveillance

Technology has a sinister side, and when intelligence is embedded into textiles, it reveals that the startling reach of surveillance even pervades the fabrics we wear. Like the body-rig devices worn by undercover cops, the cameras and recording devices embedded into fabric could easily evade detection or be used in areas where audiovisual technology has been banned. Not only can embedded electronics store information on computer circuits, they can also transmit and receive data when activated by an external signal.

Textiles that can monitor vital signs, such as those used by the military and by physicians, reveal that surveillance can play an important role in health and safety. Made into a diagnostic garment, the textiles can relay information about the wearer's health to a physician to ensure real-time assessment of the patient's health. This technology is also being investigated by the US military, as part of research into more interactive uniforms for soldiers on the ground.

Pressure-sensitive textiles enable parents to collect information about their children's whereabouts and activities. Research by Yolita Nugent into so-called abuse-sensing garments explores how a parent could monitor his or her child's clothing to ascertain if, for example, their child has been hit by another playmate or an adult.[7] The textile would record the amount of force and the time that the blow occurred.

CuteCircuit launched the Embedded Theatre, a wearable device that analyses the wearer's location and delivers audio narrative and navigational information to them via a headset. The headset exchanges information with a garment embedded with sensors and wireless network capabilities. The technology embedded in the garment contains a mobile device (like a PDA or cell phone), and headphones fitted with digital sensors. The system uses Wi-Fi triangulation to gauge the wearer's location, and its sensors identify the direction that they are facing. These two data sources make it possible to recreate the wearer's physical landscape in an ephemeral guise that corresponds precisely to real-world objects and locations. For example, the technology pinpoints where the wearer is standing and the sensors detect that he or she is looking at a particular building. At that point, the sensors trigger audio files to begin describing the building's architectural history. When the technology senses that the wearer is about to head in a certain direction, it uses audio files to advise the wearer about any unseen hindrances further ahead.

When, in 2003, it was reported that Benetton's clothing brand, Sisley, planned to embed a radio frequency identification (RFID) chip into the label of every new garment, consumer watchdog organizations protested. An RFID chip emits an electronic product code (ePC) that provide a unique ID for a garment. The ePC is intended to replace the UPC (universal product code) bar code used to tag garments. Because the ePC actually assigns a unique number to each individual item, it goes beyond identifying product categories. Once the ePC has been assigned, it is transmitted by an RFID chip embedded in the product. The chips can vary in size but are generally smaller than most fibres, comparable to the size of a grain of sand or a speck of dust. Electronic scanners or reader devices are used to detect the signal transmitted by the RFID chip. Retailers claim that RFID chips could revolutionize quality control by enabling them to retrace garment's production cycle and identify where defects could have originated.

The claim that chips are necessary to keep track of a garment's journey through production stages, shipping and retail is contested by organizations such as CASPIAN (Consumers Against Supermarket Privacy Invasion and Numbering). CASPIAN reveal that devices embedded in clothing would enable retailers to track individuals by linking the customers' names and credit card information with the serial number assigned to the garment. According to Katherine Albrecht and Liz McIntyre, CASPIAN's directors, 'Selling a pair of shoes that doubles as a tracking device without telling consumers about the RFID device it contains is essentially a form of fraud. When a shopper buys a pair of shoes, she has a reasonable expectation that she is getting shoes—not something else. Once mandatory labelling is in place, if people chose to buy shoes that can track them, that should be their free choice. But consumers must be informed of what that choice means.'[8]

21

CASPIAN, and many other consumer organizations, envision a global network of millions of scanners and reading devices along the entire garment supply chain. Not only would the devices be found in factories, seaports, transport hubs, distribution centres, warehouses and retail outlets, but even in the home.

Embedded chips also raise issues of ownership. The chips embedded in bank cards remain the property of the bank at all times, irrespective of being held by the consumer. Applied to fashion companies, who could assert ownership of the embedded chip because of its integral relationship to their data system, it could mean that the garment was merely licensed to the consumer for the duration of its lifespan.

Although the RFID system described here remains current, today's retailers are more likely to tag garments with ultra high frequency (UHF) chips. UHF tags are a new generation of RFID technology that facilitate faster data transfer speeds and longer read ranges. UHF chips were first used in retail sectors where a larger distance between the reader devices and the chip were necessary.

Embedded textiles take a radical departure from a world where distinctions between body and technology, body and dress, natural and artificial, once seemed clear. They invite social and cultural discourses about how we choose to fashion our bodies and construct our identities. While the familiar folds of traditional textiles create a second skin for the human form, the technology embedded within them makes the wearer more analogous to a machine than to a human being.

# Emotive Interfaces

The combination of tangible devices such as electronics, sensors and circuits with the ephemeral emotions of anger, fear, sorrow and joy may seem irreconcilably diverse, but there are threads that bind. The sensing and diagnostic abilities that fibres have are forming a new breed of textiles structured by feeling and mood more than by texture and motif. Because they can process data automatically and autonomously, textiles can process artificial intelligence programmes, giving them the ability to react to the wearer's visceral experiences. Information architects understand that truly user-friendly technology goes beyond adapting for the skill set of the intended user. For technological systems and textile interfaces to engage a global audience, they should be intuitive, logical and compatible with our moods and emotional triggers.

Just as artificial intelligence is rooted in rudimentary machines that play simple games and perform simple calculations, modern technology is anchored to textile production. The Jacquard loom, invented by Joseph-Marie Jacquard in 1804 to weave intricate patterns into silk brocade, created the foundations of the technology that has evolved into the information superhighway of today.[9] Charles Babbage, the Victorian scientist and philosopher, drew upon the data-storing capacity of Jacquard's loom to create the so-called analytical engine, the first instrument in the world which could store programmes. Today's sensory software draws upon both of these antecedent forms to create fabrics that can identify their wearer's feelings and respond to them.

Frison is integrated with constellations of LEDs designed to illuminate when the wearer blushes. The technology reveals the potential of using garments to convey the wearer's emotions.

Enhanced with the sensing software, such as that developed for garments such as smart shirts, textiles can discern emotion, and many other complex reaction patterns that trigger physiological responses. Textiles can identify the increased heartbeat and perspiration that accompany fear as easily as they can record changes in the wearer's health. Many other emotions are also palpable and quantifiable: anger is typically accompanied by a hot flush and muscle tension, and sadness is often experienced as a feeling of tightness in the throat and tension in the lower abdomen. Happiness is often experienced as an expansive feeling as blood rushes to the chest and induces relaxation in the arms and legs. Desire can be accompanied by heavy breathing, and increased heart rate, while embarrassment can be felt as heat in the upper chest and face.[10]

As wearable fibre-based systems identify bodily sensations and trigger responses, some emotions could be processed as a type of computation that translates into computer models, initiating a rapid automatic summary and, subsequently, an action. The interface that results reveals the potential that textiles have to acquire robotic sensory and computation abilities.

Philips Design, a private research organization based in The Netherlands, is at the forefront of combining wearable technology and sensory intelligence. Researchers within the emerging area known as emotional sensing have developed interactive garments as part of the research initiative known as SKIN. The project is based upon the integrated technology presented in the New Nomads project Philips Design launched in 2001. Philips Design established SKIN to explore the extent to which wearable technology can relate to trends emerging in fashion and other creative industries. Although emotional sensing technology relies on high tech expertise, Philips describe emotional sensing as sensitive rather than intelligent, claiming that their approach is analogue rather than a complex high tech process.

The first prototype garments developed by Philips demonstrate that electronic textiles can be used to create clothing that expresses the emotions of those who wear them. Bubelle, launched in 2007, is a dress constructed from delicate bubble-like forms that illuminate. The bubbles arrange themselves in response to the wearer's physique and begin to glow individually at an intensity related to the amount of physical contact they sense. The individual glowing areas create abstract patterns that morph into new configurations each time they detect movement or a change in surface temperature. The effect creates a visual representation of physical states; when emotions can be identified as a physical response, the dress would create a display that signified emotional states.

According to Lucy McRae, a researcher known as the 'Body Architect' at Philips Design, fashion was chosen 'as an idiom to express the kind of research we were doing, because apparel and textiles can be augmented by a lot of new functionality'. She says that 'A garment can be a highly complex interactive electronic or biochemical device. We are experimenting with devices that are more responsive to subtle triggers like sensuality, affection and sensation.'[11]

While Philips is pioneering textiles that broadcast our emotions, other practitioners are developing fabrics that alter wearers' moods or influence the emotional state of the people around them. London-based researcher Jenny Tillotson, who is exploring

In 2007, Philips Design launched Bubelle, a dress constructed from delicate bubble-like forms that illuminate in response to the wearer.

the applications of sensory, aroma and medical technology within fashion and textiles at Central Saint Martins College of Art & Design, is developing scent-infused fabrics that connect textiles with chemistry, nanotechnology, perfumery and even architecture.

Bubelle begins to illuminate as it detects temperature changes in the wearer's skin.

When fully illuminated, Bubelle creates a visual representation of physical responses, mapping and recording the wearer's emotional states.

Tillotson's research is developing a sensory platform in which individuals wear items of clothing from an emotional wardrobe capable of interacting with environmental surfaces. Called Scentsory Design, the project creates clothing capable of communicating with surfaces known as 'wellpaper', which cling to walls much like wallpaper would. 'Wellpaper' is embedded with fragrances and colours activated by wireless data signals transmitted by sensors embedded in the user's clothing. The fusion of textile and wearer constitutes a responsive, multisensory environment that bridges the distance between wearable Smart Skin and the surfaces surrounding it. Tillotson's system is intended to promote and elevate emotional states and foster a feeling of well-being by deploying fragrances and colours believed to impact positively on mental health.

Tillotson's technology is loosely modelled on the functions of the human body, which she interprets as 'a bunch of cables and intelligent cells delivering blood, signals and fluids around the body's tubing system'.[12] Tillotson is also exploring the potential to create an environment driven by olfaction, which she calls Scentimental Space. The project extends the body's olfactory system by constructing fabrics and wallpapers with a comparable network of 'colodours'. The network is powered by electronic circuitry that pulses therapeutic scents through a fluidic cabling system embedded in fabric and wallpaper. Scentimental Space loosely mimics the body's respiratory system, senses and scent glands, releasing aromas that counter stress-induced emotions.

The network is designed with a sensory interface known as a 'scentreface', which is comparable to an electronic nose. The scentreface is worn on the body to monitor the wearer's mood by detecting sudden shifts in breathing and skin temperature. It then triggers the clothing to react by releasing scents that calm the wearer. These actions initiated in the clothing are simultaneously mirrored in the wellpaper, which changes colour, sound and texture to soothe those in proximity to it. Theoretically, the system has the potential to calm victim and aggressor alike, or neutralize a situation to prevent conflict from arising.

Tillotson's Less Stress dress is an essential part of the network. The dress is woven with a network of sensors that secrete aromatherapy scents according to the wearer's mood. When sensors in the dress detects a rise in stress levels, the dress emits neroli, a flower-based fragrance believed to lower blood pressure. The dress would trigger the surrounding wellpapers to morph into 'colourways' believed to encourage relaxation. If fear is detected by the dress's sensors, for example, it would release the aroma of frankincense, and also trigger the wellpaper to change to a calming colour.

# Feel the Love

Our tactile society is a touchy-feely one that frequently indulges in hugs. We value loving embraces more than most other forms of nonverbal contact, which science claim triggers the release of endorphins that regulate blood pressure and soothe stress.[13] Now textiles can facilitate the exchange of physical sensations too. The experience of being hugged can be relayed remotely through telecommunication networks. By advancing the technology behind the Nerve sleeve mentioned previously, CuteCircuit developed the Hug Shirt, a wearable haptic interface conceived as a Bluetooth accessory for mobile phones. The shirt is embedded with sensors that can receive and transmit information to Java-enabled mobile phones. A Hug Shirt wearer can send a simulated caress to another wearer by touching sensorized areas on his or her own shirt, using it as a wearable mouse pad to activate the pressure-sensitive areas. The sensors monitor the pressure of the hug, the sender's heart rate, his or her skin temperature and the duration of the hug, and relay it to the other wearer's shirt via Bluetooth. Those without a Hug Shirt can still send virtual hugs by using a software application known as HugMe, which can create a virtual hug and transmit it wirelessly via Bluetooth.

While developing the system, CuteCircuit experimented with various kinds of textiles and materials, even lining fabric with objects such as sponges and balloons. During the test sessions, they recorded the positioning of arms and hands as people hugged each other, and mapped the positions on the textile. The most heavily trafficked areas were found to be on the upper arms, upper back, around the waist, neck, shoulders and hips. Sensors containing the hugging output actuators were incorporated into those areas of the garment in detachable pads. The pads can be removed for washing and easily plugged back into place when dry. The Hug Shirts are available in several colours and styles, and the pads can easily be interchanged from on Hug Shirt to another.

Public displays of affection, social mores and cutting-edge textiles also come together in the Love Jackets designed by Studio 5050 in New York. Led by Despina Papadopoulos, the studio set out to explore the extent to which garments could imbibe existing social interactional patterns and even promote new ones. The project was initiated to explore the ways in which technology could be seamlessly integrated into garments, without necessarily creating clothing regarded as techno fashion. The fusion of textile and technology endows garments with a new range of tactile potentials and the capacity to communicate emotive messages to others.

As a result, Studio 5050 designed a pair of jackets engineered to emit and track a signal broadcasts on a particular frequency. The jackets were equipped with a basic infrared receiver and transmitter, a speaker output, LED panels and a PIC (programmable interrupt controller) chip to control the LEDs. Instead of wires, the components were attached to the circuit board via fabric connectors. The components are all surface mounted and interwired via conductive fibres woven into the fabric. As the prototypes evolve, the technology is expected to be seamlessly integrated in the garments.

The Love Jackets are programmed to identify and track the same wave frequency they are emitting. The speaker output enable the jacket to broadcast the specific code assigned to it, and when it comes within a three-metre range of an identical code it locks onto it. The jacket responds by emitting bleeping noises—intended to mimic the cries made by mating crickets—and a pattern of LEDs begins to blink on its surface. The jackets are only programmed to identify and respond to the other counterpart in its pair. Although the jackets visibly recognize their counterparts, the infrared operates on an invisible spectrum, just as a remote control device does. The polling distance is short-range, requiring that the jackets come within sight of each other to be detected. Once the jackets have been activated, the wearers should be able to see each other immediately.

Once fully integrated into fabric, the somatic technologies described here will create the wearable interfaces that will redefine the virtual world as well as the real one. Boundaries between digital and physical space, which are as defined by feeling as they are by form, will blur and eventually merge into a single area. Textiles will become metaphors for the body, and the messages they convey about the wearer will be complex, probably telling us far more about their inner world than they will about their outer appearance.

# Feature Interview: Angel Chang

New York-based fashion designer Angel Chang is known for her conceptual clothing, techno-savvy designs and interactive garments. Fashion, for her, is a forum in which she can merge apparel with ideas that reflect her interest in art, architecture, philosophy and music. Chang uses technology to amplify the concepts underpinning her designs, imbuing many of her garments with multifunctionality and the ability to transform their surfaces. Her designs defy the boundaries between streetwear, daywear, formal and casual. Organic fabrics are gently stitched or woven to produce gossamer surfaces, while nylons and industrial plastics are used to give her clothing unexpected details. Chang's streamlined silhouettes and precise tailoring suggest a utilitarian or futuristic identity. Functional and original, Chang's clothing is designed with a high degree of comfort in mind.

Chang completed her art studies in New York and interned at Viktor & Rolf before accepting a job at Donna Karan Collection, where she was responsible for fabric embroidery and print designs. Long before she launched her own label in spring 2007, she had been exploring the potentials of smart fabrics and technologized fibres. Chang collaborated with engineers and interactive designers to develop ways of moving fashion forward and also to create garments that would solve some of the problems facing urban women. 'My generation of women is so different from previous ones,' she says.[14] 'We work harder, travel more, manage all aspects of our lives through hand-held organisers, mobile phones and the Internet.' Noting that women's lifestyles have changed drastically in recent years, Chang was perplexed to realize that wardrobes have not. Chang advocates the integration of clothing and technology to make wireless communication easier and Internet access more available, which she believes can be achieved without compromising comfort or aesthetics. 'Technology can easily be concealed within the garment's design,' Chang says, 'as it is in my metallic-finished knit hoodie with i-pod controls. And my Edwardian-inspired jacket, also made from conductive textiles, which functions as an MP3 player. I love embroidery, so it was

The motif on this dress designed by Angel Chang was printed with heat-sensitive dye. The motif only becomes visible when exposed to warmth; otherwise, the fabric appears to be completely opaque.

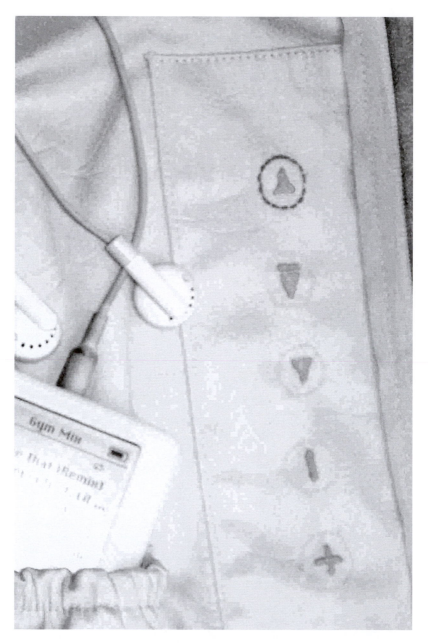

This detail from one of Angel Chang's designs shows the iPod controls she adds to certain garments.

a natural choice for me to hand embroider buttons on the sleeve that cue the MP3 player to play, stop, fast forward and rewind, and control volume.'

Chang designed a vinyl and lace raincoat hand-embroidered with LEDs and conductive X-Static silver fibres sourced from Noble Biomaterials, who also supply the fibre to the US military.[15] 'The X–static [silver] fiber is coated in a layer of pure silver permanently bonded to its surface,' Chang explains. 'The fibre remains soft after the coating process, retaining its traditional tactile characteristics. It can be made into a filament or spun yarn and used in knits, wovens and non-wovens.' The X–Static fibres enabled the raincoat to illuminate, adding an unexpected element to the decorative trim. 'Like a lot of designers, I like materials that capture light or change in different lighting,' she says. 'Trim that is a light source in itself creates new types of surface decoration because it has the potential to be changeable. For example, the light could vary in intensity or be programmed to pulsate, or even change colour.'

While Chang has a strong vision for incorporating wireless technology into fabric, her work also explores dye techniques and surface coatings. 'My interest in technological innovation is strong, and so is my desire to adapt fabric to provide the technological solutions that women need,' Chang said. 'I'm aligning with technology little by little, also exploring thermochromic inks and UV-activated motifs. They're affordable and fun, and a springboard to bigger ideas.'

# two

# Synthesized Skins

The discourse between fabric and flesh is forging fresh directions for textiles today. Fabrics, traditionally perceived as flat, unresponsive shrouds that cling lifelessly to the body, are coming to life as they mimic living flesh. Human skin is a uniquely multilayered, self-replicating organ that varies in tautness and tone. Skin is responsive and communicative, with sensors capable of surveillance so sophisticated they put even the most high tech sentries to shame. High tech textiles are mimicking skin as their designers thread them with vessels, capillaries and chemical-filled cavities. Like flesh, they are riddled with sensory membranes and pierced with fluid-emitting pores. Many are slick, soft and shiny, designed to have an erotic appeal, bringing fashion into an arena where it becomes the embodiment of fantasy and desire.[1]

The dialogue between skin and circuitry forms the cornerstone of fashion today. Designers strive to emulate fleshy textures, cocooning the body in skin soft sheaths, supple leathers and stretchy second skin materials that cling to its contours.[2] Fashion rarely forgives an unflattering figure but has been known to make excuses in the form of hard-body designs that clad the wearer in rigid materials. The allure of tactile fabrics promises to draw fashion's spectators ever closer, while rigid exoskeletons dictate considerable distance. Although the surfaces of garments can be powerfully seductive, they can also be fierce enough to keep others at arm's length.

From the dawn of the nineteenth century until today, hard materials have given feminine fashions a distinctively masculine edge. Covering the female body with rigid materials may have made it more shapely in the eyes of men, but it also brought it under male control. The bare skin and exposed bodies of contemporary fashion represented new freedom for women and introduced an organicism previously unknown in Western fashion. The advent of technologized textiles promises to be just as revolutionary—divisions between masculine and feminine, hard and soft, freedom

Fabrican's spray-on fibre technology has been developed for use in fashion but also has applications in health care, product manufacturing and interior design.

and controlled and organic and synthetic are beginning to break down, if not to collapse altogether.

This chapter examines the protective role of textiles, charting the extent to which technology can create super-strong synthetic skins and extraordinary exoskeletons. Although textiles are traditionally weakened by water, liquid gels and fluid forms are mimicking the ecology of the human body and making fabric more advanced as a result. As textile technologists increasingly turn their attention to skin, they are not as hungry for human flesh as they are for the ability to replicate its properties in fabric form.

# Exoskeletons

Warriors have been protected by armour for centuries, crafting artificial exoskeletons to shield them in combat. Associated with power, protection and discipline, armour evokes masculinity and fosters a sense of fortification. Fashion mimics it today through use of metallic fibres and rigid materials, often crafting surfaces so dense that they create the experience of wearable architecture.

Armour-like textiles mimic the dense shells of crustaceans and the hard membranes of insects, providing humans with tough exoskeletons of their own. In fashion, the body armour that such textiles represent create an impenetrable surface that masks the vulnerability of the body.

Armour began to influence contemporary fashion in the 1960s, as Paco Rabanne recreated the effects of metal mesh and chain mail in chic dresses. Issey Miyake used reinforced plastic to create a rock-hard bustier in 1983, which encased the wearer's torso with a shield-like garment. A decade later, Thierry Mugler began designing garments with steel parts and chrome surfaces that combined the reinforcement of traditional armour with the efficiency of a robot. In their autumn/winter 2007 collection, Dolce & Gabbana took armour to new heights in the guise of a shapely metal corset. The garment comprised a series of subtly tailored metal plates sculpted so close to the body that they had the appearance of lingerie.

Contemporary designers use a range of materials to evoke armour. Plastics and padded leather can be sculpted into hard surfaces or combined with textiles to create a flexible fit. Wire embroidery and jewel-encrusted surfaces can create surfaces so resilient that they are virtually bullet proof. Alexander McQueen's collections have included rigid corsets made from moulded leather that formed a tough casing around the body. Often crafted with Frankenstein stitching and fastened tightly to the wearer, they seemed to punish the body rather than protect it.

Hussein Chalayan has designed dresses made from a combination of glass fibre and resin, moulded into two smooth, glossy, pink-coloured front and back panels. The structural architecture of Chalayan's Remote Control and Dwell dresses echo the attributes of a fashioned form more than an organic body.[3] Similarly shaped, the dresses form exoskeletons around the body that arc dramatically inward at the waist and outward in the hip region, echoing the silhouette of the corset and the crinoline. This gives the dresses a defined hourglass shape that incorporates principles of corsetry in its design, emphasising a conventionally feminine shape, while creating a structure that simultaneously masks undesirable body proportions.

As metal textiles are more widely used in fashion, armour-inspired garments are becoming softer and more elastic. Metal fabric was first used in British fashion by the London-based design duo known as Vexed Generation, who began using Kevlar. They chose Kevlar for its strength and durability, and the unique weave that renders it slash and bullet proof. Their Kevlar garments combine principles from sportswear, high performance clothing and protective garments, yet create soft, sensual designs. When reinforcement fabrics such as Cordura and Schoeller-Keprotec were used to pad the knees, elbows and shoulders, the garments acquired the reinforcement of real armour.[4]

Like Kevlar, fabrics such as Aracon and Twaron are considered to be protective fabrics because off the strength of their fibres. Twaron is a heat-resistant para-aramid fibre sometimes referred to as an 'antidog' fabric since it is strong enough to withstand the grip of canine teeth.[5] Aracon is constructed from lightweight, metal-clad fibres.[6] The fabric is produced by coating a Kevlar base fibre with a metal compound often made from 100 per cent nickel or nickel/silver combinations. The textile was developed by DuPont in the 1990s and is one of the most lightweight conductive fabrics on the market.[7] Since then, Aracon has been widely used in military and aerospace applications where weight and durability are chief concerns. As well as providing reinforcement, Aracon, like many other metal textiles, is electrically conductive, anti-static, highly flexible and able to provide barriers against both electromagnetic interference and radio frequency interference. Unlike the armour-clad knight, the modern metal wearer may require protection against ambient radiation and frequencies that dampen the communicative functions of wearable technology.

Kevlar and Aracon are considered to be lightweight alternatives to metal mesh, but both lack its lustre and light-catching surface patina. Metal mesh is mostly made from lightweight aluminium, stainless steel or brass and often given metallic enamel finishes such as gold, silver, bronze or platinum. The individual metal pieces are linked together and fused by soldering or welding, and typically joined together in a spider pattern or a ring weave. Metal mesh should be able to fold in several directions and mimic the drape of chain mail, and it should also sit comfortably against the contours of the body.

Vectran, typically referred to as a 'muscle fibre', is emerging as a popular alternative to metal textiles and metal mesh. The fibre is made through a process of melt extrusion using liquid crystal polymer pellets. Vectran is popular in marine applications and aerospace projects, manufactured commercially as Superline rope used to moor ships and dock oil platforms.[8] The fabric's toughness, flexibility, abrasion and slash resistance endow it with properties far superior to those of a suit of armour. Vectran is one of the five textile layers incorporated into the new spacesuit and has also been used as a material for crafting machine parts used in space.[9] Vectran is already made into airbags deployed to cushion space landings and is expected to be used in NASA's 2011 Mars Science Laboratory.

Although Vectran surpasses the strength of most other textiles, the demand for it in garment manufacturing is limited. The attributes that make it so appealing are the same factors that limit its usage. Super strong and cut resistant, it defies conventional cutting-and-sewing operations. Because of the hardness and durability of the liquid crystal polymer used to produce the fibres, normal cutting blades are dulled instantly. The fabric can be cut by using a heat process that heats the cutting tool's blade to a temperature slightly above the zero-strength temperature of the fibre.[10]

Polyment is also an innovative, high tech fabric originally developed for space applications. The fabric is metal plated, usually in copper or nickel, and is produced in both woven and nonwoven versions. Polyment can be fabricated as a dense composite material or a thin membrane. The fabric is tear resistant, shields against high temperatures and protects against chemical contamination. The polymers forming the textile create a three-dimensional microporous structure that enables it to be cold-dip galvanized like metal.

# Robotic Textiles

Motorized mechanical exoskeletons worn to assist and protect the wearer seem to be the stuff of science fiction, but they will soon be a part of everyday life. Mechanical exoskeletons are mechatronic systems designed to follow the shape and movements of the human body.[11] Fitted with segments and joints that correspond to the natural body, they are typically made in the shape of diving suits or high performance sports gear. The suits comprise a robotic textile membrane that covers the entire body and can be controlled by normal body reflexes. The textile combines digital technologies and robotics architecture with fibre technology, which provides the system with a hardware infrastructure and makes the system wearable. As well as comprising intelligence technology systems and communication technology, the textile is designed to regulate temperature and ventilation.

When the wearer grasps an object, the fabric automatically constricts across his fingers and palm and tightens his grip considerably. As textile sensors identify more resistance, such as a pulling motion, the grip tightens even more and begins to engage fibres over the forearm, bicep and shoulder. By triggering the areas of fabric lining the muscle group to contract automatically, the wearer experiences less strain and enhanced strength.

Robotic exoskeletons are designed to protect soldiers and construction workers and to assist rescue workers as they venture into dangerous environments. Sensors woven into the fabric function like the body's nervous system to gauge pull and resistance, while mini hydraulic mechanisms distribute weight throughout the system. An article published in *Newsweek* in January 2007 highlighted the US military's new initiative to develop contemporary armour. The Pentagon granted development funds to University of Texas nanotechnologist Ray Baughman to develop military-grade artificial myomer fibres. Myomer fibres are activated electrically to contract, and as they do they increase the strength-to-weight ratio of the mechatronic movement systems in robotic exoskeletons. One of the proposed uses for robotic exoskeletons is to enable soldiers to carry more weight, enabling them to wear stronger armour and wield heavier weapons. Most prototypes are powered by a hydraulic system controlled by a wearable computer, but alternative power sources include batteries, fuel cells or internal combustion engines.

Such exoskeletons may eventually even be programmed with inherent mobility of their own so that they can bring injured soldiers back to base by themselves. The soldier could also remove them in an emergency and send them into an area considered to be too dangerous for a human. If threats such as radiation and biological agents were detected, the soldier could send the exoskeleton to complete the mission while he or she returned to safety. Robotic textiles would require strong sensory abilities to navigate such areas and handle delicate materials.

Issues surrounding robotic interaction with real objects has been the subject of research in both the robotic manipulation and haptics communities. Researchers in both areas have charted human touch-based perception and manipulation to model contact between real or virtual robotic hands and objects. To address these issues from a unified perspective, researchers are teaming up to model contacts between objects, grasp planning algorithms, haptic perception and advanced design of hands, devices and interfaces.[12]

A robotic exoskeleton prototype called the Lifesuit is being developed by a medical research association known as They Shall Walk. The Lifesuit was invented in 1986 by Monty Reed, a US Army Ranger.[13] After sustaining a sky-diving injury that left him immobilized, Reed used his personal experience as the basis for designing a wearable robot that could walk for the wearer. By 2003, Reed had advanced the prototype to the extent that it was powered by compressed air and able to record a human gait and then repeat its strides.[14] Reed's Lifesuit has advanced considerably since then, enabling the wearer to walk at the speed of about 2.5 miles per hour and even ascend and descend stairs. The Lifesuit can stand and balance the wearer unmanned, and can be controlled in a manner similar a wheelchair powered with a joystick. The future generation of the Lifesuit is envisioned to be a wetsuit-like outfit made from biosynthetic muscle fibres, fuel cells and lightweight batteries. It will be designed for wear under clothing, or made to resemble ordinary trousers or a pair of jeans.

Reed's model of biosynthetic muscle fibres is crafted from Nitinol shape memory alloy (also known as NiTinol).[15] Nitinol has an extraordinary ability to be preprogrammed to hold a shape, morph into other forms, then return to its original shape when heated. As the fibres expand and contract, they release heat, which Reed proposes to counteract with a blast of compressed air to cool them. Reed also developed a software model that uses an embedded microcontroller to activate the biosynthetic muscles. As he continues to research biosynthetic fibres, Reed is using nanotechnology to explore the potential to combine live muscle tissue with synthetic fibres.

# Sport Skins

Textile technology is playing a key role in the new generation of second skin apparel and high performance sportswear. Impact protection in sports has traditionally been provided by protective padding and rigid reinforcements. The wearable shock- and impact-resistant materials developed today provide an unprecedented combination of weightlessness, comfort and protection. A British design lab, d3o (pronounced dee-three-oh), produce impact-resistant textiles made from a specially engineered material containing intelligent molecules. The material has the high shock absorbency of sports padding, yet is soft and flexible enough to be worn comfortably over the entire body. The material, named d3o after the lab, is engineered with a structure likened to the movement of wet sand. When wet sand is allowed to flow smoothly, the grains move seamlessly together. But when pressure is applied, or the sand is gripped by a quick movement, the grains lock together. The material work in a similar way, locking together upon impact to absorb and distribute the resulting energy to protect the wearer.

The Italian research enterprise Grado Zero Espace used technology developed by the European Space Agency (ESA) to design an all-weather soft shell suit for Pia L'Obry to wear as she faced the extreme weather conditions known to occur during the Transat 6.5 transatlantic solo regatta.[16] They created the S1 survival suit for the Swedish sailor by using a shape memory membrane enhanced with alkaline sweat resistance and a noncorrosive ability to resist salt water. The outermost fabric layer remained breathable in all weather yet kept the body perfectly dry. The material's molecular structure guaranteed a constant body temperature, despite changes in weather. The textile is enhanced with a meta-aramid textile composition, making it fire and abrasion resistant.

Grado Zero Espace used their design expertise to find solutions for some of the problems that plague professional sailors. They integrated the gloves with the sleeves, eliminating the risk of them being blown off in strong winds. Keprotec, a fabric five times stronger than steel, was grafted onto the palms to heighten their antislip ability. Shock-absorber padding was produced from a visco-elastic polyurethane memory foam to cushion areas such as the knees. Electroluminescent film was attached to the back of the suit, controlled by a switch inside the pocket. To make the suit completely waterproof, the seams were sealed with Liquid Shell, whose elastic properties ensure that the seams stay supple.

# Fortified Fashion

The US military is forging new frontiers for textile research. Various arms of the US military have established development units and research partnerships specifically to enhance the protective and communicative properties of their uniforms and combat gear. Soldiers' uniforms are being engineered to change colours to match their

Nomex is a heat- and flame-resistant fibre used across a wide range of applications. Nomex fabric is a popular choice for military uniforms and protective apparel.

surroundings, making camouflage patterns redundant. Intelligent fibres can sense the impact of a bullet, and as they medicate the wearer to stop the bleeding, they also send a signal to the soldier's command base, and are also even incorporating information technology into combat clothing. The fibres are also embedded with microbial protection, thermal protection, fire retardancy, electrical conductivity and radar wave absorption capabilities.

Technology to further these advances is being developed by Georgia Tech with funding from the US Department of the Navy. Researchers use optical fibres and specialty fibres to detect bullet wounds and interconnected sensors that monitor the body's vital signs during combat conditions. The sensors monitor temperature, heart rate and respiration rate and can detect oxygen levels or hazardous gases. The Wearable Motherboard technology developed for their Smart Shirt relies on fibres to transmit information to and from sensors within a flexible data bus structure. The sensors plug in and out of T-connectors, essentially clips attached to the fibres, that serve as a data bus to transmit information from the sensors to monitoring equipment. Tests to evaluate the comfort of the garment revealed that it can be worn continuously for long periods of time, and it was also found to be easy to wear and take off.[17]

One of the most visionary research and development projects in the US military is the Future Force Warrior initiative. As researchers explore the use of innovations such as mechatronic exoskeletons and body armour based on magnetorheological fluid, they are also pioneering the applications of nanotechnology for combat wear. Nanostructured systems are generally believed to be a gateway to the technology of the future. In terms of textiles, nanofibres are more practical and economically feasible in the long run, and have proven to be long lasting, more durable and more versatile than conventional fibres. Their unique behaviour gives them sensing abilities and the ability to transmit information through their networks at rapid speeds.

Currently, combat soldiers wear bulky uniforms laden with heavy equipment, often struggling during long marches. As warfare became more technologized, soldiers were required to carry more equipment. Attempts to create a viable combat exoskeleton failed because of weight restrictions and impaired mobility. If military clothing and equipment was manufactured at the nanoscale, they would be lighter in weight and stronger but would also transmit data through their networks more efficiently. The garments that would result would be a few millimetres thick and would fit close to the body like a wetsuit. Nanotechnology would enable a variety of functions to be incorporated into the fabric at a molecular scale.[18] A network of fibre-based sensors would be seamlessly integrated into the garment, and a corresponding set of actuators would respond to injury by changing the properties of the material. If bleeding occurred, the

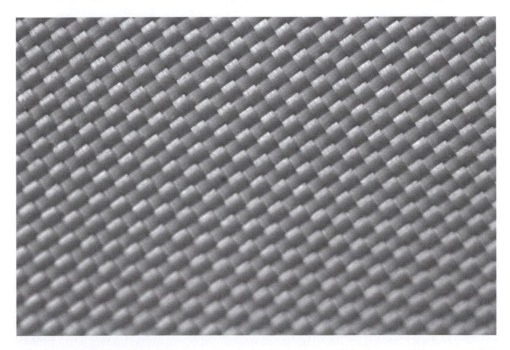

Kevlar is manufactured in a variety of fibres and yarns, that can be woven or felted into a wide range of protective fabrics.

The Kevlar Aramid fibre is lightweight, flexible and slash proof, making it an excellent choice for law enforcement apparel.

fabric would contract at strategic points to create a tourniquet. A broken leg would be instantly reinforced and supported as the fabric around it stiffened.

The Massachusetts Institute of Technology (MIT) established the Institute for Soldier Nanotechnologies (ISN) to 'develop and exploit nanotechnology to dramatically improve the survivability of Soldiers'.[19] The ISN work in tandem with the US Army Research Office (ARO), and scientists from both organizations work together

Needled felted fabric made from Kevlar fibres provide excellent resistance against injuries from sharp objects and extreme heat. Protective vests like this one helps protect law enforcement officers and military personnel.

and with other scientific communities concerned with nanotechnology. Both the ISN and the ARO believe that nanotechnology research can benefit the wider public as well as the military.

A team drawn from the faculties of chemical, mechanical, electrical and material science departments has initiated projects to fabricate nanoscale fibres and films that will be integrated with microfluidic systems. They are also developing low-temperature chemical-vapour deposition systems for polymers and other materials that could be integrated into fabric. Their so-called nanoscale origami project produced a technique for folding thin films into three-dimensional structures. Nanoparticle composites also have properties that could be used to create molecular chain mail. Individual nanoscopic pieces linked at a molecular level should have the same surface tension, drape and fold as conventional metal mesh yet be much more resilient.

Researchers working with Professor Karen Gleason have developed a process known as hot filament chemical vapour deposition (HFCVD) to waterproof ordinary cotton fabric. The process deposits nanolayers of polytetrafluoroethylene (PTFE) (also known as Teflon) onto the fibres, which remain breathable and continue to look and feel the same as untreated fabric.

Unlike conventional waterproofing processes, the HFCVD process deposits the coating during the vapour phase, which makes it possible to coat materials that cannot be immersed in a solution. Kevlar, for example, has chemical properties that prevent it from being able to be waterproofed by a conventional solution-based technique, but it responds better to the HFCVD process. Gleason's waterproofing technique is also capable of coating delicate filaments on which traditional PTFE deposition processes do not work. The HFCVD process is able to go beyond a material's external surface and coat interior cavities, such as those in porous substances like foam.

Research into nanotechnology indicates that nanotextiles have a wide range of applications beyond the battlefield. Their potentials for fashion, sportswear, aerospace and health care promise to spur a wider technology infrastructure that will make them more widely manufactured. The multilevel approach pioneered by ISN is creating a uniquely interdisciplinary area for fibre research that is securing a prominent place for nanotextiles within the growing hierarchy of nanosystems.

# Instant Armour

As researchers at MIT investigate nanotechnology's potential to produce a protective uniform, they are pioneering a textile structured by fluidic particles and magnetic fields. Researchers discovered that liquids can be manipulated by magnets when they contain sufficient quantities of iron particles. Known as magnetorheological fluids, they consist of iron particles smaller than individual red blood cells suspended in a liquid solution. The fluid is typically made from substances such as silicon oil or corn syrup, which thicken into a gel-like consistency. When exposed to magnetic fields, their properties change dramatically, instantaneously shifting from labile liquid to solid matter, and once the magnetic field has been dampened, they return to their liquid form immediately.

Gerald McKinley, director of MIT's Hatsopoulos Microfluids Lab, is exploring the potential applications for this solution in protective textiles such as bullet-proof vests. When immersed in magnetorheological fluid, woven fabric becomes completely saturated by the solution. The magnetorheological properties remain in the fibres even after the fabric has dried, making it possible to manipulate the textile when made into a garment. Varying degrees of magnetic polarity have different effects on the textile, creating levels of rigidity ranging from firm to taut and rock hard. 'What we have without a magnetic field is a very soft, very flexible fabric, and when we apply a magnetic field, the stiffness of that fabric changes by a factor of about 50,' says McKinley.[20] 'The stiffness change depends on the strength of the magnetic field. As the magnetic field gets stronger and stronger, then the stiffness change gets larger and larger.'

McKinley brings the level of rigidity under the wearer's control by equipping them with the means to create a magnetic field within the fabric. Conductive wires woven into the fabric are charged with electric currents that soldiers could switch on and off to produce electromagnetic fields, or moderate to create different levels of rigidity. When under attack or in active combat, soldiers could deploy the full magnetic strength to maximize the garment's ability to shield them.

Nanotech magnets would effectively function as valves that activate the fluids as the wearer triggers the controls. McKinley thinks it could take a further ten years of research to make the textile truly bullet proof, because scientists need time to change the shape of the iron particles. 'The particles that we're using now look like soccer balls. They're spherical,' says McKinley. 'If you were to stack a pile of those together, you don't get very far. What would be better would be to have faceted particles, particles with flat faces, or particles that look more like donuts.'

Flat-faced particles would automatically form a stacking configuration when magnetized, reacting quicker and bonding into a shape more stable than what can be created by slippery sphere shapes.

# Fluid-Based Fabrics

Fluid-based fabrics have existed for years, ever since the synthetic filament Rayon was derived from a liquid solution.[21] Textiles continue to be formed by fluids today, but their properties mimic natural ecologies more than they typify artificial fibrous forms. The human body is mostly liquid, held together by bundles of fibres and fleshy membranes. Most soft-bodied organisms are made up of fluid-filled cavities surrounded by muscle fibres, and organs like the heart maintain pressure throughout the entire system. Human skin is mimicked by mesoporous textiles, whose unique structure allows the moisture produced by the body to be released through the fabric. Like perspiration, the moisture is wicked upward through pore-like perforations and released on the fabric's surface.

Polyurethane-based gels are breathable, dimensionally stable and shock absorbent, and they strengthen a textile substrate by distributing pressure equally throughout its structure.[22] As a nonwoven membrane, the gel can be individually moulded into shapes, directly laminated with decorative materials or bonded to the fabric at a later stage with standard polyurethane glue.

Elastomeric gel is known for its ability to range from super soft to stiff, and it is malleable enough to be stretched more than ten times its length and immediately snaps back to shape without distortion.[23]

Grado Zero Espace are experts in protective, smart and multifunctional textiles, and they specialize in transforming technological know-how into wearable materials.[24]

Grado Zero Espace began collaborating with the ESA in 2000 to advance the thermal and cooling capacities of textiles. Through their work with ESA, Grado Zero Espace were able to transform shape memory materials into wearable textiles. They used the shape memory alloy Nitinol to create the first orthogonally woven fabric ever produced.

One of Grado Espace Zero's collaborations with ESA resulted in wearable cooling and air conditioning systems that would protect astronauts as they made space walks in extreme heat. One of the materials used is Aerogel, a fluidic material made with nanogel. Aerogel was developed to insulate probes and instruments sent into space, and it was consequently engineered to be virtually weightless and able to withstand extreme temperatures.[25] Grado Espace Zero adapted Aerogel technology for fashion, creating stylish jackets such as the Quota Zero jacket and the Absolute Zero jacket created for Hugo Boss. Both jackets feature a layer of Aerogel padding, making them lightweight and breathable, yet capable of unprecedented thermal performance.

The Aerogel layer is split into anatomically shaped interconnecting components to ensure cohesive contact with the body. The presence of water-based substances worn next to the body gives it another protective layer, perhaps mimicking a layer of fat, or even embryonic fluid. Because the nanogel is mesoporous, perspiration is wicked away before it has time to saturate the fibres. Grado Zero Espace and Hugo Boss also collaborated with McLaren to develop special clothing for Formula One drivers and mechanics.[26]

Gel technology was also used by Italian motorbike clothing company Spidi to develop protective clothing to keep bikers from overheating in extreme temperatures. They developed an Anatomic Intercooler System that circulates gel-cooled water throughout a custom-made vest. The system forms a base layer within a jacket that pumps the gel through tiny tubes woven across the chest and back. The system is driven by a battery-powered micro-pump that circulates approximately half a litre of fluid. The system was developed for competitive racers, ensuring that a single vest could hold enough fluid to last for a 45-minute race.

The Safe & Cool consortium set up by the ESA is also developing protective materials with fully integrated cooling systems. The consortium is coordinated by Grado Zero Espace and the Italian enterprise D'Appolonia, and it includes a range of research-based enterprises from Italy, Belgium and Poland. The objective is to develop high quality thermal-resistant material for protective clothing that will reduce the risk of heatstroke and heat-related injuries for those working in extreme temperatures. The space technology developed by ESA is enabling the consortium to find solutions on earth, resulting in protective clothing for fire fighters, rescue workers, oil-field engineers, steel workers and glass blowers.

Consortium members are pooling knowledge and experience in order to adapt ESA technology for everyday use. The garment they developed was conceived as a highly-structured design made from a complex textile substrate. As the project got underway, each research team was assigned an individual layer to develop. Grado Zero Espace's cooling apparatus formed the core of the project, and the hydrophilic

Freedom of Creation are creating a new generation of textiles that are digitally designed and manufactured. Bags like this one could eventually be download online and printed at home in a rapid-prototyping machine.

hollow fibres necessary for moisture management were produced by technical filament supplier Tirso.

Rossini, the three-dimensional-knitting specialists, developed a textile structure based on heightened thermal insulation, improved fibre distribution, weightlessness and flexibility.[27] They engineered the thermal and moisture management layer, which was made to enhance the function of Grado Zero Espace's cooling system. The cooling system

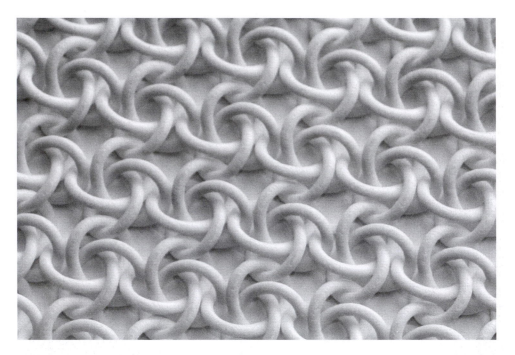

By using three-dimensional software and laser-sintered polyamide, Amsterdam-based design lab Freedom of Creation have developed a range of textiles that can be synthesised by rapid-prototyping technology.

circulated fluid through tubing pulled through custom-designed cavities in Rossini's three-dimensional knit textile substrate, mimicking the function of blood vessels. A water-binding polymer was added as both a surface coating and a powder dispersed throughout the fibres. The polymers absorbed any excess moisture permeating the textile layers, which helped to maintain the temperature moderated by the cooling apparatus. In the event of a sudden temperature increase, the polymers would release the liquid absorbed, reproducing the sweating process. The surface treatment applied to the outer layer was engineered by MTS, a textile firm with expertise in processing and finishing fabric, who coated the external surface with polymeric materials.[28]

Another Safe & Cool project developed a protective garment known as the Hydro jacket, designed with fire fighters and steel workers in mind. The Hydro jacket was engineered through use of the ESA technologies originally created to protect astronauts from the intense heat of direct sunlight in space. The jacket consists of three layers designed to maximize performance of the gel-based moisture barrier, referred to as Safe Hydrogel Padding. The inner layer is made from a flame-proof textile structure formed by combining flame-retardant hydrophobic polyester fibres with flame-retardant hydrophilic aramid fibres. Together, the fibres create suction ducts that channel the moisture away from the skin. The fabric was quilted with a layer of flame-retardant cotton that would prevent the hydrogel particles from wicking out of the fibres yet still permit moisture to escape.

Rapid-prototyping promises to revolutionize the fashion industry. Rather than managing production infrastructures, labour forces and stock quantities, fashion brands can upload garment designs on the Internet to be manufactured by the consumer.

The second layer dissipates heat and provides a thermal barrier. Like the Rossini three-dimensional knit textile detailed earlier, it provides a thermal and moisture management fabric coated with a water-absorbing polymer. If the wearer's body temperature increases, the coating will enable the perspiration to move towards the outer surface, reproducing the sweating process of human skin.[29] The external layer is made from cotton fabric treated with Antifiamma L, a flame-retardant coating. The surface reflects rays and ambient heat, and can expand up to 100 times its dry film thickness. Like the second layer, it was conceived as a coated, multilayered structure.

Practitioners working in fashion and product design are also exploring the role of fibres in liquid form. Traditionally, textiles' relationship with liquids has been limited to dyes, coatings, cleaning fluids and moulded resins, but new research is making fibre and fluid one in the same.[30] Manel Torres, the designer and researcher behind Fabrican, is based at London's Imperial College, where he collaborates with scientists to suspend textile fibres in an aerosol solution. Inspired by the aerosol bandages used in health care, Torres foresees a day when whole garments will be packaged in aerosol and sprayed directly onto the body of the wearer.

Freedom of Creation, an Amsterdam-based research lab who advance rapid prototyping processes for product design, use rapid prototyping to create textiles and whole garments.[31] The process programmes a panel of small inkjets to spray minute quantities of liquids that create layers as they dry. As the layers build, they can create flexible membranes, solid forms, objects inside other objects, objects with deep recesses or undercuts or objects composed of numerous interlocking forms. The technology has been used to create nonwoven textiles that mimic loose weaves and chain mail, all created from fluid-based fibres.

# Sensory Skins

One of the body's primary interfaces with the environment, skin plays a crucial role in keeping the body intact. Skin defines the outermost boundaries of the body as it envelopes the body's musculature and soft tissue and protects the vital systems against pathogens. Yet skin also communicates much about the body's genetic makeup, emotional states and physical well-being, and it releases chemicals that have an impact on others.

Advances in fragrance technology make it possible for many different types of scents to be formulated into fibres. Jenny Tillotson, whose groundbreaking Scentsory Design project was outlined in Chapter 1, is pioneering a new approach to the process she terms 'aroma delivery'. Tillotson initiated a project known as Scentient Beings, which integrates smell technology into multisensorial clothing. The technology heightens the impact scent has on health and well-being.[32] Tillotson interprets clothing as sensitive, aromatic surfaces that have the potential to mimic many of the functions of human skin. The Smart Second Skin Dress she developed is capable of imitating the skin's ability to create a sensory atmosphere around it.[33] Tillotson cites

Designer Jenny Tillotson creates multisensorial clothing that reflects changes in the wearer's emotional states. The Smart Second Skin Dress Tillotson developed is capable of communicating with remote systems to create a sensory atmosphere around it.

British writer J. G. Ballard's definition of fashion to describe the project's raison d'être: A 'recognition that nature has endowed us with one skin too few, that fully sentient being should wear its nervous system externally.'[34]

Like real skin, Tillotson's Smart Second Skin Dress, reflects human emotions and the individual's sensory experience. 'Using a theory that human biology can be replicated as micro mechanisms, the biological functions of skin, internal organs and the beat of the heart can be miniaturised,' she explains. 'By forming an alternative sensory communication system, it rivals nature's own capillaries.' Accordingly, Tillotson based the Smart Second Skin Dress on the body's veins and arteries, olfactory centres and scent glands. As the fabric interacts with the body, it gauges the wearer's emotional state and emits scents that correspond to her mood. The cabling integrated into the fabric streams aromatic pulses electronically to key areas in the system in order to activate the body's scent centres.

'The Smart Second Skin dress allows the wearer to enter a sixth dimension by creating a rainbow symphony of aromas,' Tillotson says. 'This makes us more aware of our own sensory universe, which has the capacity to expand our sensory repertoire towards the sixth sense. The wearer could deliver a spray of magic wellness molecules to create their own personal "smell bubble" around them.'

As sensory beings, humans respond to scent on many levels—consciously and unconsciously. Tillotson's sensory systems are designed to bring the release of scent under wearers' control, heightening their sensory experiences. 'The surfaces provide aroma molecules for the right moment for the right effect, triggering new emotions and enhancing intimate contact with other living things,' she says. 'Scent changes our feelings, our body chemistry and body odour. It transforms negative mood states into good "scentsations", releasing scents to help sleep, boost confidence, relax, energise, arouse, increase self-esteem and expand the imagination.'

A study by scientists at the University of California, Berkeley reinforces Tillotson's claims.[35] Biologists have long held the view that the chemical molecules known as pheromones exist to induce hormone release or instigate behaviour changes in other members of the species. Researchers have identified that androstadienone, a chemical released by men, causes hormonal as well as physiological and psychological changes in women, even raising their levels of cortisol, a hormone commonly associated with alertness or stress.[36] The study supports the claim that human skin has functions far beyond insulation, sensation and synthesis of vitamin D, signposting a new direction for textile technology as research into synthetic sensory skins evolves.

New horizons for sensory textiles are being forged as scientists, technologists and textile developers bind scents directly to fibres. Microcapsule technology makes it possible to seal scent particles within microscopic spheres made from ceramics, polymers or gelatine films and attach them to individual fibres. Microcapsules can be crafted with multiple layers that enable them to release a constant stream of scent over a short time period, or bonded so tightly to the fibre that they release their scents over long periods. They can be combined with sensor-like fibres to create a range of different effects, such as those that detect heightened levels of UV-radiation and release microencapsulated sunscreen to shield the wearer.

The discovery that textiles can be used to control the body's natural scent has led to groundbreaking developments. Japanese conglomerate Kanebo has conducted extensive research into antimicrobial deodorants that can be embedded within the fibre itself to destroy the bacteria responsible for body odour.[37] Scent-Lok, an American company specializing in 'scent-eliminating apparel', bind activated carbon to fibres to dampen the scent of the human body. Activated carbon is one of the most adsorptive substances used in fibre technology. In textile form, it has proven to be an effective means of masking odours by filtering away microscopic scent particles before they have a chance to travel far beyond the skin's surface. Activated carbon has millions of microscopic pores, cracks and fissures that attract scent particles and form a bond within the carbon that stops them from being released. Although the scent particles are trapped within the fabric's structure, air is still able to pass through it. Scent-Lok call this process adsorption.

The activated carbon Scent-Lok use are synthesised from coconut shell carbon. Their fabrics are able to adsorb human scent for approximately 40 hours. The fabrics can be refreshed, or desorbed in a tumble dryer. Once the fabrics have been heated to a temperature of 150 degrees Fahrenheit for 30–40 minutes, their ability to adsorb scent particles is renewed.[38] The fabric is enhanced by a wicking system that spreads perspiration over a larger surface area and repels body oils. This makes it easier for them to be completely removed when laundering, preventing any human scent from permanently bonding to the fabric.

## Soft Skeletons

The filter-like function of the skin protects the body against airborne contaminates and bacteria spread by contact. Skin triggers a response when exposed to UV-rays, ambient radiation and harmful allergens, often blistering, discolouring or breaking out in a rash. Textile technologists are striving to reproduce skin-like responses in fabric—though, hopefully, leaving blisters and rashes where they belong. Researchers are replicating the skin's antibacterial properties in antimicrobial fabrics, and endowing textiles with the capacity to react to environmental toxins and alert the wearer to their presence.

Royal College of Art researcher Anne Toomey, deputy head of the textiles department, is pioneering the concept of 'visible invisibility' to develop contamination-aware inks and dyes suitable for use on fabric. A print specialist, Toomey is exploring the potential to print textiles with patterns and motifs that change colour to indicate the presence of contamination. 'Smart surfaces react to a number of different factors,' says Toomey, 'and the materials we print on and embed into textiles can definitely contain similar sensing abilities. There is a real need for both wearable and portable warning systems that detect the presence of infectious bacteria and air pollution. Wouldn't it be good for your clothing to detect an airborne toxin and alert you before you started choking? Wouldn't it be good for a hospital gown to show that the carer—or the wearer—hadn't washed their hands properly after handling something infectious? Or indeed for the surfaces you are wearing and surrounded by to possess sensing, filtering, reactive and adaptive capabilities?'[39]

Toomey's vision of reactive surfaces would be developed in collaboration with scientists to identify the best means of bonding contaminate-aware substances to textiles. 'Ideally, the surface should be capable of renewing itself,' says Toomey, 'and able to revert back to its original state once the contaminate has been removed. Obviously the materials will have to be hypo-allergenic and environmentally-friendly. We also have to come up with a way of making it clear to the wearer what action they should take in order to utilise the window of opportunity for effective action. Maybe the contaminate will cause words to appear, such as "wash your hands" or "get the hell out of here now" so that the message is clear.'

Toomey's research adds another dimension to antimicrobial fabrics. Although they can detect and neutralize certain bacteria, they are not currently able to communicate their presence to the wearer. 'Essentially, textiles will have to have technology that delivers information about the environment in real time, giving the wearer status updates as well as warnings,' she says. 'The wearer has to develop enough confidence in textiles to trust that they will deliver the right information at the right time.'

Current research in contaminate-aware fabrics explores the potential to encapsulate the fibres with minuscule electronic chips containing live nerve cells. The cells would be capable of detecting a range of chemical, radioactive and biological contaminates and subsequently triggering a wearable alarm. The alarm system need not necessarily be high tech; a fabric woven with optic fibres and light-emitting molecules could send a simple warning message to the wearer. The fabric could also be endowed with self-decontaminating properties; for example, antibodies encapsulated in the fibres could destroy certain contaminates on contact.[40]

Toomey's research reflects wider concerns about the level of contaminates released in urban centres, which has also sparked software developers and urban planners to find wearable solutions. A research project initiated by the Centre for Advanced Spatial Analysis at University College London and the Bartlett School of Architecture and Planning is developing mobile sensors outfitted with Global Positioning System (GPS) receivers and cellular transmitters that monitor pollution levels in urban environments. Known as the Urban Pollution Monitoring Project, the initiative proposed to develop wearable sensors that would use Bluetooth technology to track pollution levels. The technology would determine the wearer's position and send text messages when he or she entered areas where pollution levels were hazardous.[41]

From his base at Siemens Corporate Technology headquarters in Munich, Maximilian Fleischer has invented miniature chemical sensors capable of detecting environmental toxins.[42] Fleischer's sensors are lightweight, durable and only a few millimetres in diameter, making it easy to embed them within thick fibres or embroider them directly onto a textile's surface. They emit a warning signal when they encounter toxins, alerting the wearer to the presence of airborne substances they may not detect otherwise.[43] The information that these sensors provide could eclipse the need for protective clothing if they could warn wearers to stay away before toxic levels became critical. Incorporated into combat exoskeletons, they would endow soldiers with an additional sensory ability. Just as Mother Nature has created a wide variety of protective shells, textile technology is creating a full spectrum of artificial exoskeletons suited to the high tech lifestyle of the modern human.

## Feature Interview: Vexed Generation

For more nearly two decades, Vexed Generation have crafted clothing from bullet-proof and slash-proof materials. Their collections pioneer new materials and construction methods, combining principles from sportswear, high performance protective clothing, and cutting-edge street style. They work with fashion not to mimic the latest trends, but to use it as a form of communication that can initiate long-term changes to the social infrastructure.

One of their most famous garments is the Vexed Parka, which they created as a commentary on the escalation of surveillance during the 1990s. Adam Thorpe, who owns Vexed Generation in partnership with Joe Hunter, explains: 'It was 1994, another aspect was the surveillance cameras going up at the time. Now there are cameras everywhere but at that time it was just starting and nobody was discussing it. So we put that on the agenda as well.'[44] The Vexed Parka is characterized by a sinister hood and collar that covers most of the head and face, closing over the mouth and nose but leaving the eye area open. 'We made the parka in 1994 and launched it in 1995. It sums up all the ideas and concepts we had about fashion and social surveillance, which we include in most of the other clothes we have designed since,' he says.

Anonymity and visibility against the urban landscape became considerations expressed in each garment Vexed Generation make. As they began exploring materials with different properties, the functions of the jackets extended beyond concealing to include weatherproofing, physical defence, and environmental hazards. 'As well as making garments for conceptual reasons, we are also making clothing that people want to wear for practical reasons,' Thorpe says. Hunter and Thorpe chose technologized materials like Kevlar and ballistic nylon for the strength and durability that makes them slash-proof, providing a shield in the event of a knife-wielding attacker.

Kevlar is regarded to be one of the most important technical fibres ever developed. Made from metal materials, the fibre is organic, and therefore imbibes principles of sustainability, yet possesses a remarkable range of properties that few organic materials have. It was first introduced commercial in the early 1970s and was subsequently used to produce cable guide wires, fishing line, marine ropes, aeroplane engine parts and protective garments. Since then, Kevlar K-159 and Kevlar XLT have been developed for body armour. They were engineered to be stab resistant, making them well-suited to law enforcement applications. They are manufactured from a new Kevlar fibre four times thinner than most ballistic yarns. The fibre can be woven into a dense textile which is five times stronger than steel of equal weight.[45]

Vexed Generation craft clothing from resilient materials such as Kevlar. The rigid structure that these textiles possess enables Vexed Generation to create cutting-edge designs that combine aspects of protective clothing with elements of street style.

When Vexed Generation first started using Kevlar, they bought it from manufacturers who produced it for use by the British Ministry of Defence and security companies. The manufacturer was reluctant to sell it to a fashion label, so Vexed Generation were forced to pretend that they were making protective clothing. 'We told them our company name was V G Security,' Thorpe says. He began buying other technologized textiles from factories in Switzerland, the United States and Italy. Using high tech materials created a unique aesthetic almost by default, because the densely textured surfaces and subtle patterns in the fabric have real impact. The properties of nonwoven textiles are ideal for creating complex forms because of their strength and ability to hold their shape.

The aesthetic this created became known as stealth utility because it defined the wearer against the pubic space, concealed his or her identity, and constituted a multifunctional design. Other streetwear labels soon began to update their look with hoods, technologized textiles and multipurpose designs. 'We never intended to become part of any fashion trend, but have noticed that much of the clothing that we originally made in 1994 and 1995 has ended up becoming a new sort of urban utility look,' Thorpe says.

Vexed Generation's uncompromising perspectives on the standards and values of their designs is a rarity in both conventional and cutting-edge fashion. Vexed Generation tend to invert superficialities like marketing clothing for its sex appeal, capitalizing on short-term trends, notions of exclusivity and product branding by placing emphasis on protection and durability. They also innovate by guaranteeing high performance standards for their clothes, achieved through high tech textiles and functional design. 'With our garments, and as a philosophy, we go against the main stream of production where the products are designed to last a determined period of time through concepts of cheapness and disposability,' Thorpe says. 'We are fundamentally against that and that's why our garments are intended to endure keeping their qualities. We'd like to think of our garments going into second hand shops and yet, being in perfect shape.'

# three

# Surfaces

A textile's surface is more than just a façade—it's a curious layer of aesthetics and identities, and a contentious site of exploration and resistance. Surfaces have acquired depth, becoming concrete, complex systems equipped with their own personalities and individual behaviours. They respond to heat, light and touch and react to mechanical stress. Surfaces connect different sites within a spatial framework, and include a multiplicity of scopic regimes and cultural forms.[1] Like a landscape, the surface constitutes a shifting topology of natural process and superficial forces. It can embody movement and express sensations, shift unexpectedly into surprising new forms or suddenly dissolve into nothingness. Surfaces are often engineered to fluctuate between disparate states, revealing that they have no fixed meanings in themselves.

Surfaces are also manifestations of social norms and moral codes, and fields of action for predatory sexuality, promiscuous styles and fleeting interactions. Surfaces reflect structures of economic power, social status and commodification, and they routinely deconstruct image and object. They represent vast territorial sprawls that extend to strange and uncertain destinations, yet they unfold locally according to culturally prescribed customs. Even if contemporary fibres seem to have broken free of traditional forms, today's fabrics remain monuments to textile history. They represent several millennia of fibres sedimented in time; although their surfaces have been constantly rewritten, they have never been erased completely.

All surfaces have perceptual qualities, their mutability enabling the body to take on chameleon-like characteristics. Surfaces represent artifice, providing the means of disguising structures beneath them or of constructing a second skin to emphasize the structure's own contours. Because surfaces are interpreted by sight and touch, physical contact with the surface initiates a complex multisensory, emotional and cognitive

Smart textiles can be controlled by woven sensors programmed to transmit data to specific circuits. The data transmissions can create changes on the surface or trigger a response within the fabric itself.

experience that provides a uniquely individual interpretation of the world. As textile technology increasingly aligns the surface with interactive potential, they provide tools for heightening the wearer's sensorial experience. Retro-reflective materials and cloaking devices may give future textiles the ability to appear to dematerialize, but they will always remain present.

Technologically enhanced textiles are advancing faster than ever before. The development of so-called switchable surfaces constructed from multifaceted molecules enables fabric to sense and respond to a wide range of conditions.

Switchable surfaces attest to the way in which textiles today are affected by scientists and engineers, who often charge high tech fibres with electric currents or magnetic fields. Technology's impact is even redefining the design process. Whereas textile practitioners once relied on geometric principles to sketch designs two-dimensionally, the application of algorithm-based programmes as design tools for textiles makes their three-dimensionality undeniable. As new textile forms begin to emerge, the extraordinary textures that result are outlining new paradigms for surfaces in the textile world.

Traditionally, the surface represents a distinction between the public and the private, but the rise of digital media has introduced them to an open domain. Virtual worlds, such as Second Life, offer textile professionals and amateur designers a limitless forum to examine textiles in a context free of preconceptions about how fibres should look and feel. Virtual fabrics may not be material, but they are real, nonetheless. As textile surfaces find new expressions in engineering, science, computer technology and other disciplines, a new textile culture is emerging. The idea that surfaces can be interactive platforms as well as vehicles for creative expression is driving both their physical and virtual components forward.

# Perceptual Surfaces

A surface does not need to represent reality; it can be a space for fantasy, imagination and individual perception. Perception is phenomenal and psychological, a process whereby we can attain awareness and understanding of sensory information. The word *perception* came into the English language from Latin, where the meaning stems from the role the senses play in receiving and collecting information for the perceiver. With the advent of switchable surfaces and wearable technology, textiles are acquiring perceptive skills as they become information hubs capable of gathering data from the environment around them. And with the ability to attract airborne particles and draw them into their fibres, textiles are now able to 'receive' and 'collect' in physical terms too.

Perception is one of the oldest fields in psychology and one of the areas with the latest theoretical applications for textiles. The oldest quantitative principle in psychology is the Weber–Fechner law, which quantifies the relationship between physical stimuli and the resulting perceptual effects.[2] It was through the study of perception that the Gestalt school of psychology emerged, and its holistic approach emphasizes the importance of touch, tactility and vision. Our senses enable us to survey the surfaces around us and construct our experiences of them. Yet reality is not always what it seems, and textiles equipped with the capacity to change shape, become invisible or dematerialize altogether are just as illusory.

The concept of a perceptual surface first emerged in architecture, but it is intriguing fashion designers on many levels.[3] Thermochromatic patterns dramatically alter the fabric's surface as heat-sensitive motifs appear and disappear on areas where they touch the body. Similarly, photochromatic motifs are invisible in the dark, only surfacing when their pigments become exposed to UV light. Colourful LED light patterns can illuminate the surface and reconfigure it into a range of motifs, creating a wearable surface that changes constantly. The responsive surface developed by Younghui Kim and Milena Lossifova for their HearWear project is embellished with LEDs and electroluminescent wires activated by the ambient sound around them. By interconnecting sound recognition sensors and microcontrollers, the HearWear garments are able to respond to surrounding noise and display their reactions on the garment's surface.

Some of the most visionary examples of shifting surfaces were designed by Hussein Chalayan in collaboration with design engineer Moritz Waldemeyer.[4] They worked

In collaboration with Moritz Waldemeyer, Hussein Chalayan encrusted this garment's surface with crystals, LEDs and electroluminescent wires. By interconnecting sensors, microcontrollers and video technology, they were able to project a video onto the garment's surface.

together in Chalayan's Airborne project, which resulted in a dress capable of projecting moving images. The front of the dresses are embellished with 15,600 LEDs and Swarovski crystals, forming screen-like surfaces. One dress projected a looped film that showed a time-lapse sequence of a rose beginning to blossom; another displayed cloudy silhouettes of sharks surfacing in a choppy sea.

A projected surface like Waldemeyer's is a uniquely creative platform for textile designers, enabling them to link physical materials with ephemeral spaces. Although surfaces created by thermochromatic pigments have ephemeral characteristics, they are essentially bound to physical space. Their reliance on the wearer's body heat and physical contact links them inextricably to real materials. Projected images represent the opposite. Since they rely on technological means to create a surface, they heighten the contrast between the organic body and the surface surrounding it.

Such surfaces are able to organize information through hyperlinks and make them visible in a spectral environment.[5] Their ability to be adaptive and continuously recalibrated transcends the performance of switchable surfaces, which are typically engineered with only a few modes of behaviour. They provide hyperscreens, surfaces able to construct virtual worlds and communicate through texts and imagery. Although

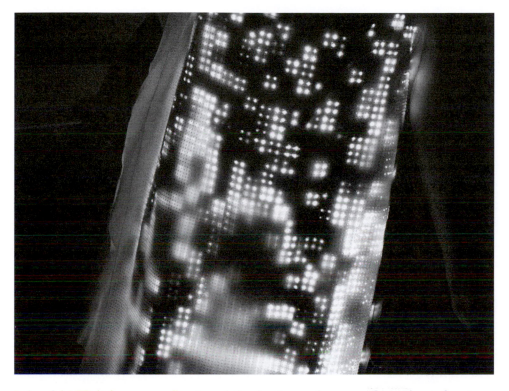

Colourful LED light patterns illuminated the dress's crystals to reconfigure the surface into a range of motifs. It created a dynamic surface that changes constantly.

French theorist Gaston Bachelard was active before the advent of the digital age, his texts seemed to anticipate the conditions that a hyperscreen would create. In the thinking of Bachelard, surfaces like these represent 'uninhabited domains', two-dimensional spaces with the potential to evoke a fantasy of a habitable shell. As the viewer watches them, the surfaces invite 'daydreams of refuge' that are at once sartorial, sensorial, architectural and material.[6]

Waldemeyer also created the technological interfaces for the so-called laser dresses Chalayan designed for his spring/summer 2008 'Readings' collection. Hundreds of motor-driven laser diodes were integrated into the garments, each attached by a custom-designed, servo-driven brass hinge that enabled it to move in several directions. The laser diodes were embellished with Swarovski crystals that would either deflect the lasers or absorb their light, depending on the angle of the beam. When the beams shone directly into the crystals, they resembled glowing embers. When they were deflected, the beams projected far beyond the surface of the garment into the surrounding space. The result was visually spectacular, creating a starburst of shifting lights that transformed the garments from static objects into animated forms that constantly changed and reconfigured. As the laser beams projected beyond the surface, they symbolically amplified its silhouette, making it appear borderless, even ephemeral.

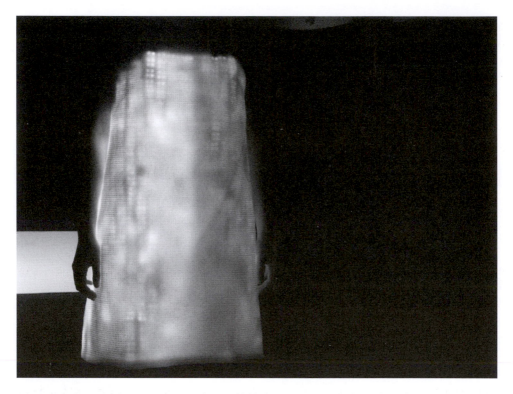

Here, Chalayan's dress projects a looped film across the surface that shows a time-lapse sequence of a rose beginning to blossom.

The surface blurred the boundaries between garment, material and space, as if the wearer was cocooned in a supernova of radiating lights.

In 2007, Waldemeyer was commissioned to design performance costumes for the rock band OK Go. Waldemeyer's show-stealing creations literally lit up the stage— thousands of LED lights were embedded into jackets for each of the four performers. The jackets were one of the first technologized surfaces to feature in menswear, which zealously incorporated electronic gadgets but has been reluctant to embrace embellishments as flashy as Waldemeyer's.

## Invisibility

Invisible textiles do exist—even if only in fiction, mythology and fairy tales. The concept of invisibility may seem to be the stuff of science fiction, but the belief was held in the Age of Antiquity. In Greek mythology, Hades (meaning the 'unseen') possessed a helmet capable of making the wearer invisible. Invisible fibres were first referenced in the Middle Ages, when a belief in invisible fern seeds was widely held.

Since ferns reproduce from microscopic spores rather than seeds, they were believed to possess magic powers. The fern cloaks of faeries prevented them from being seen, and the magical *tarnkappes* worn by dwarfs made them completely invisible.[7]

Dematerialized surfaces have been revered throughout history, often believed to possess magic powers or reflect an alternate reality. Although they may be hard to see, they are perceptible. They occur naturally as well as artificially. Objects are only visible because light reflects off their surfaces and travels to the spectator's eye. When a surface neither reflects nor absorbs light, the most natural form of invisibility has occurred—that is, light has been able to pass through it. In nature, such surfaces are described as translucent, but none are transparent enough to be truly invisible.

Laws of science dictate that opaque objects cannot be rendered 100 per cent invisible, but the development of metamaterials may enable them to be temporarily cloaked.[8] Metamaterials can deflect radio waves, which leads researchers to believe that they can be manipulated to allow light waves to pass around them also. For a metamaterial to work, the fibres that structure it must be smaller than the wavelength it targets. A human hair, by comparison, would be about 100,000 billionths of a metre across. Once engineered to allow light waves to pass around them, they would leave no visible traces of the objects they conceal. Such materials would, in theory, manipulate the relationship between light and mass to the degree that the cloaked object would not even cast a shadow.

A research team led by Xiang Zhang, a professor at the Nanoscale Science and Engineering Center at the University of California at Berkeley, fabricated objects from metamaterials with surface textures smaller than the wavelength of light.[9] Zhang's team are engineering metamaterials at the nanoscale level, striving to create artificially engineered materials that redirect light, sound and radar waves around an object. The researchers aligned nanometre-scale strands of silver and magnesium fluoride in a net-like structure and created another structure made of nanowires crafted from fibre-like silver particles.[10] The structures were fabric-like in composition, engineered to have fluid-like performance and responsive surfaces. Like a stream of water flowing around a stone, light waves would curve completely around the cloaked object so that, effectively, they flow past it. The light that an onlooker would see would have first encountered the object on the other, nonvisible side, and been artificially channelled around it before coming into view.

A collaborative project between researchers at the Imperial College in London and Duke University in North Carolina is pioneering a similar cloaking surface. Led by Imperial College's Professor Sir John Pendry, the researchers are developing a metamaterial surface that absorbs light heading towards it, and bends the light waves to make them flow smoothly past.[11] The cloaking surface would not be limited to manipulating light rays but would extend to all other field lines, including magnetic ones. Whereas the bulk of current research investigates the technology's applications for defence, the research carried out by Pendry's team indicates that the technology will also be of use in industrial and commercial applications. The strong magnetic field created by an magnetic resonance imaging (MRI) scanner, for example, precludes the use of calibrated instruments and sensitive measuring equipment in its vicinity.[12]

If the scanner could be encircled by a cloaking curtains when in use, its magnetic field could be contained within it. As wearable diagnostic technology becomes more widely used in hospitals, cloaking features would be incorporated in them in order to minimize interference from other wireless systems.

In 2006, the scientists successfully produced a cloak that channelled microwaves of a particular frequency around a copper cylinder in a route that made it seem to dematerialize. Made from metamaterials, the cloak cast a small shadow but was otherwise invisible.

# Hypersurfaces

Efforts to create wearable invisible textiles have led to developments in retroreflective fabrics, near-infrared (NIR) reflectance surfaces and adaptive camouflage clothing. The technologies used to create NIR materials and infrared (IR) filters can create textile coatings that make the wearer undiscernable to the naked eye.[13] Polysulphone plastics block over 99 per cent of the visible white light spectrum, and coatings made from them could cloak the wearer in a so-called black body surface.[14] Black bodies mask the energy radiated over the surface area (known as the black body irradiance), rendering it undetectable to radar-tracking devices. For the time that the wearer was cloaked behind the material, he or she would have a degree of radar invisibility.

Scientists developing defence technology claim that a wearable cloaking surface could be created using the technologies underpinning stealth aircraft.[15] The aircraft is equipped with jamming devices that confound remote sensors, and its surfaces are coated with radar-absorbing dark paint, optical camouflage, and systems that minimize electromagnetic and particle emissions. The combination of technology and surface coatings makes the aircraft virtually undetectable on radar screens. The effect is referred to as 'active camouflage' because it requires energy to render it undetectable. Unlike the metamaterial structures described previously, with active camouflage, electromagnetic radiation is absorbed by the surfaces rather than passing through them or around them.

Research into active camouflage technologies has led to panels and coatings capable of changing colour or luminosity to make an object or individual blend into its surroundings. Although highly technologically advanced, active camouflage systems are a close match to the wearable wireless technologies developed for everyday use. They would rely on similar user-interfaces and energy sources to operate wirelessly, and would eventually be crafted from metamaterials to create switchable surfaces.

Optical camouflage is created from retro-reflective materials, which were developed for highway paints to make them visible at night.[16] Retro-reflective textiles are also characterized by their reflective surfaces, but they also have a higher degree of translucency. They are made in both woven and nonwoven fabrics, and each type incorporates millions of microscopic glass pellets that reflect light, even in conditions when illumination is relatively low. The reflective coatings have a range of different backings, such as woven polyester/cotton, polyester/polyurethane, nylon/polyurethane and nonwoven polyester. The textiles are printed on the back side, creating a graphic surface with no diminishment of light intensity throughout the textile's structure.

The fabrics are similar to active camouflage in their coupling of technological systems and advanced surface materials, but as they do not necessarily set out to cheat sensors and confuse enemy systems, they would be classified as adaptive camouflage by military scientists. One of the best-known examples is the Transparent Cloak, designed by Susumu Tachi, a scientist at Tokyo University and the founding head of the Virtual Reality Society of Japan. Using a special type of retro-reflective fabric, Tachi created a wearable surface that acted as a photographic screen.

The garment was designed to look like an ordinary hooded grey overcoat. It is linked to a camera recording the scenes behind it, which projects the images onto the front of the garment. The effect renders the wearers virtually transparent, because the people in front of them can see the scenery that their body would normally block from view. When seen through a viewfinder, the images on the garment's surface appear to blend seamlessly with their surroundings, creating the impression that the wearer is not there at all. The inspiration behind the garment was born out of virtual reality studies, which typically create a computer-generated environment with no direct relationship to the real world. In a unique twist, the textile's retro-reflective surface places a virtual scene within a physical setting.

Such retro-reflective surfaces have numerous applications in the fields of defence, aerospace, health care, fashion and interior textiles. Tachi and his team describe how surgical gloves made with retro-reflective technology would improve a surgeon's ability to see his or her patient while performing an operation.[17] Often, parts of the patient are obscured by the surgeon's own hands and equipment, but the surfaces Tachi would like to develop would film the patient from the surgeon's palm and project the images onto the back of the hand. Retro-reflective surfaces would be useful for pilots, making the floors of their cockpits appear transparent during landing. Used in interior applications, textiles installed in a windowless room could be designed as retro-reflective surfaces that protected images from beyond the walls that brought the outside in.

In fashion, designers could use the technology to make their dresses seem several sizes smaller, by making the garment's outer edges seem invisible. Manipulating fashion textiles to this extent could also make it possible for designers to create the illusion of extreme silhouettes not normally viable in clothing design. Enabling textiles to see other surfaces would make it possible for them to style themselves and would make it possible for linings and accessories to be better coordinated with garments.

It is often said that a single surface can give rise to multiple interpretations, and the patterns covering them communicate on many different levels. The potentials of new technology promise to radically change the role of textile surfaces forever as they begin to transform them into multifunctional devices. Whereas a textile's surface used to say something about the wearer, innovations like these will probably tell us more about the future than they do about the present.

# Switchable Surfaces

Technologically advanced textiles are transcending their interactive capabilities and becoming entities in themselves. Fashion interfaces, such as those described in Chapter 1, are typically operated by the wearer or triggered by remote commands. The development of surfaces coated in multifaceted molecules enables the fabric to sense and respond to a wide range of conditions it encounters. Known as switchable surfaces, the molecules are engineered to rotate, ripple or form new configurations when they detect atmospheric changes, electric charges or magnetic fields. Like doors that open automatically and close behind those who pass through them, the textiles will sense when to perform an action, and when to return to their original form. A summer jacket, for example, could sense enough humidity in the air to switch to its water-repellent surface, without the wearer noticing any changes at all.

Such surfaces would complement embedded technology perfectly. Woven sensors currently transmit information to specific circuits in order to create changes on the surface. If the surface itself could detect a response or be activated by sensors, the pulse sweeping through it could bypass the rest of the circuitry. The effect would be that of applying a Teflon-like coating to fabric that, when connected to wireless technology, becomes a smart surface automatically. A switchable surface essentially consists of a dense molecule field known as a nanolayer, with each molecule poised to stand at an exact distance from each other. Individual molecules can be engineered to be multisided, have contrasting textures, several colours and varying degrees of pliability. They can be combined with micro-encapsulated chemicals and programmed to release them; conversely, switchable surfaces can also attract other molecules and absorb them in the fibres beneath. As they remove solid particles from the air, the surface also acts as a sophisticated filter.

Robert Langer, a chemical engineer and nanotechnologist based at MIT's Institute for Soldier Nanotechnology, began researching switchable surfaces shortly after he developed a shape-shifting plastic material.[18] The plastic can be bent or squashed into a different shape, yet it will revert automatically to its original form when heat is applied. Langer used the material to create shape-shifting fibres, such as surgical thread capable of forming stitches that tighten themselves and completely disintegrate when the wound has healed. Realizing that the technology could be used to produce whole surfaces, Langer and his team crafted wearable sensors and surfaces capable of medicating the wearer. They also began developing a textile surface that switches colours in order to camouflage soldiers as the terrain surrounding them changes.[19] If the colour of a thread can be controlled by an electrical impulse, manipulating the power frequency and source could be an effective way of reconfiguring the colourways.

Their next project was to create a surface that can change from water attracting to water repelling with the application of a weak electric field. The surface is constructed from molecules engineered to have distinct hydrophobic and hydrophilic areas. The molecules are long and lean, and arranged in a self-assembled monolayer as if they are standing on end. When a positive electrical current is applied, the charge draws the top of the molecules downward, revealing the hydrophobic surface covering their backs. Once the current has been reversed, the molecules straighten to their full height again, leaving only the hydrophilic part exposed.[20]

One of the challenges faced by Langer and his team was finding a way to create the self-assembled monolayer with enough space between molecules to give them enough room to bend forward. Such monolayers usually consists of dense assemblies of molecules packed so tightly together that they have little room to move. Since the monolayer consisted of only a single layer of molecules about one nanometre thick, roughly one-millionth the thickness of a coin, manipulating such an ultra-thin surface proved tricky.[21] The problem was solved by adding so-called hats to each molecule, creating the equivalent of a field of molecular mushrooms. When the hats were removed, the molecules stood at the perfect distance from each other, and the perfect low-density monolayer was formed.[22]

These developments are paving the way for contaminate-aware systems that could absorb or release substances from surfaces on demand. They could also lead to surfaces that are instantly made abrasion resistant, or even armour-like. They could also create a new paradigm of biocompatibility that would adapt the textile for a range of climates and environments. As Langer and his team move forward, they intend to develop surfaces that have a wider range of switchable properties. The complex surfaces that will result could activate several properties simultaneously.

# Textural Interfaces

The boundaries between textiles, product design and architecture are beginning to blur, thanks to a new interdisciplinary platform for textural interfaces. Hayes Raffle, a researcher at the MIT Media Lab, James Tichenor, from the MIT School of Architecture, and Mitchell Joachim, an MIT School of Architecture graduate, joined forces to engineer a system of multidimensional surfaces. Deciding to explore the extent to which the surface of technological devices could be improved by the addition of a textural interface, they developed a technologized membrane for use in a wide range of applications and environments.

Raffle, Tichenor and Joachim invented a new multimodal digital interface covered with an array of touch-sensitive fibre-like actuators that respond to physical gestures. The interface is one of the most groundbreaking interactive surfaces ever created, capable of tracking movement and touch in one area and relaying it among a variety of separate, but interconnected, membranes. Known as Super Cilia Skin (SCS), the membrane is constructed from a technologized surface that merges kinaesthetic input with tactile and visual output. The actuators are based on the fibre-like cilia strands found in the cells of many organisms. In humans, for example, motile cilia are found in the lining of the windpipe, where they sweep mucus and dirt out of the lungs. Each cilium resembles an antenna-like projection extending approximately five to ten micrometers from the cell body. Primary cilia are sensory strands that coordinate larger groups of cellular-signalling conduits. As they transfer information to each other throughout these pathways, they move in undulating, wave-like configurations. Collectively, they constitute an actuated, sensory interface, which is exactly the role that the SCS plays between its technologized surfaces and the environments surrounding them.

'Our early design studies explored density and aspect ratio of the cilia and their tactile responses when anchored in various kinds of membranes,' explained Hayes Raffle, Hiroshi Ishi and James Tichenor in an article written for readers of the academic journal *Textile*.[23] 'Looking to existing examples of textures and natural fields, we found consistent relationships between field and object: a forest, like a tree or a shrub, appears as both surface and structure when viewed at different distances. From an airplane, one notices the surface of the forest canopy. However, as one descends towards the individual trees one notices that tree trunks bifurcate into branches and branches divide into twigs to end with leaves. The change from field to object is an abrupt perceptual shift. We compared these visual perceptual changes to our tactile perception of material texture. By creating both three-dimensional computer models and physical models, we were able to quickly test different shapes and scales of cilia to establish an aesthetically satisfying balance between surface and texture. Since our prototype was designed to be manipulated by people's hands, we chose to make our prototype's cilia slightly smaller than our fingers and to space them with about 50% density. This gave the material a familiar feel.'

Although the SCS is described as a skin, its structure and performance resemble an artificial membrane more than they do the examples of skin-like textiles cited in previous chapters. A membrane is generally regarded to be a structure that creates a barrier between several substances, which can also obstruct certain particles and prevent them from passing through. The SCS has the protective, sensory and tactile functions of skin, but as a digital textural interface, it includes a number of different applications and regimes. As a gateway to information technology, it holds the potential to incorporate multiple surfaces, and make complex switches between information relays.

The SCS's surface is constructed from an elastic membrane covered with an array of felt actuators called 'the cilia', which can be varied in size and scale and made from a range of materials. Whether aligned in a single row or grouped into large clusters, any changes caused by external forces are sensed by the magnetic field surrounding them and are registered by the technology. As a product or clothing interface, small cilia would be engineered to respond to subtle movements created by the fingertips. Sensors would translate the gestures into computer data, which would be communicated to multiple SCS surfaces over a distance. This technology could synchronise movements along all surfaces, triggering them to create an identical response. Raffle, Ishi and Tichenor explain this through the example of a 'smart carpet' consisting of super cilia. A family of tufted carpets would be woven from sensory cilia fibres and linked to each other via a computer interface. When one of the carpets is brushed to smooth its surface, the sweeping movements would be registered in the other carpets, smoothing them also.

Large-scaled industrial-strength cilia can be designed to harness the power of the wind and convert it to electricity, linked like industrial components aligned in a power grid. 'While investigating sensing methods with our prototype, we found that movements of the cilia generate electrical power we could store…for later use,' wrote Raffle, Ishi and Tichenor. 'We imagined SCS as an exterior skin on skyscrapers that could both visualize information as a billboard size display and harness energy of the wind forces that blow over the building's facade. The idea that an alternative energy source can be a visually engaging material rather than a highly engineered object could increase the market for alternative energy.'

The SCS system provides an exciting model for a new generation of smart textiles. Future fibres may be able to collect information, communicate with remote systems and generate energy, while still maintaining the soft surfaces of traditional textiles. These textural interfaces herald an interactive future for all kinds of fabric surfaces, seamlessly united by the technologies of texture and touch.

# Textiles for Virtual Worlds

Once the stuff of science fiction, virtual worlds are becoming a real part of life. As they map out future directions for technology, design, entertainment and marketing, they are also forging new directions for textile design. Many of the software applications used to create virtual spaces are based on fibrous forms; three-dimensional modelling programmes, for example, typically include orthogonal grids that bring woven structures to mind. Software scripts that create randomly configuring animations, automated orthogonal grids and evolutionary algorithms often mimic immersive webs, and textile techniques such as felting and folding are used virtually to create infinite fractals and layered structures.[24]

Textiles' foray into the virtual domain signals a significant shift in the modes through which they are produced and consumed.[25] User interfaces make it possible to create virtual fabric and clothing without having any knowledge of textile design. As virtual textiles are produced for avatars to wear on the body and decorate their environments with, the boundaries between designer and consumer effectively collapse. For the textile designer, virtual environments represent a free space where colour-choices, styles and functionality are not limited to budgetary descriptions and practical concerns.

One of the most innovative developments in textile design has been the application of mathematic algorithms. In virtual reality environments, programmers use mathematical calculations to steer the design process towards random and nonrandom structures and shapes.[26] The textiles that result are actually mathematical descriptions of structures and shapes found in the natural world. Familiar forms such as the clustering of snowflakes, the flocking of birds, the branching patterns of trees and petals unfurling in a blossoming flowers are replicated in geometric shapes. As a grid form, the woven configuration of textile fibres constitutes a spatial index where shapes, lines, points and distances can be plotted mathematically.[27] Intersecting lines in the forms of triangular grids, meshes and orthogonal grids organize mathematical space, and corresponding structures can be found in textile design. Algorithm-based programmes enable designers to conceive textiles as three-dimensional forms, such as extruded polyhedra, dodecahedra, icosidodecahedra and zonohedra. These geometric shapes subvert the idea that a textile should be limited to a two-dimensional plane, and their virtual counterparts are outlining a new paradigm for three-dimensional surfaces in the real world.

Algorithm-based programmes are widely used to design products, interiors and architecture, and they are slowly gaining ground in textiles too. Woven textile structures require the precise manipulation of large amounts of numerical data, the majority of which is binary. Using algorithms as a design technique underpins the textile with the microcomputer data required for machine manufacturing. Despite the efficiency and uniformity with which they can be manufactured, algorithm-based textiles are not homogenous structures. Each design has an individual microstructure, and often has the advantage of structural rigidity.

Although not necessarily algorithm based, three-dimensional materials such as the warp-knitted D3 textile and the 3Weave geometric fabric resemble some of the textiles designed in algorithm-based programmes.[28] Warped-knitted fabrics produced on a Raschel machine (such as those mentioned previously in Chapter 1) are made using a single knitting sequence able to produce interesting textures and surface designs. Known as three-dimensional fabrics, they can be constructed from a variety of polymer- and natural-based fibres, with polyester, nylon, and spandex being the most popular. The space between the layers can be specified within a range of parameters, and the surface textures can be varied from centre to edge. A composite textile, 3Weave is created according to a specific weave geometry that allows for ten or more yarn layers.[29] The result is a thick preformed textile, usually made from glass, carbon or aramid fibres.

Also born out of algorithm software, the fabric patterns created by Swedish artist and designer Pierre Proske are based on evolution algorithms, intended to make the design process semiautomatic. Using software to create voice-activated, repeating visual units, Proske was able to transform voice patterns into fabric motifs. Proske engineered repeating loops and analytical frequencies to create an algorithm that identifies distinct aspects of an individual's voice and represent them visually. The process is both random and unique; it makes it possible to produce patterns that the designer/user could not create on his or her own, which are also impossible to replicate again. Involving users in the design methodology enables them to participate in the creative process and share authorship of the finished product with the designer. It also invokes questions of authorship, where the designer no longer assumes responsibility for the finished product.

The process of creating the patterns unfolds virtually in audiovisual software. Users speak into the microphone, and watch as the algorithms match their speech patterns with clusters of shapes. Technically speaking, these are abstract representations of the person's vocal frequency. The voice's basic acoustic unit is called a phoneme, and the visual equivalent is called a viseme, which is a facial expression that can represent a particular sound. Every word and turn of phrase spoken causes the clusters to move, bond together, reconfigure and overlay. The motifs that result exist as virtual structures before they become real in the form of printed textiles.

The human voice is as unique as DNA, and is capable of being translated into algorithms that encode it mathematically. The art and design enterprise known as DNA11 created a platform for transforming human DNA into bespoke artworks; Proske's forum for textile design is comparable.[30] The procedure can be of considerable help to professional designers, as it can produce patterns they would not or could not create themselves. Proske has adapted the technology to create a user-friendly interface that can be implemented with no previous preparation on the part of the designer/user. The textile that results destabilizes the accepted view that a surface motif is a fixed entity, showing that it has the potential to become animate. As today's textile designers pioneer new types of surface motifs, Proske's work outlines a new paradigm for sensorially stimulated surfaces. A garment covered in patterns programmed to move in response to the wearer's speech, movements or even heartbeat may create a hypertext that replaces the written words used in conventional languages.[31]

# Second Life

The virtual world known as Second Life, like its counterpart Entropia Universe, is accessed via the Internet, where its users, called residents, interact with each other through avatars.[32] The sites mirror the real world in many ways. Commercial enterprises, cultural institutions and governmental departments use them to create public and private spaces for communication, collaboration, market research and training. Virtual goods are designed and manufactured on the site, where they can be bought sold, exchanged and hired.[33] Avatars can buy clothing, fashion items and textiles along with a wide variety of other virtual goods such as property, vehicles, devices, art and animations.

Second Life provides users with an online platform unlike any other, where many of the best features of the Web, online gaming, community networks, user-generated content, creative applications and telecommunications technologies, merge. Easy-to-use three-dimensional modelling tools are built into the software. The scripts are typically based around simple geometric shapes that allow residents to build virtual objects and simulate three-dimensional surfaces. They can be used in combination with a scripting programme called Linden Scripting Language in order to add functionality to objects. Sculpted Prims, the algorithms used to create complex textural shapes which are colloquially known as 'sculpties', can be used to render surfaces that are not normally possible to create within Second Life's prim system. Sculpt Textures are typically used to create novel surfaces for clothing and textiles. They are similar to standard maps, but instead of encoding the default textures known as surface normals,

In Second Life, avatars can shop for fabric or experience textiles in new ways. The Multisheer three-dimensional virtual textile created by Kate Goldsworthy is exhibited at Textile Futures Island in Second Life for avatars to enjoy.

they encode complex compositions called surface positions. All events in Second Life take place in real time, giving collaborative works a dynamic edge.

A survey of the virtual textiles designed by users for fashion and interior fabrics reveals a surprising mixture of real materials and otherworldly forms. Some avatars convert digital photos and designs made in popular graphics applications into a Second Life-compatible format and import them to the Second Life servers. All images can acquire textures, or skins. Many of these reproduce traditional fabrics found in the real world, which have been altered to create alternative colourways or different motifs. Users create unique effects by uploading their own textures and manipulating them through the appearance settings built in to the Second Life creative tools set.

Many Second Life users design fashion and textiles for their own use, and some create them for others. Imbuing avatars with virtual style seems just as important as self-fashioning is in the real world. Residents flock to in-world stores to buy garments, hairstyles, avatar skins and accessories. The fabrics worn in Second Life seem to perform differently than real textiles. They generally have a higher degree of elasticity than their real-life equivalents. Form-fitting fashion fabrics cling to the wearer without straps and other supports, holding their positions perfectly despite

The practitioners, researchers and technologists active in textile research can use the Second Life platform to promote new work and expand their audiences. The London-based Textile Futures Research Group now has a global presence thanks to Second Life, where they bought their own island and built an exhibition space to showcase their works.

their gravity-defying arrangements. With their extreme elasticity, standard-sized casual wear takes on the close-fitting silhouettes of Lycra swimwear, evoking fabric technology that clings and supports. Some domains have fantastic landscapes of textured surfaces that push the boundaries of real-life design. Like the textile forms created by evolutionary algorithm-based applications, virtual fabrics can comprise a kaleidoscope of colours and surreal surfaces. Techniques seldom seen in textiles design feature in Second Life. Patchwork-like fabric designs have no overlapping seams, bringing tessellation to mind.[34]

Seams are rarely visible in Second Life, suggesting tube-like textiles that were engineered as seamless sheaths.[35] Skin itself is manufactured in Second Life and offered for sale—perhaps portending biologically engineered membranes that will be styled and sized for users by haptic scientists and textile practitioners.[36] Although the vast majority of textiles are worn skin-tight, there are also structured shapes that hold their silhouettes independently of the body—these would require lightweight, rigid fabrics. Some types of textile forms appear to have been crafted from diaphanous materials with a vapour-like consistency. Clothing made from floating spheres evoke textile

This is a close-up of a Multisheer virtual textile created by Kate Goldsworthy and animated by Andrew Sides. It is exhibited at the Textile Futures Research Group's island in Second Life.

components suspended in antigravitational fields, as do the dematerialized meshes that cocoon wearers in otherworldly silhouettes. Pieces of granite, shards of glass and barbed wire are incorporated into textiles and worn comfortably against the skin, requiring Kevlar-like fabrics that are both slash-proof and protective.

Fashion designers, textile practitioners, researchers and technologists use the Second Life platform to develop and promote new work and expand their audiences. Research-led companies such as Philips Design have established a presence in Second Life and have even formed a department in their headquarters to manage their virtual counterpart. The London-based Textile Futures Research Group now has a global presence thanks to Second Life, where they bought their own island, and designed and built an exhibition space to show their works.[37] In addition to creating a novel platform for showcasing their textiles, they have also established a global forum in which to discuss specific aspects of the member's work.

Second Life offers textile professionals and amateur designers an unlimited virtual canvas for imaginative expression. These dematerialized views of textiles enable us to examine them in a context free of preconceptions about how textiles should look and feel. Virtual space has introduced another textile domain, a delocalized in the infinity of the screen. Neither here nor there, neither then nor now, their virtual surfaces have intensively and extensively transformed the meaning of the surface as barrier.

Virtual textiles constitute an aspect of reality that is not material but which is real, nonetheless. As nontouchable, nontextural and immaterial, the fabrics in Second Life represent a kind of surface effect only visible on the screen. They are real without being actual, and material without being physical. Now that the design tools for creating new textiles are a part of the public domain, the forms that result promise to anchor virtual textures to future worlds.

# Feature Interview: Jane Harris

The spectral textiles Jane Harris designs have a powerful impact in the physical world. Although they are entirely virtual, their drape, movement and performance are life-like enough to be real. Harris uses motion capture technology to track, record and translate the movement of fabric into digital representations, taking them far beyond the limitations of the physical world.[38] As she does so, Harris is aligning textiles with a range of imaging technologies that hold the potential to create whole new paradigms of fashion design.

Harris fashions virtual textiles into realistic garments that flow with the movements of a virtual wearer, whose body remains invisible. The garments are created though software applications such as Alias | Wavefront Maya, VICON Optical Motion Capture, Photoshop and After Effects. Imaging devices, such as three-dimensional body scanners, also factor into the process. Before Harris renders the virtual garment, she uses motion capture technology to map the movements and reflexes of the human body. The data that results is used to animate the computer graphic garment later on.

'I usually work with a dancer or an actor so that I can explore a wider range of human motions than those typically seen on the catwalk,' Harris explains.[39] The motion capture process takes place in a darkened studio where a series of infrared cameras are positioned around the room. The subject wears a form-fitting black body suit with retro-reflective markers attached at the joints. The cameras pick up the light reflected by the markers and relay it to the software, where the motion appears as an animated, skeleton-like figure. The figure's movements are translated into computer data that forms a mesh-like digital grid, which seamlessly integrates the motions of a spectral body with the folds and drape of a virtual textile. 'Even though the subject is completely invisible, the data is so accurate that I can actually recognize the gait and posture of an individual we've recorded,' Harris says. 'It's such a fantastic tool.'

The forms that result resemble empathic objects, responding to their virtual environments exactly as a real garment would, reacting and adapting to touch, movement, changes in light and the addition of further layers. They reverse fashion's traditional relationship to embodiment, revealing that a garment can exist as an entity in its own right, whether the wearer is present or not.

Although textiles formed alliances with digital media several decades ago, their potential to be rendered through three-dimensional imaging technologies, motion capture and animation software has remained relatively unexplored. While conducting her PhD research at the Royal College of Art, Harris, currently Professor of Digital Design at Kingston University, identified new kinetic relationships between textiles and technology.[40] 'At the time, technology's role within fashion design was considered to be a known quantity,' Harris says, 'but I could see that many types of emerging graphics software could have relevance in the field. As I looked at the technologies used by animators, architects, filmmakers and medical researchers, I realised that they could also be used to design fashion and fabricate materials digitally, as well as create representations of historic garments. The technologies also provide a new platform for presenting garments. Just as an avant-garde garment may only be made for presentation on the catwalk, a virtual fashion "showpiece" will only ever exist on the screen.'[41]

Harris's research has culminated in a number of groundbreaking projects, such as the collaboration with designer Shelley Fox and computer graphic operator Mike Dawson. In 2003 Harris, Fox and Dawson teamed up to produce a virtual version of Fox's Balloon top, a sleekly, sculptural blouse based on a hollow, spherical form.[42] 'The virtual version of the blouse shows it evolving from a flat, balloon-like form into a 3-dimensional garment,' Harris says. 'You can see it morph from the initial shape to how it looks when worn.' The sequence reveals aspects of the garment beyond its shape and relationship to the body, giving the viewer an understanding of the inspiration behind it and the concepts underpinning its construction. 'Showing the virtual version of an individual garment or an entire collection is a new way of presenting them to the public,' Harris says. 'The virtual garment can be a dramatic showcase in itself, providing the viewer with a unique alternative to the catwalk presentation. There's also huge potential for designers to explore creative ideas digitally in ways they can't do physically. Virtual or real time spaces such as Second Life or Entropia Universe can also provide alternative presentation and commercial showcases for fashion and textiles.'

The technologies used to create the Balloon top's virtual counterpart have advanced dramatically in recent years, but at the time, it took more than three months to complete the garment. 'Shelley was generous with her time, because this was a new field for her and it took a number of discussions to achieve the right approach,' Harris explains. 'It would be fantastic to collaborate with her again, or a designer such as Boudicca or McQueen. Although the technology is still in development it is moving forward quickly. The process can still be labour-intensive, meaning that a challenging digital collection pushing the boundaries of the software would have to be conceived of months in advance in order to finish the virtual work in time for an event like Fashion Week.'

Harris's work can breathe new life into old textiles, creating virtual versions of historical garments too delicate to be worn or too fragile to be exhibited. With funding from Britain's Arts and Humanities Research Council, she recreated an eighteenth-century Spitalfields silk dress from the Museum of London's collection, modelling it virtually so that visitors could see how it would appear when worn.[43] 'I wanted to make the garment move exactly as it would have in the eighteenth-century,' Harris

Jane Harris created a virtual version of Shelley Fox's Balloon top. The virtual version of the blouse shows viewers how the design evolved from a flat, balloon-like form into a three-dimensional garment.

explains, 'so for the Motion Capture sequence we dressed the subject, Ruth Gibson, in a corset, crinoline and wooden two-inch heels to emulate what Georgian women wore. The dress itself consisted of five fabric layers involving a crinoline, underskirt, side panels, lace trim and a train. It was technically quite challenging to recreate such a complex, five-tiered form virtually, because each layer had to be rendered individually. As the garment moved, the crinoline constantly touched the inside of the fabric, and the lace trim at the sleeves fluttered continuously. It took a lot of skill to recreate those movements, because computerised cloth simulation tends to behave like cling film, and the garment we were representing was characterised by volume and drape. So to emulate the interaction of these layers accurately, all five surfaces had to recognise each other mathematically, otherwise the entire dress would not function recognisably.'

By taking textiles into a virtual space, Harris is mapping the past and charting future directions for fashion. Harris's work makes it possible to use textiles as a means of exploring space and time and establishing new rapports with practitioners in a wide array of disciplines. Her virtual fabrics are not mere simulations of objects that exist

Jane Harris uses motion capture technology to track, record and translate the movement of fabric into digital representations. The garments she creates are entirely virtual, but their drape and movement are lifelike enough to be real.

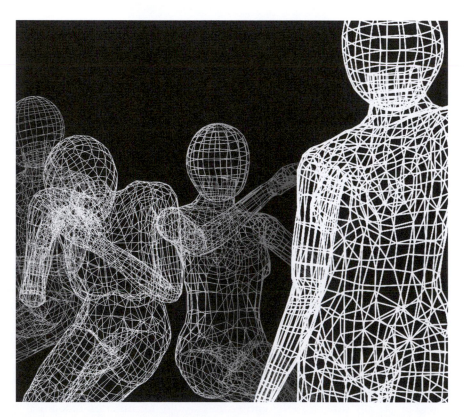

Harris also uses motion capture technology to translate the movements of the fashioned body into an animated skeleton-like figure. The subject's movements are translated into computer data that forms a mesh-like digital grid, which seamlessly integrates the motions of a spectral body with the folds and drape of the virtual textile.

but creations that challenge perceptions of what is real. As Harris strives to make her virtual fabrics lifelike, her work reflects the role of artifice that pervades fashion on so many levels. 'Fabric and form have beguiling qualities that intrigue the designer and onlooker alike,' she says. 'The challenge was never to make virtual garments seem real, but like fashion itself, believable.'

# four

## Vital Signs

Textiles are having profound effects on our lives today, radically reinventing the way we fashion our bodies and decorate our interiors. One of the most revolutionary developments is taking place in health care, where textiles are sculpting bodies from within, delivering medication through the skin and even diagnosing ailments. Fibre-based implants take medical textiles to the extreme, dramatically altering the body's texture and shape. Fabrics, in the form of subdermal mesh and knitted vascular grafts, are promoting new tissue growth and replacing human arteries. Medical textiles are improving patient care and speeding up recovery, and textiles are now capable of saving life too.

Health care textiles and smart bandages are beginning to shrug off the clinical aesthetic that characterizes medical fabrics. Collaborations between physicians and textile designers are resulting in bandages and braces that resemble mainstream fashion more than forensic instruments. Patients want to resume normal life as soon as they can, without the uncomfortable bulk and clinical look of bandages. The shift from sickness to wellness can happen more quickly when patients focus more on recovery than on illness. Studies have shown that mental attitude is an important factor in the healing process, and bandages that enable patients to look normal allow them to see themselves as well rather than sick.

Patients need to recuperate in comfort, and advances in health care textiles are creating fabrics that perform efficiently and look good. Textiles used in seating and bedding to reduce discomfort and promote improved circulation can also wick away perspiration and heal wounds. The development of diagnostic fabrics makes it possible to monitor a patient's condition remotely and check their vital signs in an unobtrusive way. Sensors can be integrated into clothing, cushions, mattresses, blankets and wheelchairs, where they record temperature and heart rate and detect changes in the

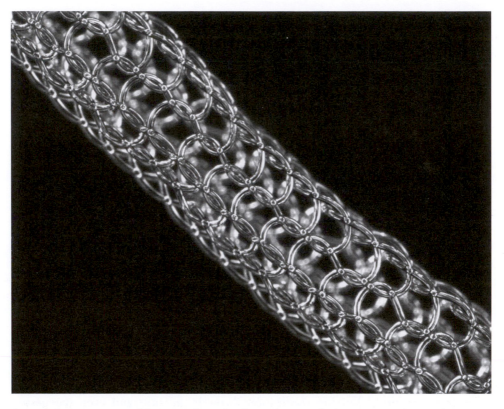

Australia's Commonwealth Scientific and Industrial Research Organisation (CSIRO) promotes biocompatible fibres for neural repairs (such as the knitted microtube shown here) and re-growth of human tissue.

patient's condition. Diagnostic textiles also have applications as blood pressure cuffs and wearable scanning devices, and they can be crafted into splints, braces, bandages and operating theatre fabrics.

Colour is finding a new role in health care textiles as the medical profession accepts that it can have healing properties. Hospital environments are usually characterized by soothing pastel tones, but now they promise to imbibe tenets of colour therapy. As such colours brighten up health care centres, they promise to lift the patients' spirits and help their bodies heal quicker. The regenerative effects of colour are transforming clinical environments, making them look—and feel—better than ever before.

## Antimicrobial Fabrics

Killing off deadly bacteria may have kept biologists busy in the past, but today, textile practitioners are the ones repelling bugs.[1] The integration of antibacterial and

antifungal substances into fibres imbues textiles with powerful antimicrobial properties, enabling them to repel germs or kill them completely. The fabrics that result can
neutralize odours and deodorize the wearer, create antiseptic environments and even
enable the textiles to clean themselves. Effects like these are created by processes that
coat polymers and monofilaments with silver ions and incorporate biocide agents
such as triclosan into the fibres.[2] Filaments may also be bonded with zeolite molecules,
a process that forms a molecular sieve to trap impurities.

Antimicrobial textiles were first developed for medical applications, such as surgical
smocks, hospital gowns, sterile fabrics, bedding and bandages. Biosafe, one of the first
antimicrobial fabrics to be widely used, was woven from nylon filament yarns embedded with microscopic ceramic spheres bound chemically to the fibres.[3] Biosafe's fibres
release a constant stream of silver ions that destroy some harmful bacteria on contact
or inhibit the growth of others. Because the antimicrobes are embedded deep within
the fibres, they withstand repeated washing. Their applications for sportswear and un-
derwear brought them into mainstream fashion, where they are typically mixed with a
range of other natural and synthetic fibres. Similarly, AgUARDIAN fabric, developed
by Sommers in collaboration with AgION Technologies, contains microencapsulated
silver embedded in knit polyester fibres.[4] The silver is bound to a durable polyurethane coating that makes it antimicrobial and antifungal continuous.

Many other antimicrobial textiles are also treated with coatings that kill bacteria.[5]
A coating of nanoparticles derived from silver oxide, for example, is especially effective against staphylococcus germs, killing them within thirty minutes of contact.[6]
Compared to the toxic arsenic- and cyanide-based biocides that may be used otherwise, nontoxic silver oxide is a much more environmentally friendly material. The
high-performance X-Static fibre is silver coated, created by binding silver to nylon
yarn. The fibre that results is conductive, reflective, antimicrobial, anti-odour, antistatic
and insulating.[7] Depending on the application, the fibres may contain up to 15 per
cent pure silver. X-Static has been tested for medical uses by major institutions, such
as the US Environmental Protection Agency, the National Institutes of Health, Johns
Hopkins University and Cornell University. X-Static has been shown to eliminate 99.9 per cent of bacteria in less than one hour of contact, and its antimicrobial
performance does not diminish after 250 washes.

When nanostructured silver is combined with titanium, the synergy between them
considerably heightens their individual antimicrobial qualities. When titanium dioxide (TiO2) is exposed to light, a photocatalytic effect is created that breaks down dirt.
The nanostructured silver is antimicrobial on its own but is even more effective when
exposed to a light source to increase the photocatalytic effect. The antimicrobial
impact of the silver and titanium combination becomes even stronger when they are
bonded with voriconazole, making the fibres virtually bacteria resistant.[8] The compound is usually applied to a mix of synthetic fibres. When added to a polyester and
spandex mix, the fabric may be washed over 50 times with no loss of antibacterial or
self-cleaning properties.

Known for their powerful antimicrobial properties, submicrometre silver particles
made from nanostructured silver compounds are widely used in medical textiles.

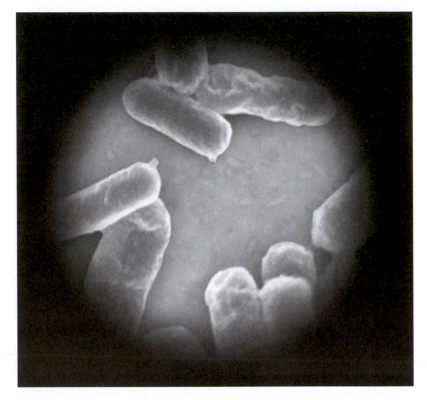

DuPont's DNA-based BAX system can be combined with fibre technology to detect the presence of bacteria, enabling food industry workers to identify strains such as E. coli (shown here) which can cause food poisoning.

Silver particles are chemically bonded to the surfaces of textiles to prolong the efficacy of the protection, making the antimicrobial effect permanent. The small size of the particles creates a larger surface area than most other compounds, providing more protection for the textile's surface even though less antimicrobial material is used. The SmartSilver range of antimicrobial additives for polyester and 100 per cent cotton produced by NanoHorizons is one of the most popular antibacterial surfaces for textiles, upholstery and other flexible materials.[9]

The demand for alternatives to metallic antimicrobial compounds has inspired researchers to explore a range of other substances. Crabyon fabrics are a blend of natural and synthetic fibres intermixed with chitosan, a product derived from chitin, a natural extract from crab shells and shellfish.[10] The similarity between fibrous cellulose and chitosan makes it possible to blend the two together easily. The cotton and viscose fabrics that result are easy to dye and retain their soft textures even after the antimicrobial processing is completed.

BamBreeze is a four-way elastic textile made mostly from bamboo fibre synthesized from hydrolyzed bamboo pulp. Initially developed to be a hypoallergenic fabric, the bamboo's enzymes imbue the fabric with antibacterial and anti-odour textile

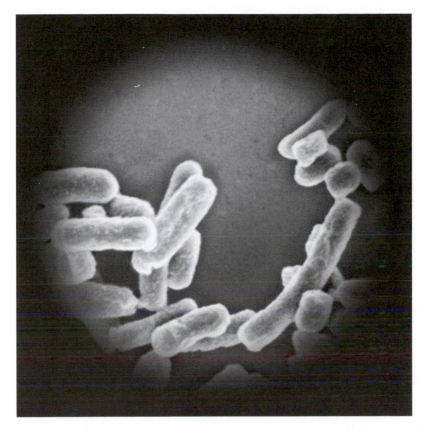

A range of nonwoven textile surfaces and environmental filters combined with DuPont's BAX system were able to detect the Listeria bacteria (shown here) and treat it with a safe sanitizer before it spread.

properties. The bamboo fibre is typically mixed with 48 per cent cotton and 2 per cent spandex, and can be dyed almost any colour. The fabric's antimicrobial properties, together with its allowance for moisture absorption and release, make it a perfect choice for swimwear lining and intimate apparel.

Textiles researchers at the PSG College of Technology in Coimbatore, India have identified naturally occurring antimicrobes in neem, pomegranate rind and chaff flower and incorporated them in fibres.[11] By drying them and reducing them to fine powders, then treating them in a methanol process, these researchers created active antimicrobial substances that limited the growth of microbes on textile substrates.

As well as being made antiviral and antifungal, antimicrobial fabrics can also be embedded with nanocapsules to render them insecticidal.[12] ZeroFly waterproof sheeting is woven from flat, high density polyethylene (HDPE) yarns and coated with a low density polyethylene (LDPE) laminate on both sides. The sheeting is impregnated with insecticide throughout, so that the chemical can constantly migrate to the surfaces. UV protectors ensure that the chemical maintains its effectiveness even in

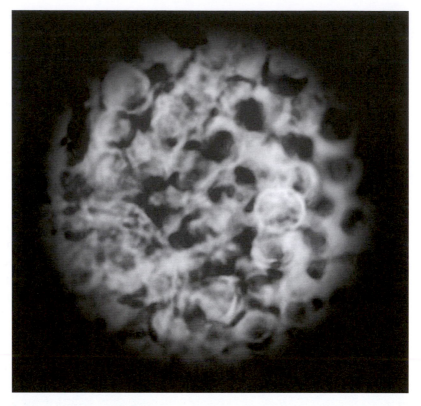

DuPont is developing fibres for use in food production and packaging that can combat the yeast and mould cultures (like those shown here) that cause food products to spoil.

hot temperatures and strong UV conditions. ZeroFly is also waterproof, tear proof and lightweight, making it a good choice for use in disaster relief. ZeroFly was mass distributed in the Indian Ocean tsunami in 2004, the Pakistan earthquake in 2005 and widely used in refugee centres in Darfur.[13]

As textile designers broaden their knowledge of science to create sophisticated textiles, the microorganisms they're tackling are developing the intelligence to out-smart them. Microbial intelligence (also known as bacterial intelligence) is the term used to describe the complex adaptive behaviour shown by single microorganisms and the collaborative colonies that large populations of them create. Complex cells, like protozoa or algae, show remarkable abilities to organize themselves in changing cir-cumstances, but even bacteria, which have limited abilities as isolated cells, can adapt and evolve to counteract the substances that combat them. In a manner similar to how molecules link to create the unbroken membrane of a switchable surface, bacteria form a biofilm to garner strength in numbers and create a protective barrier.

Making textiles that are continually bacteria resistant may prove to be a difficult task, since in the long run, antimicrobial compounds will have to change as the bacteria become immune to their effects. The discovery of Strain 121, a deadly single-cell bacteria that survives autoclave temperatures, has lead scientists to conclude that there are other bacteria, viruses, fungi and spores that are not destroyed by autoclaving. This has made antimicrobial textiles a huge growth area for scientific researchers, health care specialists and textile practitioners. Researchers at Japanese enzyme laboratory Rakuto Kasei are pioneering new paradigms for antimicrobial textiles by developing fibres coated in friendly bacteria to deter toxic ones.[14] By incorporating strains such as the bacillus subtilis natto, which has natural antifungal and antibiotic properties, to fabric fibres, a uniquely contaminate-resistant textile may result.

# Biotextiles

High tech fibres have a radical reputation. Textiles are credited with redesigning the world around us, but few realize that they are restructuring the human body too. Fabric is literally getting under our skin, where it creates artificial organs and synthetic body parts. Biotextiles are used to construct implants, repair hernias, create arterial grafts and grow artificial skin. Surgical sutures are made from biofibres, and nanofibres are used to build the fibrous scaffolds that facilitate the growth of human skin.

The development of biocompatible polymers has made it possible to create inert fibres that the human body recognizes as its own. Biocompatible fibres are used in regenerative medicine, such as for neural repairs and regrowth of human tissue. The interdisciplinary science of biomechatronics, which aims to augment the body by integrating mechanical elements in it, comprises aspects of biology, mechanics, electronics and fibre technology. Artificial hearts contain metallic parts but also textile membranes, polyurethane tubes and woven filaments. Pacemakers are also fitted with fibres to form the atrial and ventricular leads that connect electrodes to the main part of the unit.

Surgical mesh is also used to synthesize artificial skin products and has drastically improved burn victims' chances of survival. Sheets of flexible mesh are placed over open wounds to encourage growth of the bottom layer of skin, which does not regenerate under normal circumstances. Surgeons can then transplant small pieces of the patient's epidermis, the top layer of skin, which grows and spreads over the newly-grown dermis beneath. Nanotechnology is creating breakthroughs in the creation of living tissue, leading researchers to conclude that it will soon be possible to transplant masks of live skin directly onto a burn victim's face. Electro-spinning, a technique for creating nonwoven fabrics with nanoscale fibres, creates customized shapes that support the growth of cells that produce new skin.[15] By grafting the patient's own skin onto a mask moulded on the shape of his or her face, the skin could attach more easily.

Endowing implants with neurosensing abilities decreases the risk of them being rejected by the body and enhances their ability to establish sensitive connections with the body's nerves. Fibre technology is being used internally to augment the body's primary transmission lines to improve joint mobility and muscle activity. Externally,

The Flex-Foot is a high performance carbon-fibre prosthetic foot suitable for all ages and levels of activity. Carbon fibre surpasses other materials in flexibility and support, enabling the user to move quickly and comfortably.

Orthopaedic specialists Össur use bionic technology and carbon fibres to make modern prosthesis more advanced, subsequently imbuing them with a level of performance that was previously unimaginable.

fibres are being engineered to create prosthetic devices. The most sophisticated model produced to date is the Cheetah Flex-Foot carbon composite prosthetic, worn by amputee world champion sprinter Oscar Pistorius, who is the first ever Paralympian to win gold in each of the 100-, 200- and 400-metre sprints. Pistorius's carbon fibre prostheses were so sophisticated that in 2008, the International Association of Athletics Federations banned him from competing against able-bodied runners on the grounds that the prostheses give him a technical advantage.

Muscle reinforcement techniques use synthetic fibres to create mesh prosthesis. Meshes made from polypropylene and polytetrafluoroethylene (PTFE) fibres are used to support weakened tissue so that they do not over-stretch and disintegrate further.

PTFE mesh combines a high degree of strength with a high degree of suppleness. It is soft to the touch and conforms easily to three-dimensional profiles. In the case of anterior repair, the mesh is inserted over the injured muscle to support it. In the case of posterior repair, the mesh is placed underneath the muscle to prop it up. The application of mesh pulls the muscles together without relying on tension to hold them in place, creating a uniquely tension free method that has a lower percentage of injury recurrences and a faster recovery period than what was possible with older suture repair methods. Mesh fabrics are also used to manufacture devices such as hernia mesh, stress urinary incontinence slings and vaginal prolapse suspenders. Polyester felt and PTFE felt fabrics are used to craft suture pledgets, suture line buttresses, septal defect plugs and catheter cuffs.

Use of fibre technology contributes to the development of advanced prosthetic devices for sports, such as running and sprinting.

Biotextiles can sculpt the body in a number of ways. Although they were initially restricted to reconstructive surgeries, biotextiles have found a bigger market in breast augmentation today.

Textiles sculpt the body in a number of ways. Reconstructive surgeries use polyester mesh to reshape damaged tissue and create a framework to facilitate the growth of the body's own cells. Knitted mesh fabrics are composed of multifilament and monofilament yarns to produce small textiles that reinforce veins and arteries. Polyester mesh fabrics are also used in medical device applications, such as surgical mesh and wound dressing. The polyethylene filament know as Dyneema Purity provides high strength fibres for medical implants and sutures.[16] Dyneema Purity is an oriented, crystalline polyethylene continuous filament yarn. Tensile strength-versus-denier comparisons have shown it to be fifteen times stronger than drawn steel wire. Because Dyneema

Maxi Mounds holds the Guinness World Record for the World's Largest Augmented Breasts. Miss Mounds's implants are formed by polypropylene string, one of the fibre-based implants that provides an alternative to silicone.

Purity is resistant to most acids and alkalis and does not absorb water, it is a perfect material for implants. Its fibres are thinner than filaments made from metals or polymers, resulting in faster recovery times.

Breast implants are a big area these days, and researchers are exploring the extent to which fibre-based implants can provide alternatives to silicone. Textiles have formed a part of breast implants since the Cronin-Gerow implants were developed in 1961. They were made of pear-shaped silicone rubber envelopes filled with viscous silicone gel. They were with lined with Dacron in order to attach them more firmly to body tissue, and therefore reduce the risk of the implants rotating.[17] In the 1970s, breast implants were redesigned to be softer and more lifelike by diluting the gel and using thinner shells. They had a tendency to rupture, and subsequently received a polyurethane foam coating. Polyurethane implants were briefly banned in the United States when researchers thought polyurethane implants may have had carcinogenic effects.

Polypropylene is used to create the highly controversial breast implant known as polypropylene string implants, developed in the late 1990s. The implants were designed to produce extreme sizes, resulting in cartoon-like, super-size breasts popular among some women active in the adult entertainment industry. Yarn-like polypropylene fibres are used because they cause irritation to the implant pocket, initiating the production of body fluid, which fills them on a continual basis. The polypropylene fibres absorb water very slowly, causing continuous expansion of the breast after surgery. Due to the medical complications associated with them, the implants have been banned in the European Union and United States.

# Diagnostic Textiles

The demand for textiles capable of monitoring the body's vital signs has created a new direction for fibre technology. Diagnostic fabrics provide an unobtrusive method of recording temperature, heart rate, respiration and blood pressure, and they can also track the patient's movements. As researchers develop techniques that incorporate sensors into fabric seamlessly, they are also pioneering wireless garments that monitor the wearer in a range of everyday situations. In the case of patients who have been immobilized, diagnostic fabric could be used as bed linen or made into upholstery, transmitting the patients' vital signs to medical personnel in real time. They may even be able to detect critical conditions and activate an emergency alert system that sends help to the patient immediately.

The conductive filament known as Textro-yarn is crafted with a Lycra fibre at its core, encircled by fine strands of conductive metals such as copper wire and silver-coated nylon. It can be woven or knitted and still retain its conductive properties after being subjected to normal textile processing. The fibrous cables known as Textro-interconnects are embedded with electronic wiring.[18] They are made with commercial conductors and standard connectors and are washable, sewable and stretchable. Several versions of the cables are available, some with as many as six conductors per inch, and in widths ranging from one-half inch to fifteen inches. As the Lycra fibre stretches, it pulls the conductors into a straight position, giving the yarn maximum elasticity without breaking the conductive wiring. Textro-interconnects performs well in virtually every wearable application; the cables' extreme durability enables them to withstand twisting, stretching, bending, folding and vibrating.

Sundaresan Jayaraman, the researcher behind the Georgia Institute of Technology's SmartShirt described in Chapter 1, created an electronic fabric by blending natural filaments and gossamer wires with optic fibres. Sensatex, a life science technology company focused on the development of electronic textile systems, acquired the rights to develop the SmartShirt specifically for medical applications.[19] The garment features a patented conductive fibre/sensor system designed to monitor and transmit biometric information from the wearer to a base station. Heart rate, respiration and body temperature are all calibrated and relayed in real time for analysis by medical staff.

The SmartShirt promised to be the first wearable wireless monitoring device. Its technology enables the conductive fibres to form a network into which sensors and electronic devices can be connected. They form a flexible bus structure that widens the range of applications that can connect it to. Not only could the data bus transmit information to monitoring devices such as an EKG machine, it can also be linked to environmental controls that will enhance the patient's comfort levels.

The SmartShirt provides an interface between medical personnel and their patients that promises to revolutionize health care. Just as the data bus can relay information between the wearer and the base, it can also transmit data back to the fabric's sensors to effect changes in the wearer's condition. Because patients can be monitored remotely, they will have greater privacy and be able to convalesce in their own homes.

Diagnostic textiles may someday be able to prevent sudden infant death syndrome (SIDS), the phenomenon commonly known as cot death. A collaboration between Belgian company Verhaert Design and Development and the University of Brussels has resulted in a new type of pyjamas that continuously monitor a baby's vital signs.[20] Known as the Mamagoose pyjamas, the garment has five fabric-embedded sensors positioned over the chest and abdomen to monitor the baby's heartbeat and breathing. An algorithm frequency is transmitted through the sensors to scan the baby's breathing pattern. Breathing abnormalities are detected immediately and relayed to a control unit to activate an alarm. The system was developed from the wearable pulmonary plethysmographs created to monitor astronauts' vital signs while in space, which researchers adapted especially for health care use.

The emerging field of remote care known as telemedicine makes it possible to monitor patients, athletes and combat soldiers via telephone, the Internet or other networks.[21] Telemedicine was initially developed for the purpose of consulting, but trials have proven that remote medical procedures and examinations are also possible and successful. The systems rely on wearable sensors fitted in exact positions to monitor patients in postoperative recovery. The technology can also be used to detect injuries in astronauts, athletes, law enforcement officers and combat soldiers. The SmartShirt can be sized to fit individuals of all ages. When worn by babies, it could alert carers to the symptoms of SIDS in time to take action.

Textronic Inc, a leading developer of wearable sensors for fitness and health monitoring, created the NuMetrex range of heart-sensing sportswear.[22] The garments are made from fabrics that incorporate heart-sensing fibres seamlessly into the textile. The Heart Sensing Sports Bra, introduced in 2005, was the first garment in the NuMetrex range to be released. The bra resembles a sleeveless tank top, and features a fabric support shelf where electronic sensing technology was integrated to monitor the heart rate. A small transmitter was fitted into a pocket in the shelf to transmit data to a monitoring device. The next NuMetrex garment to be released was the Heart Sensing Racer Tank, a sports top made of nylon Lycra with a second-skin fit. It provided the same seamless heart rate monitoring capabilities as the Heart Sensing Sports Bra, also providing a comfortable alternative to the belts, straps and other heart-sensing devices that position hard components against the skin.

Textronic Inc also produced the Cardio Shirt for Men as part of the NuMetrex range. The shirt provides men with an alternative to the cumbersome chest straps that monitor heart rate. It was constructed from a high tech wicking fabric made with integrated sensory fibres. The shirt is sleeveless and can be worn alone or as a first layer. The shirt's conductive fabric moves comfortably with the body, detecting the heartbeat and sending it to a compatible cardio machine via a transmitter inserted into the shirt's pocket. The NuMetrex range includes a variety of transmitters that can be attached directly to the garments or worn as wristwatches.

Garments such as the Heart Sensing Sport Bra, the Heart Sensing Racer Tank and the Cardio Shirt for Men could also be used by athletes to monitor fitness levels during training and sports competitions. They would create a better understanding of how to maximize endurance levels and would emit warnings if an athlete's vital signs became critical.

## Wearable Technology

Health care researchers regard robotic exoskeletons to be the prosthetics of the future, anticipating that they will provide mobility assistance for the disabled and infirm, and even replace prosthetic limbs. The wearable diagnostic technology outlined in the preceding section could be adapted for garments that monitor movement and the wearer's physical position. Individuals prone to falling could wear garments woven with a network of sensors capable of communicating with each other and transmitting information to remote systems. The sensors would issue an alert if they detected a fall.[23] In the case of patients susceptible to strokes or liable to have seizures, the garment may even be able to detect an episode in time to stop it.

Thurmon Lockhart, of Virginia Tech's Grado Department of Industrial and Systems Engineering (ISE), runs the Locomotion Research Laboratory, where researchers are trying to identify a biomechanical basis for human slips and falls. Lockhart and his team designed an experimental setup to monitor human gait. Using a walking platform, a harness apparatus and a wearable sensor array, they measure muscle and joint activity in the hips, legs, ankles and feet. The data they amass enables them to create computer models of gait patterns.

The ISE is collaborating with the department's e-Textile Laboratory, where researchers are integrating conductive materials, processors, sensors and actuators into fabric. Together, the research teams created a diagnostic garment they call the Hokie Suit, composed of a pair of trousers and sleeveless top.[24] The suit is equipped with a so-called gait matrix in order to analyse the wearer's strides. The matrix includes accelerometers to detect changes in the wearer's speed and direction. The electronic components are powered by a regular nine-volt battery connected in the pocket. The initial prototypes enable the matrix components to be removed when the garment is washed, but researchers are developing ways to waterproof and seal them so they can remain permanently embedded in the garment.

The technology could be worn long-term by patients considered to be at risk or by those undergoing prolonged treatment. The garment could also be worn for short diagnostic examinations to determine the patient's progress. Children suffering from cerebral palsy, for example, could wear the suit to have changes in their condition detected. As they walk around naturally, their gait is measured, while heart rate, blood pressure and temperature are recorded simultaneously. The researchers plan to develop the suit for environmental sensing applications. It provides fresh hope for asthma sufferers, who could wear the device to determine which factors in their environment trigger their attacks and thereby take steps to counteract them.

# Medicating Fabrics

Textiles are traditionally known for their ability soak up liquid, but advances in fibre technology reveal that they have the capacity to release substances to. Absorbent fibres are being developed for the health care industry, where their ability to discharge drugs and release medical preparations at controlled rates is making them an important part of many new treatments. Their ability to administer substances transdermally has also attracted interest from the cosmetics industry, who now use fibres to beautify the skin or protect it.

Transdermal drug delivery relies on absorbent fibres to release medication through the skin. Health care practitioners prescribe specific doses of drugs in the form of medicated adhesive patches placed directly on the skin. The patches release the medication over time, administering a steady dose that seeps into the bloodstream through the skin. Because it provides a controlled release of the medication, transdermal delivery has an advantage over traditional oral methods.

Often, the transdermal method is more effective in treating a specific area, such as an injury. Because such a wide variety of pharmaceuticals can be delivered transdermally, medications that cause nausea when taken orally can be administered without unsettling side effects.[25]

The most widely used transdermal drug today is the topical nicotine patch designed to help smokers quit. The patch places nicotine-coated fibres against the skin, where they are held in place by a protective plastic membrane coated with adhesive. Transdermal patches for the treatment of acute pain due to strains and sprains are said to be more effective than analgesics taken orally. Nonprescription drug preparations such as Cordran tape, a steroid-based anti-inflammatory treatment impregnated with fludroxycortide, can be bought without a prescription, as can transdermal analgesics such as Fentanyl. Transdermal patches are also widely used to administer estrogen, nitroglycerin and lidocaine, and treat conditions such as fibromyalgia and arthritis.[26]

Japanese textile manufacturer Fujibo is pioneering the concept of wearable vitamins, made possible by saturating fibres in soluble vitamins for transdermal delivery.[27] Known as V–Up, the fabric includes cellulosic fibres containing a solution of vitamins C and E. As the skin's natural oils come into contact with the fibres, the vitamins begin to break down for transdermal absorption, encouraging the growth of silkier, smoother and healthier skin. V–Up has a similar effect to vitamin skin creams, but with the advantage of delivering doses of vitamins to the dermis over prolonged periods. The fibres can also be saturated with the Q10 enzyme, which is believed to boost the wearer's energy levels.

Bioactive textiles function in a similar manner, but deliver herbal preparations or minerals instead of vitamins. Spa treatments have long extolled the virtues of sea vegetables, and now textile experts have found ways to use them too. Fujibo's Slimwish fabric is infused with a solution of kelp extract. A sea vegetable, kelp is said to help break down fat cells while moisturising the skin. The SeaCell range of fabrics produced by SmartFiber Ag incorporates seaweed cellulose into fibres for apparel textiles. Seaweed cellulose is dissolved and blended with other plant material and then converted into fibres using the Lyocell process.[28] Minerals and other active substances found in the seaweed are also incorporated into the fibres, imbuing the fabric with anti-inflammatory and antipruriginous properties known to exist in seaweed.[29] The minerals leach into the skin continuously over time, with 80 per cent of the original percentage of minerals still remaining after washing. The fibre's tenacity is comparable to viscose and has proven to be durable in both wet and dry conditions.

Grass-roots medicine is marrying cutting-edge technology in the form of fabrics derived from folk remedies. Fabric embedded with capsaicin, an enzyme found in chilli peppers, boosts the wearer's circulation. As the capsaicin is absorbed by the skin it stimulates the blood flow, increases body temperature and can give the wearer extra warmth in winter. Another natural remedy found in the Carpathian Mountains led researchers to discover the antiseptic properties of spider silk, which contains unique healing proteins. The locals used to cut up tubes spun by the *Atypus* spider and cover wounds with their inner linings. The fibres facilitated healing, and in some cases were even absorbed directly into the skin.

One of the benefits of textiles is the protection they offer. Cosmetic companies are collaborating with textile technologists and pharmaceutical researchers to endow clothing with the ability to protect the wearer from environmental hazards. Fujibo found a way to coat the skin against damaging UV rays by binding factor 50 sunscreen to fibres. They went a step further by adding polymer beads, which reflect harsh rays so effectively that they even lower the surface temperature by several degrees. Asics, another Japanese company, produce their own version of a cooling shirt. By coating fabric with xylitol, a natural sweetener used in chewing gum, they have been able to make shirts that cool and refresh their wearers.

# Smart Bandages

Transdermal drug delivery, antimicrobial activity, bioactive fibres and protective fabrics come together in the emerging field of smart bandages. Super absorbent fibres make it possible to wick fluids away from infected areas and disperse them throughout the bandage's structure, enabling more oxygen to come in contact with the wound. Other fibres automatically release medication and combat bacteria, resulting in bandages that stay fresher longer and need replacing less frequently.

Smart bandages have moved far beyond the strips of woven gauze wrapped around wounds and the adhesive compression bandages applied to the skin. Today, bandages developed by researchers at the University of Rochester in Rochester, New York, can change colour to warn that there is a risk of infection.[30] By reading the colours shown on the bandage, physicians will be able to identify which bacteria are present.

The smart bandage is actually a thin sensor strip made of crystalline silicon and layers of porous silicon. The porous silicon contains a liquid solution that includes probe molecules engineered to bind themselves to molecules found on the surface of bacteria. When the bandage is placed over a wound, bacteria from infected areas are drawn into the porous silicon, where they attach to the probes. The process alters the silicon enough for the changes to register when illuminated by a handheld laser device. The colours picked up by the laser reveal which kinds of bacteria are present. Because health care practitioners will be able to identify the bacteria immediately, they won't have to wait for lab results.[31]

Conventional bandages are being upgraded and improved as new types of clinical fabrics are developed. Apertured films made from polymer mesh are lightweight, nonwoven fabrics made from a unique extrusion, embossing and orientation process. The mesh is sterile, durable and nonstick, giving it the performance required for a textile brought into contact with infectious tissue. It also has a symmetrical hole pattern that achieves precise rates of permeability and filtration. Specialty thermoplastic netting fabrics such as Conwed are ideal for applications where open mesh substrates are required. The fabric is sterile, lightweight, flexible and breathable.[32] Not only has it proved effective as a bandage, but its germ-resistant properties make it well-suited for produce bags designed to keep fruit and vegetables fresher longer.

Bandages for chronic wounds often include hydrophilic polyurethane foam, such as the biocompatible and sterilizable Vivo produced by Corpura.[33] Vivo is highly flexible and soft to the touch, making it ideal for cushioning. It does not shed fibres or stick to other surfaces. The material offers controlled release of active antibacterial ingredients and can be integrated with odour-reducing substances or cooling agents.

Thanks to advances in technology, textile treatments like these promise to be a new staple in health care. As bandages become more technologically advanced, they are becoming slimmer, sleeker and less obvious. While the bandages of today continue to look like medical implements, the bandages of tomorrow could resemble fashion accessories more than surgical supplies.

# Colour and Well-Being

The power of colour is profound, and its impact on human behaviour has intrigued health practitioners for several millennia. The art of using colour and light to treat physical and psychological symptoms is believed to be rooted in Ayurveda, an ancient form of Indian medicine, still practiced today. The ancient Egyptians confined patients to solarium-type rooms fitted with coloured panes of glass, flooding their vision with a particular colour. Early European hospitals draped sickrooms with red cloth, believing that the colour could draw disease away from the body.

Chromotherapists claim that colours create physical and emotional reactions in people, and they treat patients by applying colour and light to specific areas of the body.[34] Colour therapy is based on the premise that the human body is made up of vibrations, which create interconnected fields of energy throughout the body. Colour can be considered to be a form of energy; it is created by the distribution of light energy versus wavelength, essentially creating a vibration made visible as the eye discerns different intensities. When chromotherapists determine that one or more of the body's energy fields has become unbalanced, they counter it by applying a colour that has a complementary vibrational resonance. Therapeutic colour can be administered in a number of ways and is often combined with hydrotherapy and aromatherapy. Colour has been proven to affect the body at the bimolecular and cellular levels, and conventional medicine is beginning to see the benefit of its effects.

The colour of a textile, like all surfaces, is a complex result of how it transmits and emits electromagnetic radiation in light. A viewer's perception of a textile's colour depends on more than the spectrum of light leaving its surface. The eye relies on contextual cues, such as texture, sheen and movement, giving the beholder a deeper awareness of its properties. When colour can be described as soothing, its therapeutic effects are being felt at many levels of awareness.

Although some scientists, colour psychologists and colour consultants are radically rethinking how the medium impacts on human behaviour, an overview of the clinical associations traditionally assigned to colours provides a useful benchmark. The colour blue is associated with relaxation and has been shown to have a pacifying effect on the nervous system. A colour therapist may prescribe blue-painted bedroom walls and blue-coloured textiles and for sleep problems and may recommend dressing hyperactive children in blue clothes. The colour purple is said to balance emotional problems and bring relief to sufferers of rheumatism, epilepsy and bone pain. Red is associated with heat, energy and blood, and is said to literally stir the blood by inciting strong emotions. Therapists may recommend red for individuals who need more arousal and vitality. Red's complementary opposite is blue-green, used in surgical scrubs and operating theatre textiles to dampen the intense hues of human blood and soothe the surgeon's eye.

New findings indicate that the particular tone and value of a colour, more than the actual colour itself, may stimulate the eye, producing an unexpected effect. Field research conducted by colour expert Ptolemy Mann, for example, showed that vibrant blue colourways could prove refreshing rather than relaxing, and that red could promote womb-like relaxation rather excitement.

When textile designer and colour therapist Louise Russell presented the collection she titled 'Philosophy: Fabrics for Health and Wellness' in 1997, health care textiles had not previously been designed with therapeutic properties in mind. The collection was produced by New York-based Carnegie Fabrics in 1997, who intended to introduce a new dimension to textiles made for the medical industry.[35] Recognizing that the patients' surroundings were critical to their well-being and recovery process, Russell decided to explore the healing properties that textiles have. 'I believe textiles can have direct healing powers,' says Russell.[36] 'Everything around us emits energy—be it positive or negative. We are surrounded by energetic fields and tapping into them can have a profound effect on our health and personal sense of balance and harmony. Nowhere is this more apparent or powerful than in the healthcare environment.'

The collection was coloured in soft pastels printed on high-sheen reflective yarns that added brightness and light. Russell drew patterns in large-scale repetitions, some of which depicted plants with healing properties such as bamboo, eucalyptus, and jasmine. Russell used images of the plants, which were scanned and printed on fabric by using a special photo process, to bring natural remedies into the patients' awareness. 'Everything resonates,' says Russell. 'I'm creating a product that will influence the environment and that will have an influence on the individuals within the environment.'

## Feature Interview: Ptolemy Mann

Choosing colour comes from feeling as much as it does observation. Apart from its powerful visual effects, colour can influence mood and even affect behaviour. As a medium it has tremendous impact, and in the hands of artist and colour consultant Ptolemy Mann, it is brightening the tone of health care environments. Mann's pioneering approach promotes colours that have a feel-good factor, and her vibrant palettes give clinical spaces a kaleidoscope of chromatic cool.

Mann collaborates with architects and interior designers to develop colour schemes for a range of environments, but her work has had the most impact in hospitals and clinics.[37] From her studio in London, Mann conducts extensive research on colour theory and its effects on human behaviour. 'I'm not a scientist or a psychologist,' she says.[38] 'Although I respect what they do, my approach is different. Many years of working as an artist submerged in a practical dialogue around colour has taught me to use a more instinctive and sensitive approach. Colour is a deeply emotive issue and this must be considered. Observing reactions to my artwork informs how I use colour in my architectural projects. For example, I've noticed that people like the transition point created when two or more colours merge together. It stimulates the eye and engages the viewer.'

Mann works on projects worldwide, and collaborations with foreign architects sometimes yield surprising insights into how clinical colours are perceived. 'A new hospital opened in the United States and it became apparent that many visitors and patients felt unwell when spending time in the building,' she says. 'A specific shade of lavender had been used throughout the scheme. It took a while for the staff to realise that the colour was affecting how people felt. It was eventually pointed out that it was not the shade of lavender itself but the after-image people were reacting to.'[39] After-images occur when the eye has had a concentrated burst of a single colour for a period of time. It triggers the optic nerve to create a brief flash of its complementary opposite, so fleeting that it hardly registers. Ever wondered why surgical scrubs and operating theatre textiles are blue-green? It's because the colour is the complementary opposite of blood red. It prevents the surgeons from getting an after-image when

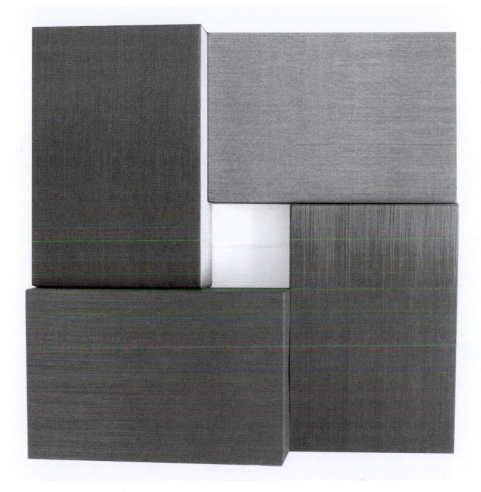

Textile designer Ptolemy Mann conducts extensive research on colour theory and its effects on human behaviour. Her research indicated that the transition points that form when two or more colours merge together stimulate the eye and engage the viewer more than solid blocks of colour do.

they look away from an open wound they are operating on. Because the optic nerve recognises the complementary colour when they look up, it doesn't recreate it as an after-image. In this case, it turned out that the complementary colours of lavender were the colours of vomit and bile—which was enough to make anyone in that environment feel ill.'

For another project, Mann was briefed that American hospitals are moving away from clinical pastels, opting for neutral tones instead. 'The architect, a partner at Swanke Hayden Connell Architects USA, said "American healthcare is suffocating in beige" and desperately wanted to try and change the trend,' Mann says. 'I could see why he was upset, since most healthcare fabrics and colour schemes are rooted

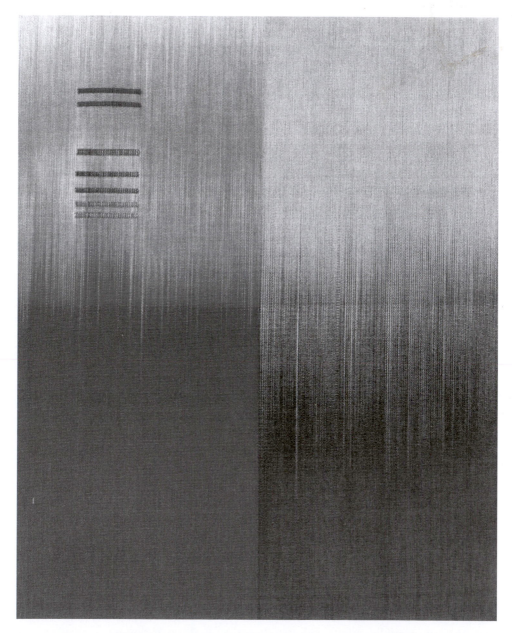

Ptolemy Mann uses textiles to brighten the tone of health care environments. Mann promotes colours that have a feel-good factor, giving clinical spaces a kaleidoscope of colours that soothe and uplift.

in earth tones. Brown is believed to be grounding, and beige is said to be reassuring, even soothing. My projects in the UK revealed the opposite, showing that patients and staff at British healthcare facilities appreciate colourful environments. They especially like a gradation of colours, which evokes a sense of movement in an otherwise sterile

Architects Swanke Hayden Connell commissioned Ptolemy Mann to create a colour palette for the entire façade of King's Mill Acute Care Hospital in Nottinghamshire.

environment. A palette of beautiful colours creates a sense of harmony, and in many cases, momentarily distracts the patient from what's bothering them.'

One of Mann's most exciting projects to date was a commission to create the external architectural colour scheme for King's Mill Acute Care Hospital in Nottinghamshire, designed by Swanke Hayden Connell.[40] Mann was brought into the project relatively late in the development process and asked to create a colour palette that would be used across the entire façade of the scheme. 'The building had already been designed and the process of choosing colours was intended to complement the existing by design making the hospital's identity as dynamic as possible,' Mann explains, 'but that aspect of the project had already been finalised when I came on board. It's a rural hospital, so I looked at the scenery surrounding it and talked to the landscape architects, and felt inspired to use greens and blues to help anchor the building's outer edges to the landscape. The "hottest" colour I specified was a vivid orange at the entrance. Many children visit the hospital, so I wanted it to be welcoming, but also vibrant enough to lead visitors back to the entrance if they got lost. In other parts of the hospital, I used colours to guide people through the space. There are three towers, and each has a distinct palette of seven tones of a single colour that change in value. If someone is looking for the green tower, they will see green details to guide them towards it.'

The nonclinical colour choices Mann prefers are partly intended to help patients overcome the 'threshold anxiety' that they feel when entering a care facility. 'I am an advocate of many tones or subtle spectrums of soft tones rather than one dominate colour,' she says. 'A mono-colour approach is the hallmark of an institution, while a balanced range is associated with domestic settings.' When a fertility clinic at St Mary's Hospital in London was refurbished, they commissioned Mann to create fifteen fabric panels to decorate the walls.[41] 'The clinic's director wanted to include my work because she wanted the unit to feel comfortable and like home. I developed a strong colour scheme to create an uplifting sense of optimism. Colour is an extraordinary tool, and when used deliberately, it can help people feel so much better.'

# five

# Sustainability

Yesterday's textiles are tomorrow's toxins; an estimated 1 million tonnes of fabric waste ends up in landfills each year.[1] Right now, fashion manufacturers use bleaching, dying and printing processes that place clothing fabrication on a par with petro-chemical production.[2] Clothing can take decades to decompose, all the while leaching deadly chemicals and harmful gases into the soil around it.

The growing movement to produce sustainable textiles advocates environmentalism, economics and social responsibility. A holistic, cradle-to-grave approach is emerging, which considers the impact of the textile's entire life cycle. Campaigners draw attention to the impact that textile production can have on the environment, recommending the use of new production methods that reduce the industry's carbon footprint. They criticize the fashion industry for using textiles known to create harmful emissions, and they actively discourage the use of chemical processing to finish the fabrics. The economic formulas many fashion conglomerates adhere to encourage overproduction in order to reduce the unit cost per item. The result is a shocking amount of unsold garments, which are subsequently discarded as waste.

Textile specialists and fashion designers are working together to encourage manufacturers to use environmentally friendly materials and develop socially responsible methods for clothing production. Some designers use recycled materials, while others prefer organic fabrics such as hemp, bamboo, Ingeo and raw silk. Popular inorganic choices include biodegradable textiles, recycled plastics and renewable melt-processable fibres that can be woven into fashion fabrics and made into nonwoven interior textiles.[3] Melt-processable fibres offer a sustainable alternative to existing polymer textiles. Fabrics such as Alcryn and Duracryn, produced by Advanced Polymer Alloys, are already commercially available.[4] Manufacturers such as NatureWorks and Cargill Dow Polymers are developing polylactic-polymer

This striking black and white motif was created for Becky Earley's Top 100 project, an initiative to salvage discarded tops and remake them in themed sets of ten.

technology that will make it possible to create fibres from renewable agricultural resources, such as corn or sugar beets.[5]

But while technologists are engineering the fabrics of the future, textile designers are the ones cleaning up the mess left behind. While the practitioners described in this chapter are supporters of sustainability, none of them see the production of more materials as a viable solution. Some tackle the growing problem of postconsumer waste, devising methods for recycling the garments that result from overproduction, and reusing the vast numbers of items worn for only one season. Others are finding ways to transform discarded industrial fabrics into textiles that are as beautiful as they are sustainable, making sure that the processes used to recycle them minimizes water pollution and chemical waste.

A handful of textile designers are forging alliances with science to create sustainable textiles, exploring the extent to which biomimetics, biochemistry and epigenetics can create new solutions. Evolution has enabled animals, plants and microbes to create a plethora of techniques and materials that could significantly improve textile design. Plant fibres, pine cones and peacock quills have provided inspirations for new types of textiles, and the potential to harvest spider silk has aligned fibre production with genetic engineering.

The growing market for sustainable textiles has reclaimed organic materials and found cutting-edge expressions for traditional crafts. As craft skills are being revived, whole communities have been regenerated by forming artisan cooperatives and re-establishing textile workshops. Embroidery, appliqué, beading and hand stitching are becoming as popular today as high tech prints, smart fabrics and responsive surfaces. As interest in sustainability grows, these two areas of design are working side by side. They show the economic and environmental value of recycled resources, revealing renewed respect for the artistry required to produce beautiful textiles.

# Biomimicry

The distinctions between nature and culture are not sharply drawn. Boundaries between the high tech habitats of the modern human and the nifty know-how of nature are being redrawn as mankind learns to mimic the natural world. Thanks to the science of biomimicry, which studies animals and plants, their models, systems and processes, nature's ways are being adapted for human use. And as biomimicry begins to unlock the secrets of evolution, new horizons for textile design are beginning to emerge.

Although the science of biomimicry is new, the principles behind it are not. Mankind has long used technology to imitate nature. Leonardo da Vinci's flying machine mimicked outspread wings, and airline jets take their aerodynamic shape from bird's bodies and beaks. The telephone receiver is modelled on the anatomy of the human ear, and animal dwellings and plant life have inspired architectural shapes and surfaces for many centuries.[6] In 1948, the Swiss naturalist George de Mestral invented Velcro by recreating a natural phenomenon in fibre form. After detaching burrs from his trousers, de Mestral examined them under a microscope and discovered they had tiny hooks that clung to fibres. De Mestral reproduced them in the form of a fabric fastener designed with tiny hooks on one side and fibre loops on the other, then collaborated with weaving experts to produce cotton tapes that fastened in the same manner. The fastener was patented by a Swiss company, Velcro S.A. in 1952, and continues to be known as Velcro today.[7] The synergy between the burr seed and plant fibres are the result of millions of years of evolution, and exchanges like theirs has inspired models of sustainability for future design.[8]

One of the first researchers to recognize nature's ability to provide sustainable solutions was Janine Benyus, an American science writer.[9] Benyus coined the term *biomimicry* from the Greek word 'bios,' meaning life, and 'mimesis,' which means imitate. Benyus is the author of *Biomimicry: Innovation Inspired by Nature,* a book that startled scientist by claiming that technologists, chemists and engineers abound in the natural world.[10] According to Benyus, more than 3.8 billion years of natural selection have enabled animals, plants and even microbes to create marvels that modern science can only dream of. Benyus also revealed that nature has perfected a plethora of ordinary materials and techniques that could significantly improve the human world.

Benyus gives the example of the peacock, whose colourful plumage is widely regarded as the most resplendent in the world. Its feathers are unique in that their colours are not created by an array of pigments, but by light-catching barbules—minute filaments projecting from barbs on the surfaces of the quill's spine. Although the feathers appear to be multicoloured, the only pigment they contain comes from melanin, which is brown. Their brilliant colours are due to an optical phenomenon created by the barbules. The barbules form a lattice-like pattern of melanin granules. The lattice's patterns vary, affecting how light waves pass over them, and therefore which colours are caught and reflected back to the eye. Because the colours are created by the barbules rather than by an array of colourful pigments (which oxidize over time), they never fade. Barbules create lasting colours, revealing that texture can be a viable alternative to the use of pigments, enabling textile designers to create colourful fabrics without chemical processing.[11]

Morphotex is a leading example of a colourful textile made without using any dyes or pigments at all. The fabric is named after the South American morpho butterfly, an insect characterized by its deep, jewel-like hues of blue.[12] Although richly coloured, the butterfly's wings do not actually contain any pigment. The insect's wings are covered by microscopic scales that reflect light in a manner similar to a photonic crystal, angling and refracting it in a way that reflects the blue wavelengths found in ambient light. Japanese fibre company Teijin used nanotechnology to mimic the varying thicknesses of the butterfly's scales, and created the world's first laminated chromogenic fibres as a result. The textile is woven with varying arrangements of polyester and nylon, making it seem to be blue. The fabric can also appear to be red, purple and green, depending on how light is shining on the material. Because no energy is spent on dying it, fewer resources are used to produce it. Morphotex is also completely recyclable without producing any contaminated liquid waste in the process.[13]

Morphotex has proven to be suitable for a number of high performance applications. In 2000, Nissan used Morphotex to upholster the front seats of the Silvia Convertible Varietta. As the fabric is pigment-free, there is no danger of it fading when exposed to strong UV light. Two years later, sportswear company Descente used Morphotex to produce skiwear designed by award-winning costume designer Eiko Ishioka for the Swiss, Canadian and Spanish Olympic alpine teams.[14] The fabric broadcasts an environmentally friendly message heard by sports enthusiasts around the world.

Unlike human skin, the exoskeletons of insects and crustaceans and the shells of molluscs have slick, durable surfaces that enable them to move through water with ease. When wet, they perform much better than human skin. Humans, in comparison to other organisms, experience much more friction when moving through water and air, which slows them down. Exoskeletons and shells, on the other hand, have evolved to enable fluids to flow around them in a geometrically consistent centripetal swirling pattern.[15] Exoskeletons and shells, together with the soft tissues and membranes inside them, create a system of layers that absorb impact, minimizing the friction they experience as they move through water. Layered structures like these have shown designers how to give materials added shock absorbency by intermixing hard layers with soft ones, and pockets of air in between.[16]

The abalone sea snail is being studied by material scientists around the world in order to replicate the shell's shatterproof structure in ceramic fibres and textile armour. Angela Belcher, a specialist in material science and bioengineering at MIT, identified how the abalone's proteins provide complex building blocks to generate its shell, which bind themselves to calcium present in the ocean to become stronger. Belcher explored the extent to which the abalone's structure could be applied to create a nanowire that would be strong and conductive and, to a certain degree, self-replicating. Belcher found a bacteriophage that resembled the abalone's ability to bind the proteins in its shell to semiconductive materials, and she set up a growth process that caused the virus to build nanowires.[17] Belcher is developing ways to reproduce the process by combining semiconductive materials with self-replicating organisms capable of assembling complex structures at a molecular scale. In the future, Belcher's process may be capable of producing nanofibre devices that can be fully integrated into fabric.

Fascinated by how easily fish slip through water, scientists and sportswear designers alike have examined fish skins at the molecular level to determine why they have less friction than humans. Researchers were surprised to discover that shark skin, which is rough enough be used as sandpaper when dried, is one of the animal skins with the least friction. Shark skin is covered by small, V-shaped protrusions, made from the same material as the sharks' teeth. The rough surface actually reduces drag as the shark glides through the ocean, because the protrusions efficiently channel the water away from the surface. Replicated in fabric form, a shark skin–like system of ridges and grooves woven into a textile's structure causes the water to spiral in microscopic vortices, giving the fabric a hydrodynamic advantage.

Grado Zero Espace mimicked dolphin skin to create a low friction, high performance waterproof textile known as Freeskin. The two-way stretch textile was woven with microchannels that improve the hydrodynamics of the surface. Like dolphin skin and shark skin, the fabric has a variety of ridges with different heights, wavelengths and frequencies, which minimize the friction between the surface and the water.[18] These parameters can be varied to suit individual body shapes, creating a custom-made swimwear textile that heightens the swimmer's performance.

In 2008, Speedo launched the LZR Racer suit (pronounced 'laser racer suit') made of high tech fabric that mimics the skins of sharks, dolphins and porpoises.[19] Known as LZR Pulse fabric, the textile is composed of lightweight woven fibres coated with polyurethane to reduce drag. The fabric was developed in association with NASA and the Australian Institute of Sport, and it was given a cutting-edge surface motif designed by Comme des Garçons. The swimsuit is made with an anatomically shaped core stabilizer that adds corset-like support to the fabric's structure. The seams of the suit are ultrasonically welded to further reduce drag. The design of the LZR Racer suit has had an impact on other areas of sportswear: all-in-one suits, seamless surfaces and polyurethane coatings are now common features of high performance design.

The dolphin and shark skin technology developed for high performance textiles is also found in other areas of aquatic design. Boat hulls are based on the shapes of dolphins and fish, and propellers are now designed with slicker surfaces that perform like shark skin. As a result, new marine vehicles have less drag, more efficient propulsion and consume less fuel. When it comes to bonding surfaces under water, a waterproof glue based on the substance blue mussels secrete to bind themselves to ocean rocks is the strongest underwater adhesive known to man. Mussels are even able to bond themselves to Teflon, indicating that the substance will also be capable of welding fabric seams together permanently.

The tough shell of the Stenocara beetle, native to Africa's Namib Desert, was the inspiration behind a textile able to create drinking water out of air. Andrew Parker, a zoologist based at the University of Oxford, noticed that the beetle's shell contains a sophisticated system of hydrophilic and hydrophobic textures. The insect's back is covered with microscopic ridge-like bumps that attract moisture, and wax-coated crevices between them that repel water. When the beetle senses fog in the atmosphere, it lowers its head and tilts its back into the wind, enabling its hydrophilic bumps to attract the moisture in the air. Miniscule drops of water gather on the tops of the ridges, and when they become heavy enough, they roll down the sides. As they fill the crevices between them, they are channelled around the beetle's shell and into its mouth.

The beetle's shell can be reproduced in fabric form as a plastic textile covered with tiny glass beads coated with hydrophobic wax. The textile would assist farmers in arid areas by enabling them to harness the moisture in the air to water their crops. Parker says that the textile could also be used to make a tent capable of transforming ambient moisture into drinking water, and may one day be efficient enough to lift fog at airports.[20]

Another example of hydrophobic wax can be found on the petals of the white lotus flower, which grows beneath muddy waters and blossoms on the surface without a single grain of dirt clinging to it. Wilhelm Barthlott, a botanist at the University of Bonn in Germany, discovered that lotus petals are not as smooth as they appear to be. At a microscopic level, the entire surface is covered with jagged points that resemble the teeth of a saw.[21] The points are formed by the petals' coating of wax crystals, which is so dense that there isn't enough space for water molecules to stick. As the surface causes water to form droplets and run off, they pick up dirt along the way. This makes the flower uniquely nonstick, and its ability to repel water and dirt gives it a self-cleaning surface.

Barthlott's findings enabled a German manufacturer to develop Lotusan, a spray-on exterior paint, that creates a similarly rough exterior coating that makes surfaces self-cleaning in the rain.[22] Technologists are pioneering a nanoparticle coating that may one day be applied to textiles and leather. Used in apparel and soft furnishings applications, clothing and interior textiles could wipe themselves clean when a jet of water is sprayed onto the surface.

Researchers at the University of Reading's Centre for Biomimetics are pioneering an impressive variety of biomimetic designs.[23] Their research has revealed that penguin feathers contain miniscule hooks, making them similar to Velcro. When the penguin dives into the sea, the pressure forces the air out of the feathers, compressing its coat to make the penguin's body more streamlined and hydrodynamic. As soon as the penguin rises out of the water again, the hooks immediately pull the feathers back into place so that they can quickly absorb the bird's body heat. Otherwise, a wet penguin would be unable to survive the sub-zero temperatures it lives in. The penguin's unique system of feather hooks is inspiring new types of insulative materials and waterproof fabrics. Down-like insulating fibres could be engineered to store energy when dry and repel water when submerged, enabling them to perform efficiently whether wet or dry.

Pine cones are providing researchers at the Centre for Biomimetics with an inspiring model for responsive fabrics. As pine cones mature on the tree, their surfaces remain closed. But as they ripen and fall to the ground, they expand and open in order to release their seeds. The researchers discovered that the pine cone's scales open because they are divided into separate layers, and that each has a different response to moisture. After the pine cone detaches and it begins to dry out, one of the layers releases moisture at a faster rate, causing the scales to bend and flex.[24] Researchers believe that by creating a reverse effect in fabrics, fibres could expand to ventilate the wearer when they detect perspiration and close again when dry. The effect would be created by a multilayered textile constructed with miniscule flaps that open automatically when the wearer starts to sweat, and wick moisture upwards away from the skin. When the skin returns to its normal condition, the flaps would close and the surface would be smooth again.

Stomatex is a lightweight, ultra-thin, nonporous polyester textile that is weatherproof and breathable.[25] Stomatex was engineered to mimic the transpiration of plant leaves. The fabric has a pattern of dome-shaped cells that allow body heat and perspiration to exit through tiny pores on the surface, maintaining a microclimate between the skin and the fabric. The pore-like punctures are placed in the centre of the cells, which are made in a dome-like shape to draw excess body heat and perspiration inside. The cells are a part of the fabric's structure, flexing and stretching with the body's movements, enabling excess heat and perspiration to be pumped out through the pores as cooler, drier air is pulled in from the outside. The fabric has a unique pumping action that increases and decreases according to the user's level of physical activity. The fabric is truly unique, being the first material able to maintain a perfect microclimate between the skin and the fabric during physical activity. It is designed to be worn for long periods of time to prevent overheating.

According to fashion futurist Suzanne Lee, director of the BioCouture research project, manmade fashion fabrics may someday be replaced by textile membranes that produce themselves.[26] In 2004, Lee teamed up with David Hepworth, a scientist and codirector of biotech company Cellucomp, to determine the extent to

The BioCouture research project used bacterial cellulose to produce clothing. When dry, the bacterial cellulose can be cut and bonded to produce garments, such as the indigo-dyed faux denim jacket shown here.

which garments could actually *grow* from bacterial cellulose. Together, they launched BioCouture as an initiative to develop sustainable fashions that would be eco-friendly throughout every stage of their production cycle. By cultivating harmless bacteria that bond active enzymes and cellulose fibres into a textile-like material, they developed a plant-based membrane without using any manmade derivatives.

The BioCouture membrane is grown in a tea and sugar solution, similar to the kombucha bacteria culture.[27] As the bacteria synthesize the sugar nutrients, they expel

As bacterial cellulose dries, chains of glucose join together in repeating units that form micro-fibres as they build. As a result, the dried bacterial cellulose is strong, giving garments like this jacket durability and strength.

compounds that form the cellulose fibres. Once the membrane has been extracted and dried, the microorganisms are deprived of their nutrients; they immediately become dormant, but not dead. In dried form, the membrane behaves like a nonwoven textile and can be pattern-cut like conventional fabric, coloured with vegetable dyes, printed, layered and sewn into a garment. When the garment is ready to be discarded, it can be composted just like any organic food item.

117

One of BioCouture's long-term ambitions is to grow seamless, ready-formed clothing by immersing a garment mould into a vat of liquid containing the bacteria. As the bacteria attach themselves to the mould they would assume its shape, almost mimicking a felting technique as individual organisms meshed themselves into a single membrane. Lee's quest to create sustainable garments is aligning textile production with science more than industry; as her fabrication techniques resemble the self-replicating RNA enzymes engineered to create new molecular models, her textiles evolve much like natural ecosystems do. But unlike self-replicating enzymes, which tend to mutate into unexpected forms, bacterial-cellulose is stable and reliable. It is produced commercially for a variety of nonfashion applications, where it performs with the same durability of conventional fibre-based fabric, yet it possesses unique regenerative properties. Once the material is reimmersed in a solution of nutrients, it begins to grow again, enabling it to repair itself or be re-moulded in another form.

As a living membrane, the BioCouture textile is unlike any other fabric used in fashion today. Lee points out that BioCouture is closer to the field of biotechnology than it is to the science of biomimetics. 'We are manipulating biological organisms and systems to shape biological materials into applications for the body,' she says. 'BioCouture is exploiting a biological material which we harvest for use as a textile. Biomimicry, on the other hand, is when design is *inspired* by nature. BioCouture is not inspired by nature, it *is* nature.'[28]

# Spider Silk

Spider silk is one of the world's toughest fibres. It is lightweight, flexible, waterproof and sustainable, and gram for gram, it is five times stronger than steel. Before scientists discovered its strength, they had noticed its ability to absorb energy before breaking. A spider's web is powerfully elastic, stretching up to 40 per cent of its length before it breaks. In doing so, it absorbs and disperses a lot of the energy created by impact. The fibres' unique energy-absorbing process is what makes spider silk so tough.

Spider silk is mostly derived from the complex protein molecules found in the insects they catch and eat. They begin spinning their silk by secreting a gel-like protein similar to keratin, the fibrous protein found in hair and nails. The proteins present in the silk harden as they are exuded, forming elastic fibres almost immediately. Electron micrographs show that the fibres are uniform in cross-section—roughly fifteen μm in diameter—and have a smooth, slick surface. Some fibres are produced with a sticky coating, making it easier to form joints and make attachments.

Spiders produce a range of different fibres for a variety of applications, and each of them has a distinct property. Each species of spider has unique glands to produce its own types of silk for the tasks at hand. Soft fibres are created for the inner lining of the egg sac, for example, while their toughest fibres are used to form the sac's outer layer. Spider silk has been classified in five main types, each assigned to a specific task. Minor ampullate silk is a medium-strength fibre used to construct temporary scaffolding as the web is being built. Dragline silk is the type of fibre used to manufacture the web's outer rim and spokes; it is the lifeline that keeps the spider connected to the hub. Capture-spiral silk is sticky, stretchy and tough, and is spun within the radius of the web to catch prey. Once prey is captured, the fibre known as aciniform silk is used to secure the prey and wrap it. The aciniform fibre is nearly three times tougher than the others, even dragline. Tubiliform silk, the fifth type, are the fibres used to make protective egg sacs.

Although Kevlar, Twaron, Vectran and carbon fibres are some of the strongest fibres made today, their production involves extensive processing that impacts on the environment. Kevlar's production involves heating oil to over 700°C, and then extruding long, thin fibres under enormous pressure in vats filled with sulphuric acid. Because it takes several centuries for Kevlar fibres to biodegrade, they have the potential to occupy a landfill for a long time. The fibres would have to be subjected to further processing to be recycled efficiently, making them a poor choice as a sustainable textile. Spider silk, on the other hand, is produced without creating any toxic waste, and is entirely biodegradable.

Reproducing spider silk is notoriously difficult, because few scientists have been able to decode its protein DNA and determine its sequence. Research into spider silk first began at the University of Wyoming, when a team led by Randy Lewis mapped the genes responsible for the spider's silk in 1989.[29] They recorded the properties of dragline silk produced by predator spiders. When researchers discovered that the thinnest fibres were the strongest, they realized that spider silk held the potential to emerge as a lightweight alternative to heavy filaments. The research team discovered that spiders bond large numbers of small fibres together to create long, thin, strong strands, and produce single filaments when strength is less of an issue. The fibres consist of a polymer that has two areas, each with its own distinct property. One area is supple, soft and elastic, while the other forms miniscule, hard crystallites.[30] Researchers presume that these unusual polymers are the secret to spider silk's remarkable properties.

Researchers realized that if spider silk could be harvested, its strength would make it ideal for military and medical applications. It proved to be tougher than Kevlar and weighs three times less, making it a viable alternative for bullet-proof vests. Medical tests revealed that it has antibiotic properties, and its strength makes it ideal for sutures, artificial ligaments and artificial tendons. Farming the material proved problematic, because spiders are much more predatory than organisms such as silkworms, which have been successfully bred in captivity to produce fibres. Spiders are territorial and aggressive, with cannibalistic tendencies that make them difficult to domesticate. Even when farmed, silkworms continue to spin large amounts of fibres. Spiders won't produce significant amounts in captivity, and when two or more spiders are confined together, one of them will eventually eat the others.

Inspired by developments in genetic engineering, the research team explored the potential to introduce spider genes into other species. They set out to identify the gene that produces spider silk and introduce it to bacteria culture, hoping the colonies would acquire the ability to produce silk proteins.[31] Although they identified the right gene, they realized that it would not be cost-effective to use bacteria in large-scale spider silk production. The researchers subsequently embarked on a collaborative project with Canadian biotech company Nexia to marry spider silk production with transgenic goat technology. The spider genes were introduced to the goats in a way that would only permit them to be synthesised in the milk. They believed that by harvesting the spider silk proteins from the milk they could extract quantities large enough to produce the amounts of fibres needed for commercial applications.[32] Subsequently, Nexia genetically modified goats to make them capable of producing the protein in their milk, and they plan to create larger quantities by breeding them.

For enough of the goat's milk containing the silk proteins to create a viable substitute for Kevlar, 600 gallons (2,271 litres) would be needed to make a five-pound bullet-proof vest. Producing a single vest would require a day's milk production from 200 goats. The University of Wyoming research team decided to explore the viability of using a genetically modified crop to create a cost-effective alternative. Researchers are introducing the spider silk proteins to alfalfa, hoping that super-strong fibres will result.

Biomimetic fabric and genetically engineered filaments may seem worlds apart from organic fibres and traditional textiles, but they share a common ground. Some of the most sophisticated textiles are engineered to reproduce what nature does naturally, while many organic fibres are cultivated through technologized means. Not only are the natural and the manmade overlapping, they are folding one into the other. As they do so, the sophisticated abilities of biomimetic fabrics remind us less of science fiction, and more of colours, designs and capabilities borrowed from the natural world.

# Upcycled Chic

The unspoken assumption of all textile practice is that it results in a finished product. Yet designers are developing new methods of constructing and consuming textiles that challenge traditional ideas about their use, function, life cycle and disposal. As designers find ways of reusing textiles for the whole of their lifespan, they try to identify the point at which a textile can be considered wholly complete. Innovations to create new fabrics from recycled synthetic materials are transforming thermoplastic waste into interim textile products. The interstitial fabrics that result reveal that even ragged, unusable fibres can be used to produce new textiles.

The concept of life-cycle textiles is inspiring a new paradigm of manufacturing processes. Among them, upcycling, a process whose name was coined by William McDonough and Michael Braungart in their book, *Cradle to Cradle,* advocates refurbishing waste items to reintroduce them to the top of the consumer goods chain.[33] As all discarded fabrics are seen as having the potential to acquire fresh life as a new form, the concept of textile waste is disappearing. The processes collectively known as 'resurfacing' describe the studio-based practices and digital technologies used to reprocess the textiles and give them new surface motifs.

The sleek shapes Mark West creates are formed through use of inexpensive polyolefin fabrics, known for their slick, nonadhesive surfaces, chemically inert properties, high strength and low cost.

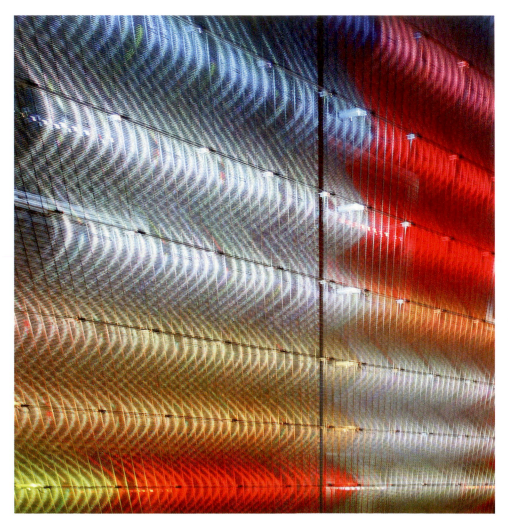

GKD's Illumesh metal textile is interwoven with electrical components that enable it to be illuminated in a wide spectrum of colours. Illumesh enables a building's façade to change colour with the press of a button.

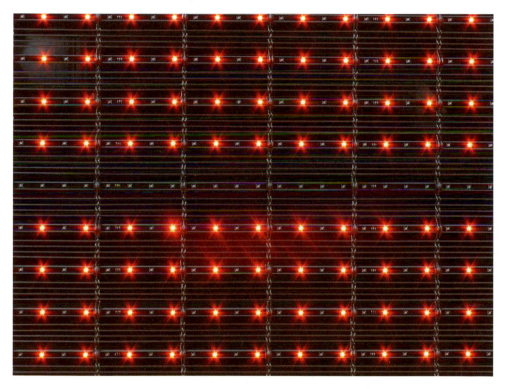

Some of GKD's fabrics can project animations and films across a building's surface. Mediamesh (shown here) integrates LEDs, surface-mounted devices and conductive fibres into the weave, enabling the textiles to illuminate and pulsate with colour.

This close-up reveals how LED units and digital circuitry are interwoven into Mediamesh architectural fabric.

Dutch design group Demakersvan used textile techniques to imbue a chain link security fence with a lace pattern, giving a purely functional object an eye-catching decorative detail.

This yacht is powered by FLEX10G laminate sailcloth, constructed from strong fill and warp yarns. FLEX10G sailcloth has unprecedented shape and retention characteristics, designed to cope with multidirectional stress from six different directions by dispersing it evenly across its surface.

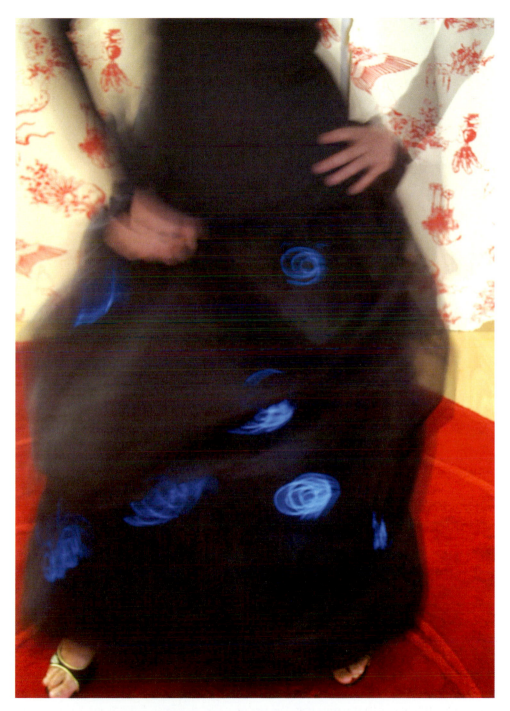

CuteCircuit embedded their KineticDress with sensors able to capture the wearer's movements. As the wearer moves, sensors activate the electroluminescent embroidery spiralling throughout the dress and illuminate its patterns.

Identifying the acoustic properties that 100 per cent felt wool can have, Anne Kyyrö Quinn developed a range of layered textiles engineered to dampen sound or absorb it altogether.

Loops and folds in the surface motifs adorning Anne Kyyrö Quinn's felt textiles create tiny cavities that wick sound waves into the layer of fabric underneath.

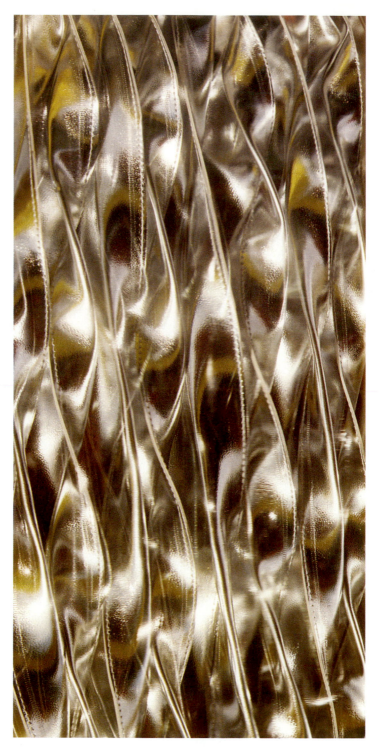

For a residential architectural project, Driessen + van Deijne created a textile print inspired by rippling water. The print was manipulated digitally and transferred onto 750 glass sheets, which they installed instead of balcony railings.

Textile designer Sophie Mallebranche is also a material innovator. She created this metal fabric by combining brass filaments with strands of bronze.

Sophie Mallebranche's Champagne fabric is made from fibres woven into a gossamer mesh that appear to glow in the ambient light.

Like hot air balloons and life rafts, the inflatable structures designed by Veech Media Architecture rely on air contained within fabric membranes to provide volume and strength.

This textile mould was designed by Mark West to cast architectural columns in concrete. After the wet concrete is poured into the top of the mould, corset-like lacing is pulled tight to compress and shape the concrete as it dries.

Márcia Ganem's exquisitely-crafted gowns are made from textiles she commissions from artisans in northern Brazil. Ganem has been instrumental in reviving the region's forgotten textile traditions.

Grethe Wittrock's Aqua wall hanging is a vertical sea of shining threads which catches the light, generating a clear blue glow. The textile is crafted from forty-two kilometres of translucent fishing line, and each strand was knotted by hand.

A commission from the local council in Kolding, Denmark inspired Astrid Krogh to embroider the façade of a historic building with neon tubes.

Astrid Krogh named the large-scale architectural motif Flora, referencing the simple floral shapes featured in the motif.

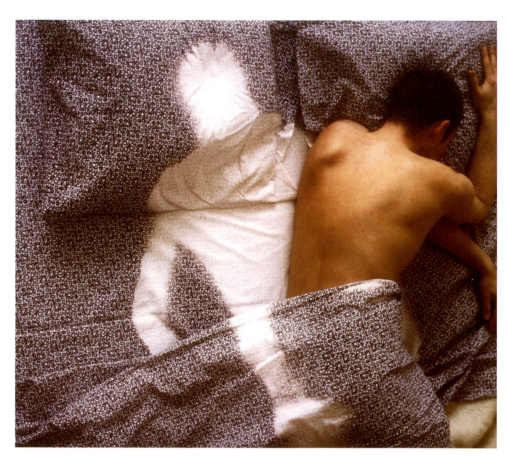

Jürgen Mayer designed thermochromatic bed linens with motifs that react to the sleeper's body heat. They form temporary impressions on the fabric that mark out the outline of the sleeper.

Luminex is a light-emitting fabric woven with optic fibres. The textile can be powered by a rechargeable mobile phone battery, which enables it to operate wirelessly.

Monica Förster created the Flow seating system for auditoriums and theatres by using shape-memory alloy materials in the seat's construction. When those seated rise to leave the auditorium, the seats merely morph back into their original form.

Förster covered the seat's steel frame in cold-pressed, fireproof polyurethane foam padding, then added shape-memory alloys. Since the shape-memory materials morph the backrest back to its upright form, no springs are required to return the seat to its original position.

Janet Echelmen's sculpture 'She Changes' is one of the biggest public sculptures in existence. Measuring forty-six metres in diameter and nearly fourteen storeys high, thousands of kilometres of Tenara fibres were used to create its shape.

'She Changes' is designed to interact with the blowing wind and changing light. The sculpture is constantly changing and reforming in response to weather conditions and the movement of the sun across the sky.

This detail reveals how nuanced and layered Natalie Chanin's designs can be. Quilting techniques borrowed from traditional Southern quilt making underpin most of Chanin's output.

Natalie Chanin's designs are some of the most lavishly embellished garments ever made from recycled materials. Many hours of work are devoted to each garment, resulting in a level of craftsmanship rarely found in the fashion world today.

Guerra de la Paz create works of beauty from discarded textiles that they scavenge and sort, take apart or use whole. Brown clothing was used to craft this tree trunk and branches, and create roots that anchor it to the ground. Green garments form a canopy of leaves overhead.

At first glance, it is hard to believe that this installation is fashioned out of discarded garments. Guerra de la Paz sort reclaimed textiles according to colour and motif, then shred, cut and sew them into a sculptural forms such as these.

The Slow Furl project aligns textile technology with the emerging field of robotics. Made of textiles, robotic membranes are sensory materials that can be programmed with the potential for movement and actuation.

Slow Furl's mechanized internal structure is covered with a custom-made textile skin woven with conductive copper fibres. When two parts of the textile touch each other, the conductive fibres trigger the mechanical system to change the structure's surface and shape.

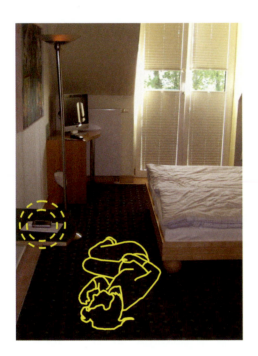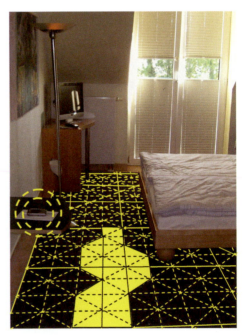

Sensfloor's sensory textile underlay is embedded with a network of integrated sensors that detect movement on the surface above them. As well as tracking footsteps, they can detect falls and relay the position of an injured person to a remote monitor.

Peter Testa and Devyn Weiser, principals in the Testa + Weiser architectural firm, are pioneer-ing a paradigm of carbon-fibre architecture that uses weaving and braiding techniques to construct multistorey buildings.

Computer modelling tools enabled Testa + Weiser to design and build the architectural proto-type of the carbon-fibre high rise shown here. The streamlined structure is lightweight, crafted from carbon fibres, carbon-fibre composites and shatterproof glass.

The printing techniques Becky Earley pioneers create motifs that are as elegant as they are edgy.

Ideas and methodologies like these are gaining ground in many areas, especially in fashion, interior design and contemporary art. London-based designer Becky Earley reprints fashion textiles to make them wearable again, transforming textiles that would otherwise end up in landfills into garments that women want to continue wearing for years to come. Earley was one of the first designers to print onto light-absorbing fleece made from recycled plastic bottles, and she broke fresh ground by developing eco-friendly printing processes.[34] Earley advocates garment recycling in many forms: upcycling, remaking and swap-shop sessions among friends.[35]

Earley is committed to addressing the growing problem of postconsumer waste, determined to come up with a method of recycling the millions of garments that are worn for one season and cast off when trends move forward. 'From working in the industry, I knew that Marks & Spencer have researched micro-fibre polyester and produce blouses that are long-lasting,' Earley explains. 'But I also knew that they dated quickly and end up in the rubbish. So I order them from textile recycling plants outside

Becky Earley's designs demonstrate how added value could be given to discarded fabric forms so that they can be worn again. Earley outlines a new paradigm for prolonging the lifespan of clothing by reconfiguring and redying them.

London, where I buy them by the bale. They're almost always in perfect condition, occasionally they're be a balsamic vinegar stain or something, which doesn't make any difference because I over-print them anyway. Many of them are also re-cut by sonic slitting that reconfigures the seams or incorporates a few new design details.'[36]

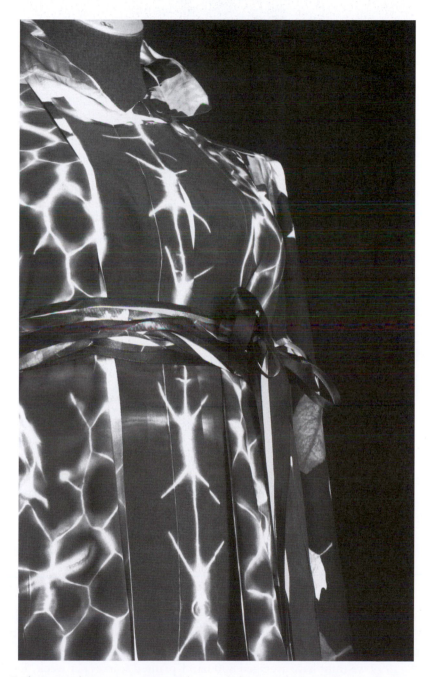

Becky Earley started experimenting with recycled materials, low impact printing processes and PET-based fabrics in 1998, she was one of the first fashion and textile designers to do so.

Becky Earley's heat photogram print shown here uses a palm leaf and reactive dyes to create an overprint that masks any stains remaining from the garment's first life cycle.

Earley's career began in 1994, when she launched the b.earley label assisted by funding from the Prince's Trust and the British Crafts Council. Earley leased a tiny studio in London's Brick Lane, where she made space to produce substantial orders. 'By 1998–1999 we must have averaged 800 hand-printed scarves per week,' Earley remembers. 'Which were distributed to 26 stockists worldwide.' Earley produced many of the garments with her own hands, which quickly showed her how toxic textile production could be. 'Everything was filthy all the time,' she says. 'It was uncomfortable for the people working there, and damaging to the environment. At one point in

Becky Earley's Worn Again project upcycled garments by using exhaust printing processes and new dying techniques. Making the garments new again means that they are worn rather than left in a landfill to decompose.

1999 I looked around and thought "What can I clean up here?" and so I started developing my "exhaust printing" process.' Exhaust printing is similar to exhaust dyeing, reusing the original dye solution for each garment in the production run. It recycles the solvents and chemicals, reducing water pollution and minimizing chemical waste. 'None of my clients wanted to buy a whole production run at first because the image fades in the process and gives each garment a unique colour-way,' Earley says. 'To me, that was a major selling point, because the production run created a group of unique items to sell rather than just a series of multiples.'

Earley holds the position of reader in textiles at Chelsea College of Art & Design, where she initiates research projects while continuing to develop her own label when she is not at college.[37] 'I teach and co-ordinate research projects in the college and outside it,' Earley says. 'When I'm there I'm analysing how other design disciplines are finding ways to become more environmentally-friendly and seeing what textile designers can learn from them.' Earley is preparing her research for publication in a book that proposes seven strategies for eco-friendly textile design. 'When I'm not at the college you'll probably find me in the wooden eco lodge at the bottom of my garden, sitting in behind my computer. It's a great place to think. I think a lot about the future of textile design and I want to develop new strategies to minimise the amount of waste.'

Kate Goldsworthy is also based in London, where she is a faculty member of the MA Design for Textile Futures at Central Saint Martins College of Art & Design. Like Earley, Goldsworthy is not afraid to tackle textile waste—in fact, she has even made a name for herself by taking textile design to places where other designers fear to go.[38] When it comes to the materials she uses, Goldsworthy describes them as, 'in themselves, completely unremarkable. In fact, it is actually their extreme "ordinari-ness" that I find so appealing. I work with non-woven polyesters and the robust felts used to make carpet underlay, insulation, household textiles, medical bandaging and geo-textiles. These materials are the unseen "work-horses" of the textile world. Because they are rarely used as outward-facing materials, they are almost always hid-den from view.'[39]

Goldsworthy's methodology takes waste as the starting point, efficiently con-verting it into a base material. 'The processes I'm developing are inspired by the traditions of lace making, appliqué and marquetry, but also the hi-tech polymer re-cycling technologies that use experimental surface treatments to "upgrade" samples of mixed-fibre waste,' she explains. Goldsworthy resurfaces mixed-fibre felt by layer-ing reclaimed nonwoven materials on its outer surface. The finish it yields gives the surface a uniquely structured texture that looks as good—if not better—than many bonded fabrics. 'New technologies make resurfacing a viable and sustainable method of producing "up-cycled" textile products,' she says.

The types of waste textiles that Goldsworthy works with are manufactured in large volumes, providing a remarkably reliable secondary resource for industrial recycling. 'Whether you realise it or not, these materials are a precious resource, and I treat them that way,' Goldsworthy says. 'By revealing their hidden beauty, I can elevate them to a higher status and make them more desirable to consumers.' Goldsworthy is challenged by a system in which materials have been devalued to the point of disposability, but she is optimistic about the way forward. 'I am really encouraged by the discussion emerging around the new luxury created through eco-design,' she says. 'I would love to think that the future holds a culture of rediscovered delight in the value of recycled resources, and a renewed respect for the time and care it takes to produce beautiful textiles.'

Goldsworthy makes the paillette-like recycled polyester discs that feature in her MultiSheer pieces individually, using laser technology, plastic processing methods and heat-bonding tools rather than a sewing machine or print table. 'I wanted the fabrics' decorative elements to be removable, updatable and recyclable,' she says, 'so that their replaceability would be an essential quality of the design.' Goldsworthy's works mostly feature thermoplastic materials such as polyester, which she says represents over 50 per cent of global fibre production today. 'Thermoplastics have very specific properties that yield to heat by melting, expanding and contracting, and this can be used to form them in a way which isn't possible with natural fibres.'

The textiles in Kate Goldsworthy's MultiSheer series are lightweight, recycled fabrics that are as environmentally friendly as they are beautiful.

Kate Goldsworthy used a heat-photogram printing process to create this motif on a recycled polyester shirt.

Some of Goldsworthy's works feature natural fibres alongside upcycled materials. 'Natural fibres follow the laws of nature,' she said. 'They are grown, processed and can biodegrade to fuel future growth as part of an agricultural cycle. Synthetic materials are not part of this cycle and need to be processed separately.' Goldsworthy's resurfaced materials address this problem, because they can be mechanically recycled through further life cycles when needed.

One of Goldsworthy's sources of inspiration is the *Cradle to Cradle* theory espoused by McDonough and Braungart. 'Much of my work explores the "mono-materiality" advocated in *Cradle to Cradle,* with the intention that products can be recycled through multiple life-cycles,' she says. 'Technology is beginning to provide alternative

Guerra de la Paz use multiple layers of cast–off clothing to construct life-sized families of char–acters. Although the figures are gendered and ascribed an age range, their generic appearance enables them to transcend notions of nationality or race.

answers and systems especially in the field of recycling. For example, the Eco–Circle process that repolymerize 100 per cent polyester fabrics into virgin-quality polyester fibre is overcoming some of the problems associated with mechanical textile recycling, because it results in better fibre quality.'

Guerra de la Paz also create artworks from salvaged neckties. These are shaped like snakes poised to strike their prey.

While the upcylced products created by Earley and Goldsworthy are made with functional roles in mind, the reclaimed textile works created by Guerra de la Paz are intended to be transcendent. Guerra de la Paz is the collective name of the collaborative Cuban-born artists, Alain Guerra and Neraldo de la Paz. They initially worked individually while sharing a studio in Miami, and eventually they embarked on joint projects.[40] That was quite a few years ago, and their collaborative efforts have evolved into an ongoing body of work spanning more than a decade.

The material they use is reclaimed fabric, and they create works of beauty from textiles that they have scavenged and sorted, taken apart or used whole. They sort lengths of textiles according to colour and motif, then shred, cut and sew them into a variety of sculptural forms. In site-specific works created in museums and art galleries, they have reconstructed whole landscapes out of reclaimed textiles and created sculptures from assemblages of fabric carefully layered by colour. Textiles, as a tactile material, invite the viewer to experience the work more intimately through the experiences and associations they have had with fabrics in various forms.

Many of their works are figurative. Guerra de la Paz construct life-sized families from reclaimed textiles, which are richly nuanced on many levels. Gloves are attached to suggest hands, and layered textiles are used to create facial features. Body contours are shaped by multiple layers of fabric. The figures typically represent the traditional roles of parents, grandparents and siblings and remain true to typical body proportions. Although the figures are gendered and ascribed an age range, their generic appearance enables them to transcend notions of nationality or race. The body images that result wholeheartedly reject the iconic bodies of visual culture, which are often represented in contemporary art as sylph-like supermodels, the superheroes of action films and cosmetically enhanced stars of stage and screen.

Guerra de la Paz also use textiles to create nonfigurative works that represent flora and fauna, or natural phenomena. Playing upon the neckties' role as a constricting object, they constructed nooses from salvaged neckties, and crafted them into snakes poised to strike their prey. Both snakes and nooses alike are universal forms that are feared in many cultures, but when replicated from colourful neckties, they represent whimsical, tactile objects that have fresh meanings.

As Guerra de la Paz, and practitioners like Earley and Goldsworthy, create new directions for textile waste, they are turning fabric scraps into high end objects. Whether crafted into chic garments, stylish interior accessories or spectacular works of art, the striking forms that result showcase the colours, textures and motifs that abandoned textiles can create.

# Weaving Social Links

In an industry characterized by style over content and image over substance, the movement to infuse fashion with social responsibility is one of the most radical changes in fashion's history. The eco-friendly fashion movement is on the rise, promising to put an end to practices that harm the environment. Many consumers now place sustainable clothing on the same agenda as organic food, recycled waste products and environmentally friendly transport. Fashion designers are slowly gaining the confidence to opt for organic fabrics and ethical manufacturing, and if their success is anything to go by, sustainable fashion seems here to stay.

Much is written about textiles' ecological impact on the landscapes they are produced in and the landfills where they usually end up. Little is said about the communities that were lost as industrial production took hold, and even less is being done to rebuild them. This section features Natalie Chanin, Márcia Ganem and Anita Ahuja—three visionary designers on three different continents that are pioneering one vision for rebuilding local communities. Each has made textiles the starting point for sustainable development and economic regeneration of their communities. With textiles as their material and sustainability as their methodology, these designers are making a difference to local economies and individual lives.

### NATALIE CHANIN

Alabama-based fashion designer Natalie Chanin established a couture line crafted from recycled textiles, and as she did so, she sparked a movement that introduced American fashion to sustainable ideals.[41] Chanin also introduced ethical standards to the production process, refusing to produce her garments under sweatshop conditions. Accounts of her commitment to sustainable methods have rippled through the

Natalie Chanin transforms reclaimed materials into cutting-edge designs. Her garments are hand-made and typically feature embroidery and appliqué.

fashion world and far beyond, where her model of using reclaimed textiles as a source material has inspired new ways of working.

Chanin had lived in Europe for more than a decade before she relocated her business to New York. In one collection, Chanin decided to combine couture techniques and recycled fabrics, but she couldn't find a local labour force capable of reproducing

Natalie Chanin uses scraps of recycled fabric to appliqué new motifs on items of clothing she has salvaged and made new again.

the sewing techniques that featured in the collection. She flew home to her native Alabama, because that was the only place she could think of where there were groups of women who could sew. 'I couldn't find people to hand-sew the samples for fashion week, and the deadline was looming,' she said. 'I came home and placed an ad in the local newspaper to find seamstresses. I had practically forgotten how in the South women of all ages get together and form sewing circles, where they socialise, sew, swap stories and teach each other techniques.'[42] Chanin realized that she had tapped into a unique labour force and that her garments could be distributed just as easily from the South as any other part of the United States. She found a rural three-bedroom ranch-style house in Florence, Alabama, that suited her needs and relocated her business there.

As word spread that Chanin was recruiting part-time seamstresses, women of all ages and from all walks of life contacted her. 'My label almost immediately evolved into a widespread community of women,' Chanin says. 'There are retired ladies working for me because they like to stay active. There are women in full-time employment who sew during their lunch breaks and free time to earn money for their kids' education. There are college students who sew to support themselves while they study. And the ranges of skills they have are amazing. I can give you several examples where three generations of the same family are sewing my clothes, and the older generation thinks that it's just as cool as their granddaughters do.'

133

This close-up reveals how intricately Natalie Chanin's garments are stitched and embroidered. Chanin encourages seamstresses to focus on good wishes when threading the needle. As Natalie Chanin told the author, 'Use your thread to add love to what you sew.'

Recycled T-shirts are used as the base material for Chanin's designs. She buys them in bulk, removes the sleeves and opens the seams to create a fabric length. 'On average they measure around 70 cm x 90 cm,' Chanin says. 'After making a garment out of them we sew on appliqués that are also cut out of T-shirt fabric. Every part of the process is done by hand, and as a result, there is hardly any waste at all.' Using reclaimed T-shirts as an inexpensive base material has a number of practical advantages. 'I like it because it doesn't matter if someone doesn't want it or if one of the seamstresses makes a mistake,' Chanin says. 'After all, it's just T-shirts we're talking about here.'

Although Chanin uses inexpensive materials, the clothes that result are expensive to buy. 'Our labour overheads are huge compared to the cost of producing in the Far East, but the quality is higher and it sustains local women economically,' she says. 'I don't think that my business model is necessarily the best one for a sustainable business because relatively few people can afford my products.' Chanin found a way to spread her design philosophy and methodologies to individuals and local labour forces by publishing a book to teach people how to make some of her best-selling items themselves.[43] Chanin offers the readers simple, step-by-step instructions that guide them through the process of making some of her signature designs. 'I tell them that if they don't know how to sew, they can source some recycled fabric locally and pay someone in their community to make it,' she says.

While Chanin's work connects locally and globally with other individuals committed to conserving resources and eliminating waste, it also reflects local tradition. 'You know, taking cast-off clothing and transforming it into beautiful garments is something rare in the fashion world,' she says, 'but in Alabama, clothing has always been recycled for several generations. Down here, even sackcloth was printed and made into clothing. Historically, Alabama was a poor area. There were never any leftovers to throw away. Not only did my grandmother not have a garbage can, she didn't even have the word in her vocabulary. Throwing something away was unheard of.'

When Chanin was once wrongly accused of trying to regress fashion back to the homemade methods used by her grandmother's generation, she countered the criticism by saying: 'I don't want to do that because without UPS, Fed-Ex, the Internet and my iPhone, I couldn't distribute my work globally from Alabama. But I can tell you that my grandparents were the most sustainable people I ever met: they grew their own food and recycled everything. My grandmother once said that she was poor but she didn't know it, because there was always just enough of everything to go around. So here I am, two generations later, at a time when the United States has become the world's biggest exporter of garbage. I'm doing what I can to recycle a small part of it.'

As Chanin expanded her range of designs she added a jewellery line and a home collection to her portfolio of products. She also developed a new technique that enabled women to custom-order her garments. 'I've developed a completely new way of producing my designs. I make a series of "bodies" each season in sizes ranging from extra-small to extra-large, and produce swatch books of sample fabrics. The retailers can then choose what they think their customers will buy and place an order, or request bodies for their customers to try on and let them choose the fabric styles themselves. The long dresses have to be made from new T-shirt jersey but the appliqué is still recycled.'


## MÁRCIA GANEM

The excesses of fashion are legendary. Many designers are likely to lavish money on overpriced silks, expensive beads and exclusive leathers, but the materials used by Brazilian-based fashion designer Márcia Ganem are nothing less than priceless. Ganem takes the precious gems, polished stones, facet-cut crystals and pieces of pure gold harvested from the Brazilian landscape and integrates them into textiles.[44] Mixed together with natural fibres and reclaimed materials, and crafted in the textile techniques characteristic of Brazil's Bahia region, Ganem's designs are vibrant emblems of craft production.

Ganem combines these precious materials with recycled synthetic Polyamide fibres synthesised from worn-out tires, inner tubes and other vehicle parts. Ganem was drawn to polyamide because it has the tenacity of coconut fibre but is even easier to

Márcia Ganem's fabrics are characterized by their rich textures, as shown here in this double-breasted sleeveless top.

work with. 'Polyamide is easy to recycle and excellent to work with, so it became the base material for the textiles used to produce my couture line,' Ganem said. 'It's easy to create a surface with it by using handcraft techniques. The appeal of the couture range isn't just that the garments are meticulously-fitted, it's also because the fabrics themselves are made by hand.'[45]

This dress and fabric were conceived as one. Márcia Ganem knotted hundreds of sparkling citrine crystals into polyamide fibres to create this unique couture dress.

The foundation of Ganem's work is anchored to a variety of textile techniques that brings fashion fabric into dialogue with craft traditions, fine art and jewellery. 'Handmade techniques are literally the heart of our work, pulsating, generating energy and making our inspirations flow into beautiful creations,' Ganem said. 'Our Brazilian identity, our understanding of our textiles, fashion, culture, and history are united in the garments we make. And when you wear them, you feel it.'

One of the best examples of Ganem's process is the textile technique inspired by the *xequere,* a percussion instrument crafted out of a dried gourd and strung with a knotted weft. 'I developed a method of making a knotted weft from Polyamide fibres which I studded with gems and adapted for clothes,' Ganem says. 'The textile is knotted by hand over a dress form, so you can imagine it took a lot of time to perfect the technique. But it was worth it, because now I can truly fuse fashion and jewellery.'

Ganem used the technique based on the *xequere* to design and make a dress embedded with 7,200 carats of polished citrine, each attached to the fabric in a setting made from gold. Although Ganem's garments could be mistaken for pure luxury, every aspect of their production is intended to revitalize local communities of traditional artisans. Using the artisans' craft techniques as her starting point, Ganem finds ways to adapt them for new types of materials and contemporary designs. With each new collection, Ganem explores the possibility to revive a traditional technique in order to add something novel to her designs and find fresh ventures for the communities she works with. 'My Dândi collection, from autumn/winter 2006, used techniques such as macramé, Nhaduti, bobbin lace and knotted-weft,' Ganem says. 'The textiles were produced in partnership with artisan communities such as the group of embroiderers known as 25 de Junho, and a group of women from Saubara who formed a 120-member association of lace-makers. For the Dândi collection, they combined traditional bobbin lace techniques with Polyamide fibres. I believe that working with the textile traditions from the Northeast in this way maintains a link between modern innovation and Brazilian cultural identity, and, at the same time, it sustains marginalised communities.'

## ANITA AHUJA

Anita Ahuja is based in New Delhi, where she transforms trash into trendy textiles. In 1998, Ahuja established a nonprofit organization to protect marginalized peoples and regenerate pollution-threatened environments, and she aptly named it Conserve.[46] The organization comprises teams of people who reclaim the polyethylene bags dumped on the streets on New Delhi and deliver them to her workshop, where they are sorted, washed and subsequently compressed by heat in an oven-like apparatus. Together with a team of traditional tailors, Ahuja and her staff cut and sew the nonwoven fabrics they create, producing fashion accessories such as handbags, evening bags, beach bags, totes, shoppers and belts.

Although Conserve is a brand of products made from sustainable textiles, the goods themselves are only a by-product of what Ahuja set out to do. Ahuja intended to find a means of helping the caste of people assigned the title of 'rag-pickers', who

Conserve India's nonwoven fabrics are made through a special heat process that fuses recycled plastics together. As different colours are overlaid and bonded together, unique varieties of striped textiles are created.

live solely on what others throw away. They are often marginalized within Indian society, and many only have limited access to education and health benefits. The wages they earn in Ahuja's employ enable them to maintain a stable household, send their children to school and buy medicines and health care treatment when needed.

Although Conserve has already made a big difference to her employees' lifestyles, Ahuja hopes that the project will enable the workers and their children to eventually move on to bigger and better opportunities. 'Conserve contributes to a development of a new consciousness for the rag-pickers, which enables them to progressively become aware of their value as they have opportunities to become more prosperous individually and as a community,' Ahuja explains. 'Conserve is not limited to clothing the body or creating stylish products. We want our fabric to be beautiful and amazing in a way that empowers the mind and elevates the spirit. Conserve is not a part of a contemporary textile movement, it is the beginning of something bigger. Beginnings

Because each of Conserve India's textile lengths is made from a variety of recycled materials, different colour combinations constantly emerge. No two fabrics or products are ever the same.

are always small. Go to Gangotri where the Ganges river begins and you'll see a few drops trickling. And one cannot believe that these trickling drops are going to create the Ganges, but they do.'[47]

Ahuja believes that textiles in general have the potential to uplift those who make them and buy them. 'Textiles are based on the fundamental human values of love, integrity and joy,' she says. 'Hand-spun Indian textiles were once loaded with emotion, but today, because of industrialisation, there is an emotional hollowness towards them. We need to stir passions about textiles, and recycled fabrics do that.'

## Feature Interview: Carole Collet

With their interactive motifs, responsive textures and technologized interfaces, the surfaces designed by Carole Collet are some of the most dynamic expressions of textiles today. Since establishing the MA Design for Textile Futures at Central Saint Martins College of Art & Design in 2001, Collet has gained a reputation as one of the most visionary figures in the field today.[48] She set up the course at a time when textiles languished in the shadows of other disciplines, and she shone a spotlight on their potential to radically reinvent our world. At a time when many textile

Carole Collet's Suicidal Poufs were constructed to explore the textiles' capacity to create new shapes as they biodegrade.

specialists were interpreting sustainability in terms of cold wash cottons and hemp-heavy weaves, Collet was busy forging alliances with biochemists, material scientists and biomimetic engineers.

When asked for her views on sustainable textiles, Collet returns a blank, slightly perplexed look before replying. 'Well, for me, sustainability is just a natural part of textile design,' she says.[49] 'Not something that you try to add to the process later on. Managing resources, minimising waste and staying away from harmful chemicals is second nature to textile designers, especially these days. I can heighten the sustainability that's already there by designing textiles that don't drain any resources at all. Fabrics that actually generate the energy they need to perform, textiles capable of replicating themselves and self-cleaning surfaces are good examples of this.'

Collet is keen to dispel the idea that the future of textiles has to be based in technology alone. 'Technology holds exciting applications for the future, but so does Mother Nature,' she says. 'I love being surrounded by nature; it's a source of inspiration for me personally, but also for textile design in general. To me, the sun and the

Carole Collet constructed these poufs from materials such as hemp, jute, abaca, paper yarn and sisal that would quickly biodegrade when composted.

wind can be expressed in textile form as solar energy and movement. Look at how the sunflower can open and close, and lock onto the sun, moving its face in sync with the sun's movements in the sky.[50] I found out from Richard Bonser, a biomimetic scientist I collaborate with, that the sunflower is able to perform these movements due to the passage of water through its cells.[51] I realised that osmosis could be mimicked by a textile as well, providing a model that could inspire a design for sustainable fabric in future. It has provided a starting point for the biosurfaces I'm developing for the Future Home project supported by Central St Martin's College of Art & Design.'

Just as alliances with scientists have informed Collet's views about subjects such as biomimicry, the field itself has shaped her vision for biodegradable design. 'My contribution to the Nobel Textiles initiative was a project based on the concept of "suicide cells" that shape our body,' Collet explains. 'It made me think about labile forms that morph into new shapes as they biodegrade.'[52] Collet's Nobel Textiles project was developed in collaboration with John Sulston, an award-winning human genome scientist whose research into the cell death process identified the first mutation of one of the genes participating.[53] Cell death research examines the process whereby cells

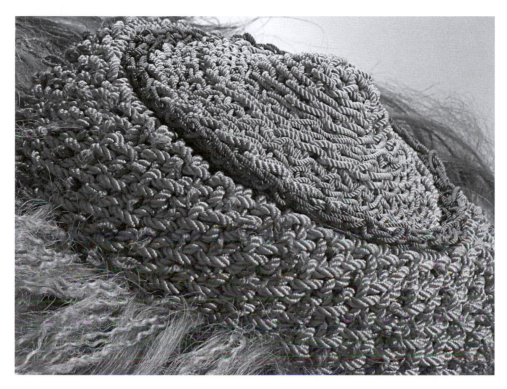

As materials begin to biodegrade they reveal the pouf's final shape. This is intended to echo the apoptosis process of cellular development whereby certain cells die to promote growth in others, thus contributing to the final shape of a growing organism.

on the periphery of a developing foetus die off voluntarily so that cells generating the body's surface can function more fully.[54] 'I was fascinated by John's discovery that all organisms produce more cells than they need, which made me think that some textiles have more fibres than they actually need,' Collet explains. 'John talked about programmed cell death and the notion of obsolescence in humans and worms, which I interpreted in a piece of furniture designed for the garden—which, you know, is an environment shared by humans and worms.'

Collet designed a macramé pouf constructed with abaca, jute, sisal and nylon rope. The combination of a biodegradable surface and a resilient nylon core resulted in a fibrous form that would change shape but not disappear completely. Jute, abaca and sisal were looped across the poufs' surfaces, giving them shaggy exteriors; as they de-grade and disappear, the textured surface underneath becomes more visible, and the cylindrical shape of the nylon core comes more clearly into view.

The enthusiasm with which Collet embraces science is pioneering an exciting new direction for textile practice. As she straddles the divide between nature and science, moves between playful expression and intellectual discourse and works within a vast repertoire of materials, Collet seems to be creating a new discipline where design, science and sustainability meet. 'Well, I did establish a master of arts degree course and call it Textile Futures for a good reason,' she says, 'meaning that the focus would always stay on what's next to come. But I don't believe textiles' future is limited to sustainability or science. Designers are producing new materials, exciting ideas and fresh horizons. We are creating future worlds.'

# six

# Contemporary Art

Torn fabric, shredded selvedges and trailing threads are hallmarks of the textile trade, but in contemporary art practice, they are also materials for some of the most exciting artworks produced today. Many types of artists are using fibre-based materials to produce their artwork, and as they do so, their works take shape as soft sculptures, woven installations and embroidered paintings.

For several decades, initiatives to elevate fibre-based practices to the high status of fine art were routinely overturned. Although contemporary art venerates time-honoured traditions such as painting, textiles, despite their long history, were routinely dismissed as decorative expressions or functional items. The two disciplines have a long history of mutual exchanges, with painting actually based in fabrics such as canvas and linen. Themes from nature, figurative works and abstract expressions are expressed in both mediums, and styles such as avant-gardism, realism and surrealism are common to each.

Modern art movements such as feminist art, fluxus, process art, performance art and land art placed fibre-based works on contemporary agendas for the first time. American artist Robert Morris pioneered a new direction in 1958, when he layered felt fabrics, slit them horizontally and mounted them on a gallery wall. Morris cited cutting and draping as artistic processes. Avant-garde Japanese artist Atsuko Tanaka embedded a textile with multicoloured flashing lights to wear in a performance and made a billowing dress from crimson-coloured satin with sleeves that spanned more than nine metres wide. Beat generation artist Bruce Connor incorporated textile objects into his pop-culture protest art pieces, while artists such as Judy Chicago, Mimi Smith and Barbara Kruger transformed fibrous materials into hallmarks of feminist art. Louise Bourgeois, who expressed her lifetime affinity with textiles relatively late in her career, uses textiles as potent metaphors for mothering and nurturing. Radical

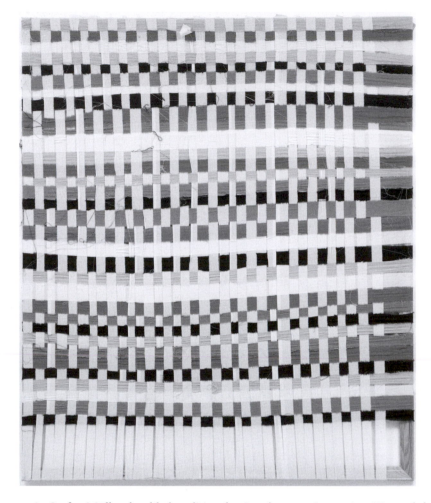

German artist Stefan Müller shredded traditional painter's canvas into strips. He used the torn pieces to create a warp, through which he threaded a weft of shredded cloth.

land art duo Christo and Jeanne-Claude treat textiles as mega-materials, revealing that fabric has the ability to reshape whole landscapes.

At the twenty-first century dawned, textiles were reclaimed by a new generation of artists. Practitioners such as Tracey Emin, Andrea Zittel, Annette Messager, Lucy Orta, Rosemarie Trockel, Do-Ho Suh, Ernesto Netto and Yinka Shonibare explored textiles within a diverse range of media, often pioneering innovative tactile forms as a result. One of the most radical approaches seen in recent years is that of German art- ist Stefan Müller, who shreds traditional painter's canvas into strips and uses the torn pieces to weave a new surface. By using the stretcher strips as a makeshift loom and winding a warp of torn canvas lengths from top to bottom, Müller threads a weft of shredded canvas through his loom. The effect is that of a woven artwork, where torn selvedges and hanging threads create a richly textured surface. The slashed canvases

American mixed-media artist Jim Drain creates fabric forms and textile-based installations. Working with yarn, fabric and beads enables him to express harsh narratives through soft materials.

and woven textures invert traditional perceptions of how a painterly surface should appear and contribute to the widening debate about how a painting can be defined.

The exchanges between textile practice and contemporary art are developing a dynamic rapport today, initiating a whole new dialogue between the two disciplines. This chapter charts the relationships between them in three sections that reveal how the synergy between them is resulting in unexpected new forms. As textiles find a fresh voice within contemporary art, their new roles reveal that the cutting edge of art may not necessarily be the shock of the new, but the soft, sensuality of fabrics inspired by traditional techniques.

## Textile Installations

Exciting exchanges are taking place between textiles and space. Their fascination for one another seems to centre around their mutual desire to transmute the space surrounding them into art. Just as contemporary artists explore a textile's tactile allure,

Jim Drain's installations dramatically alter the viewer's relationships to the spaces around them. Drain uses colours, materials and textures to create physical environments imbued with strong elements of fantasy.

they discover its intrinsic ability to demarcate space, absorb sound and create decorative elements that combine the poetics of art with the aesthetic features of design.

From his base in Providence, Rhode Island, Dave Cole creates textile installations so massive that they can seldom be contained indoors. Cole is a sculptor who encountered knitting while he was studying fine art at university. His work takes knitting to new heights by creating fibrous sculptures that can reach extreme proportions. 'I've been knitting my art work for a number of years now and I'm always trying to make things on a larger scale,' Cole says. 'I want to push boundaries and see what's possible in knitting, and so far, I haven't found anything that proved to be impossible.'[1]

Cole is known for his use of unconventional materials, textile-based practices and his ability to work in a variety of scales. Smaller works tend to reference emotive themes, such as the tenderness of childhood or the brutality of adult behaviour. For example, Cole knitted an unusable baby blanket out of spun silica, a high performance fibre so robust it can withstand temperatures above melting point. He also knitted a jumper from Kevlar yarn and crafted toy teddy bears from slices of metal, which he cut into thin strips and then knitted into a teddy bear shape. Cole used rolls of fibreglass insulation to create another nontactile teddy bear, a large-scale installation piece that took several days to complete. The artwork was commissioned by the

American artist Dave Cole knitted a huge American flag by attaching five-metre-long aluminium poles to the mechanical arms of two excavating machines. The poles performed like
knitting needles, and the machines manoeuvred them like a pair of hands would.

Decordova Museum of Contemporary Art and constructed on-site, and it measured
more than four metres high and nearly six metres wide. To mimic knitting, Cole bent
and looped the fibreglass strips by hand. Although he wore protective gloves and an
industrial Tyvek boiler suit, friction from the fibreglass cut through the protective
fabric and came in contact with his skin. 'It was an itchy experience,' Cole says. 'To
knit the teddy bear's belly, I had to jump inside it and push the stitches out. That created friction between the suit and the fibreglass that wore holes in the tyvek.'

On the first anniversary of the 9/11 tragedy in 2002, city officials in Provincetown,
Massachusetts, commissioned Cole to make a giant American flag to memorialize the
event. Cole began by attaching five-metre-long aluminium poles to the mechanical
arms of two John Deere excavating machines. The poles functioned like knitting
needles, and the excavating machines provided the power to manoeuvre them in knitting motions. Cole was suspended high above them on a boom, and using a flexible
fishing rod, he fed thirty-centimetre-wide felt strips into the needles below him. The
flag that resulted was more than four metres wide. Cole says the flag was laden with
personal memories and private emotions that followed his own experience of the
9/11 attacks in New York. 'I spent the week after the attacks in New York where I
volunteered to do search-and-rescue work,' Cole says. 'At the time, I felt like I'd never

Dave Cole used rolls of fibreglass to create an enormous teddy bear measuring more than four metres high and nearly six metres wide.

be able to get my head around what had happened. So I went down to New York to get my hands around it. That's how I understand things.'

Jim Drain, another American mixed-media artist with an interest in knitted textiles, also creates fabric forms and textile-based installations. After completing his studies at the Rhode Island School of Design in Providence in 1998, Drain used a knitting machine for the first time. The technique enabled him to produce forms that perfectly communicated the messages he wanted to express: harsh narratives cocooned in soft textures. Drain works with yarn, fabric and beads but also includes a range of materials described as 'gaudy' by his critics. Strings of brightly-coloured plastic beads, lengths of silver fringe and terry cloth bath towels depicting images of a topless women have featured in his art pieces.

Drain uses textile forms to explore how identities can be created, dissolved and reformulated. His critique of America's consumerist, celebrity-crazed culture is executed in appliqué and embroidery, together with some of the trashy elements of mainstream American style. Drain's works are grounded in the ordinary and the everyday, using societal mores to spark a cultural commentary. The installations radically alter our relationships to the spaces around them, deploying colours, materials and textures to create real places imbued with strong elements of fantasy.

Multimedia artist Bayard goes by only one name. Based in New York, he crafts installations using soft materials and textile methodologies. Bayard's artworks give textiles a new platform in contemporary art practice, where they express themselves

New York–based artist Bayard crafts installations ranging from small, intimate pieces to site-specific installations made on a monumental scale.

American artist Piper Shepard creates lace-like panels that are architectural in scale, which she hangs from the ceiling to designate architectonic enclosures.

in a sculptural, sometimes architectural guise. His installations and sculptures range from small, intimate pieces to site-specific installations made on a monumental scale. Bayard's diverse styles and different locations are united by his consistent use of fibres and his vibrant sense of colour. Many of Bayard's works can be characterized by three different textile forms: mohair yarn, which is typically wound through wooden frames to make hanging installations, brightly coloured yarns and silicon-coated rip-stop nylon, which creates inflatable sculptures. The bellicose foam-based works that Bayard refers to as 'poems' also include rhinestones and acrylic yarn. Bayard's eye-catching textile forms create a momentary pause in a high speed world.

Bayard's artistic range is not limited to visual art; he is also a writer with more than 150 short stories published worldwide and is the founder of the avant-garde literary journal, *Happy*. Although he is willing to articulate the narratives underpinning his works, Bayard is also passionate in his belief that art should speak for itself without making declarations of meaning. His works are intended to be immediate and easy to understand, drawing the viewer closer and encouraging them to interpret the works in any way they choose.

American artist Piper Shepard is forging fresh dialogues between textiles and interior architecture. Shepard's textile art pieces unfold three-dimensional structures that sometimes appear architectural in scale. Simply shaped and elegantly designed, the lace-like panels Shepard makes are suspended from the ceiling to designate architectonic enclosures. Shepard makes both sides of the textiles visible at once, blurring the boundaries between inside and outside, structure and surface, front and back. Shepard projects diffuse light over the panels to create areas of contrast on the textiles' surfaces. The light effects cast elaborate shadows over the area around the textiles, amplifying their impact as they mesh with the space surrounding them.

Despite their architectonic scale, Shepard's work is delicate and hand-made. Shepard uses traditional processes such as cutting, printing, sewing and dyeing to create textiles unconventional in their proportions and designs. Shepard's work has the delicacy of fine-boned lace patterns and is often mistaken for it. Unlike a traditional lace practitioner, Shepard doesn't rely on threads, bobbins, pricking cards and needlelace pillows to create her work. Shepard coats long lengths of cotton muslin with graphite, then smoothes the fabric across a work surface to hand cut an exquisitely detailed lace pattern into it.

Shepard's works seem to reference textiles' long history, harkening back to a time when textiles were fabricated into tents to create domestic enclosures and when fabric panels were attached to the walls as a source of insulation and decor. The textiles can be regarded as small monuments to architecture, yet they form grand testimonials to intricate textile techniques.

# Second Skins

The growing symbiosis between textiles and art is generating a new body consciousness. Just as textiles play a key role in moulding the body's shape into stylized second skin apparel or in crafting rigid garments that define space around the body, they also lend themselves to the creation of sculptural shapes that explore new representations of the human form.

Sensory skins are a point of fascination for Chicago-based artist Nick Cave, who is probably best known for his Soundsuits, wearable sculptures he constructs from fabrics, found items and recycled objects. A fine art graduate, Cave is currently the chair of the fashion department at the Art Institute of Chicago. Cave's creations blur the boundaries between surface design, performance art and costume design. Cave's Soundsuits are literally larger than life; they almost cover the entire body, sometimes only revealing the eyes. Although they are worn as ritualistic costumes for live performances and video recordings, they are also mounted in galleries as sculptural installations. In both cases, the Soundsuits provide extravagant showcases of painted fabric, intricate jewellery and collages of reclaimed objects. Cave has said, 'I believe that the familiar must move towards the fantastic. I want to evoke feelings that are unnamed, that aren't realised except in dreams.'[2]

When the suits are worn in Cave's ritualistic dance performances, they seem connected to African ceremonial costumes. The labour-intensive, highly skilled techniques used to construct them also forge links to couture techniques. The flea market finds that embellish them, such as plastic beads, fake flowers, costume jewellery and key chains, imbue them with retro nostalgia and pop-culture ciphers. Cave describes this aspect of his work as 'the act of collecting and reconfiguring', a concept that brings contemporary art closer to the recycling ethos pioneered by textile practitioners such as Becky Earley and Kate Goldsworthy.[3] Cave's use of recycled materials has been likened to quilt making, a practice which may also fabricate decorative and functional textiles from discarded cloth. Likewise, Cave reclaims unwanted materials and transforms them into resplendent surfaces.

Masking the wearer's identity is central to Cave's work. An African American male, Cave claims that he encounters prejudice virtually every time he steps onto the street. The Soundsuits can provide a symbolic disguise that poetically thwarts the prejudices some African Americans encounter. Some of the materials appliquéd onto the suits, such as twigs and bottle-caps, are discarded objects that have little value. In Cave's eyes, these items represent society's view of African American males. The Soundsuits are intended to represent something beyond skin by taking the wearer to a space free of class, race or gender.

Although Cave's work explores personal identity from the perspective of his cultural background and racial makeup, his art intends to reflect some of the universal tropes that characterize human experience today. As such, parallels can be drawn between Cave's work and the art of the late Brazilian artists Hélio Oiticica and Lygia Clark, who examined the mutability of the body through its relationship to signifiers beyond it. The Parangolés, Oiticica's best-known works, were wearable structures fabricated from textiles and plastics. Similar to Cave's work, the Parangolés were also explorations of the individual's role in collective experience as 'a participant, transforming his own body into a prop, in a ludic experience that becomes an expressive act'.[4]

Pia Myrvold is an artist and fashion designer who transforms modern technology into wearable fabric. Originally from Norway but based in Paris, Myrvold began her multifaceted career as a textile artist before pursuing a career in fashion. Her first major art commission was for a series of ten outdoor fibre sculptures in the 1985 Nordic Textile Triennial, and in 1992, Myrvold stretched scaffolding and textile panels for five hundred meters along the L'Ourcq canal at Parc de la Villette to create an interactive textile structure that visitors could move through. Today her artwork pioneers new relationships between textiles and performance art, giving her a platform to challenge traditional ideas about clothing construction.

Myrvold's ambitious 'Female Interfaces' performance, held at Centre Pompidou in Paris in September 2004, was a triumph of technology and performance art. Myrvold took centre stage wearing clothing embedded with wireless technology that enabled her to interact with audio-visual media. The technology enabled her to trigger sound and image loops, control volume and activate voice effects. Myrvold stepped onto the stage at Centre Pompidou, and carried out a tour de force of personal expression and technological interaction. Her performance clothing contained memory circuits with six sound and image loops controlled by performance movements. Each loop was activated by a sensor embedded in the clothing or footwear. Flexible sensors in the garment's elbows controlled the volume, while sensors in Myrvold's gloves also

In Pia Myrvold's ambitious 'Female Interfaces' performance, she took centre stage at Centre Pompoidou wearing clothing embedded with wireless technology. The wearable circuitry enabled her to activate sound and image loops, volume controls and trigger voice effects.

activated sounds. A slight bend of her index finger made Myrvold's voice resonate softly, while a sharp crook of the finger amplified it into an echo.

The feedback Myrvold received after the performance at Centre Pompidou made her realize that 'Female Interfaces' presented a platform that the public could easily relate to, and one that enabled them to grasp the trinity of identity, individuality and interactivity that she advocates. 'I want to take Female Interfaces to new levels by designing a collection of ten interactive suits, each fabricated with state of the art technology that includes sound and image loops,' she explained.[5] The two first segments were titled Female Interfaces 1.0 and 2.0, and as the series evolves, the next segments will be titled Female Interfaces 3.0, 4.0, 5.0, and so on, until all ten interfaces have been realized.

'Female Interfaces will continue to be a fashion performance that uses a catwalk format and live models to wear the garments,' Myrvold explained. 'It's possible to perform an individual interface segment on its own in a small venue or all of them together in a big event like a rock festival. Each interactive suit will challenge the social conditioning that we are shaped by and offer alternative ways of thinking about individuality and creative potential. I hope that this project will introduce new models of thinking about real life interaction. It could even launch a new art form and a new way of thinking about integrating technology into fashion.'

Myrvold's performance costumes are made in a range of synthetic fabrics to which wires, connectors, sensors, switches and batteries have been added. 'I have a vision for the seamless integration of fashion textiles and technology,' Myrvold explains. 'But right now, there aren't fabrics durable enough to be interwoven with cables and circuitry and still be worn comfortably on the body. In the meantime, my "Female Interfaces" collection provides me with a means of experimenting with how hardware can be integrated into fashion, so hopefully, phasing in software will be the next step.'

Before she began engaging with technology, Myrvold looked for fashion materials in unlikely outlets such as yachting supply wholesalers and interior textile shops. The fabrics were customised by dye and paint, or subjected to specialist processes such as printing, laser cutting, stitching or embroidery. 'When it comes to hand-finishing, these days I like to melt PVC into tulle, or cut up plastic bags and sew them onto toile. I'm also developing a silkscreen technique using concrete or metallic paint.' Myrvold often incorporates light effects into her garments by including reflective materials and shining surfaces. 'Reflective PVC has a dynamic surface that reacts to light and movement,' Myrvold says. 'By combining it with tulle and denim, or using it as trim, it transforms matt materials into lustrous surfaces.'

Tokyo-born artist and designer Kahori Maki roots her prints in the natural world, capturing both the exotic and the everyday in stylized expressions that seem to hover between dream and reality. Few would believe that Maki's love of nature could be attributed to an earlier life sandwiched between the glass and concrete canyons of New York. 'Paradoxically, living in Manhattan made me realise how much nature pervades urban life in Japan. When I moved back to Tokyo, I rediscovered how present Shintoism is in the city. I felt like nature was a part of the human soul, something

Japanese artist Kahori Maki has a distinctive style. Her textile works juxtapose black graphics against a white background, carefully sketched out in crisp outlines and velvety details.

eternal, something poetic and beautiful. You could say I work in response to urban life, yet express myself by depicting nature. The extremes of nature and urban life continue to inspire my work today.'[6]

Since she returned to Japan, Maki's prints have adorned a wide variety of media, knitting together the worlds of art, fashion and graphic design. Her work has spun threads between Japan and the West—strands navigated by Maki with the grace of an acrobat. Installations at the galleries in Tokyo and New York showcased her dramatic style: black graphics are juxtaposed against a white background, carefully drawn in swirling outlines and detailed etchings. Maki's work often features crisp outlines of verdant leaves and velvety flower petals, seductively intertwined with looping vines, forked foliage and lazy insects. 'I find beauty in things like spiders and caterpillars, forms that many would regard as grotesque or macabre,' Maki says. 'I can study an insect forever, noticing the gossamer textures of their wings and the soft fibres that cover their shells.'

Although most of us would regard insects as poisonous pests to be kept at a distance, Maki is not afraid to get up close. She depicts beetles with a dark lustre that

Many of Kahori Maki's motifs explore natural themes. Here, she depicts an insect's view of the world, guiding a beetle through intertwining flowers and looping vines.

evokes mystery, darkness and melancholy, and meandering snails that happily inhabit serpentine shells. Thick black strands outline the robust shapes of Maki's caterpillars, who trail alongside weightless butterflies gently opening their wings. 'I'm not afraid of looking into the shadows,' Maki says, 'and shedding light on the beautiful creatures that live in twilight worlds.'

'The figures I draw are about beauty more than anything else,' Maki explains. 'There is much more to beauty than just a look. Beauty is about elegance, style and strength, but also innocence too.' Maki's figures gaze outwards with eyes that have no pupils, a detail she likens to the slit pupils that reptiles have. She says: 'The position of the eyes and the shape of the pupils may suggest how people see the world around them. Reptiles are supposed to be scary, but their eyes have an uncanny innocence about them.'

Maki's artwork was first worn on the human body when she collaborated with Comme des Garçons, who printed her illustrations on a special collection of coats, jackets and skirts. 'I enjoyed that collaboration tremendously,' Maki says. 'Comme des Garçons treated my works like art and photographed them in a context that fused together fashion and fine art.' As Maki continues to translate the fashioned body into organic forms and edgy abstractions, her work reveals the unexpected power that beauty can have.

# Subversive Stitches

Needlework has a revolutionary reputation. William Morris famously used it as a symbol of dissent in his protest against industrial production. He wanted his textile designs to continue to be produced by hand, so he rebelled against industrialists to protect the Royal School of Needlework. Morris succeeded, and it is said today that he single-handedly revitalized the art of tapestry weaving in Britain. Another rebellion was sparked a century later when feminist artists incorporated needlework into their artwork. The artists challenged the distinction between art and craft that divided fibre art and fine art. Because needlework was considered to be a hobby or a domestic skill, it was not yet recognized as an art practice, and the presence of sewn objects, samplers and needlepoint in art provoked the American art establishment. Needlework was eventually acknowledged as an art form, but for many years sewn textiles and stitched surfaces continued to rank below the established art forms of painting and sculpture.

The new generation of emerging artists look to textiles as a source of innovation more than as a means of rebellion or political dissent. Fibres imbue artworks with colour, texture and tactility and incorporate techniques that provide a means of creating radical expressions, subversive imagery or simply beautiful motifs. Embroidery threads, in the hands of San Francisco-based artist Benji Whalen, are used to create unique surfaces that would be difficult to reproduce by hand and virtually impossible to reproduce mechanically.

After gaining a master's degree in painting at the San Francisco Art Institute in 1997, Whalen discovered embroidery on a visit to see his grandmother. Noticing that most of her interior textiles had been embellished with elaborate needlework, Whalen felt inspired to learn his grandmother's craft. He quickly learned the basic embroidery stitches, and since then, he's been embroidering cloth, making dummies and creating textile-based installations.

Whalen says that part of embroidery's appeal is that every individual stitch is unique. Extrapolated to the human body, tattooing is one means of enhancing the body with a unique motif. Like embroidery, tattooing is a needle-based practice used to create a wide range of styles and designs. Whalen reconstructs arms out of padding and lines them with a fabric skin that he can embroider tattoo motifs onto. Whalen's tattoos feature religious iconography, biker emblems, Goth symbols and sexual images. The

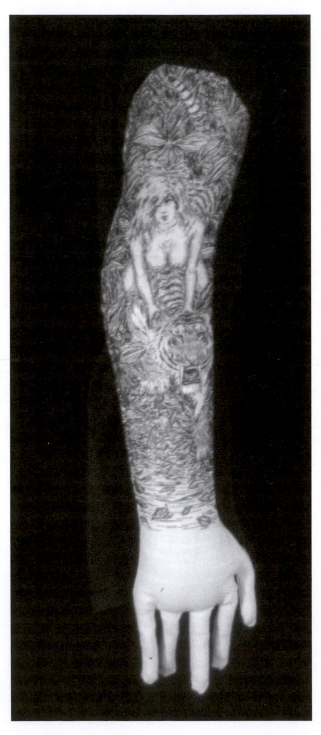

San Francisco–based artist Benji Whalen discovered embroidery on a visit to his grandmother. He quickly learned the basic embroidery stitches and began embroidering cloth to resemble cult tattoos.

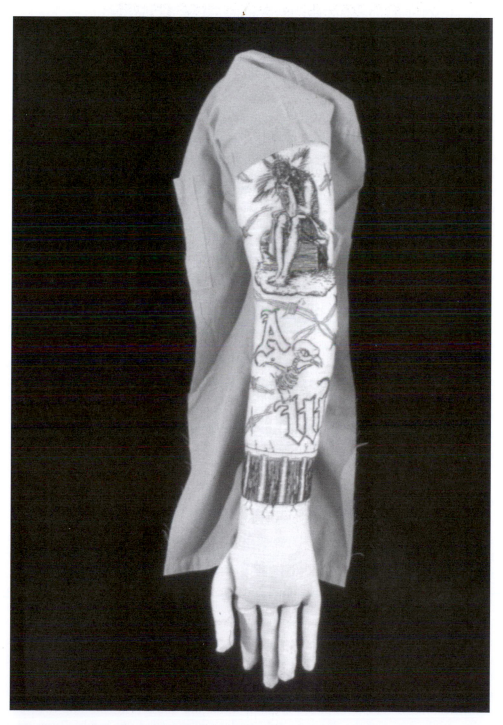

Embroidery techniques enable Whalen to create unique surfaces that would be difficult to reproduce by hand and virtually impossible to copy mechanically.

emblems Whalen embroiders reveal how human skin, like a textile surface, can be a compelling signifier of identity and can transmit powerful messages about the individuals who inscribe their bodies. Whalen's artworks show that textiles bridge diverse narratives more easily than many other types media do, and they invite interpretations that are both literal and metaphorical.

Sabrina Gschwandtner, a New York-based artist, works with sewing, crochet and knitting, which she combines with film, photography and video. In 2007, Gschwandtner created an interactive installation titled 'Wartime Knitting Circle', which consisted of nine machine-knitted photo blankets that chronicled the role of knitting during times of war.[7] Gschwandtner gathered images from ephemera, periodicals, historical societies and library archives that depicted how knitting had been used during wartime as a form of civic participation, protest and, more recently, as a way for families to remember relatives who had been deployed to Afghanistan and Iraq.

A previous work, titled 'Phototactic Behavior in Sewn Slides', features threads stitched onto slides Gschwandtner had taken with a 35 mm camera. As the slides were projected, the projector's fan blew the threads randomly, causing its automatic focusing mechanism to fluctuate as it tried to focus on the threads attached to the slides. The movements of the threads created an effect Gschwandtner likened to random animation, and the holes made by the sewing needle created a repeating pattern when they were projected.

Advances in digital technology provide textile practitioners with novel methods that liberate them from tedious, repetitive stitching. Yet some fibre artists prefer the homespun appeal of stitched surfaces, using the craft practice to create beautiful, often thought-provoking works. Dutch artist Annet Couwenberg, formerly chair of the fibre department at the Maryland Institute College of Art in Baltimore, merges both processes in works created through a method she describes as digitized embroidery. Repetition is a theme in Couwenberg's work, and digital technology enables her to replicate a single motif in different stitch patterns, sizes, orientations and palettes. Couwenberg cites seventeenth-century Dutch samplers as an inspiration behind her methodology, rooting them in the tradition of creating popular motifs or precisely stitched ciphers that are usually easy to decode. Using digital scans to outline a pattern to work from, Couwenberg rejects their uniformity by making random stitches or integrating unexpected materials into the work.

Anila Rubiku is Albanian but lives in Milan, where she combines needlework with artificial light sources to create luminous fabric installations. Rubiku uses techniques based on traditional Albanian embroideries to depict contemporary, often autobiographical, motifs. Rubiku stitched images depicting a journey she made from Milan to Tokyo across fifty linen surfaces and fastened them inside wooden embroidery frames. Rather than document the journey with photography or video, Rubiku decided to document her experiences in a textile archive. Rubiku also uses fabric to constructs fabric sculptures in the shape of miniature houses, embellishing their exteriors with scenes of the domestic tasks traditionally carried out inside. By using a domesticated craft practice to evoke the experience of domesticity, Rubiku brings the private world of family life under public scrutiny.

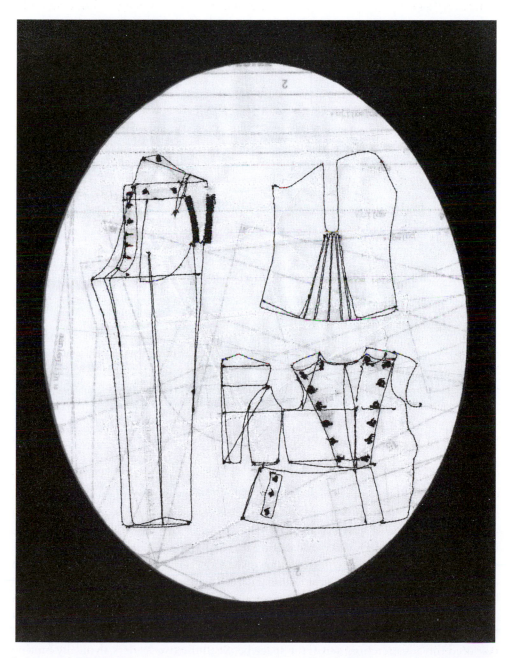

Baltimore-based Dutch artist Annet Couwenberg uses digital scans to create works inspired by seventeenth-century samplers. Couwenberg rejects their uniformity by making random stitches and integrating unexpected materials into the work.

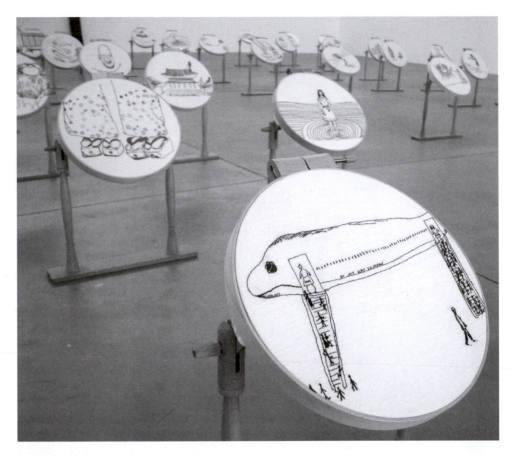

Anila Rubiku uses techniques based on traditional Albanian embroideries to depict contemporary, often autobiographical, motifs. The works here record memories from a journey to Japan.

Xiang Yang, a political activist and artist from Beijing who emigrated to America, stretched embroidery through space to create three-dimensional works. Yang began producing art based on political and social themes at a time when Chinese artists were forbidden to do so. He was arrested during the Tiananmen Square protests, when the authorities discovered his cynical portrait of Mao Zedong. Today, Yang continues to clash images of disparate political leaders, such as Saddam Hussein and George Bush, by embroidering their portraits onto clear plastic. Placing them back to back, with one a short distance behind the other, Xiang Yang pulls the threads from one embroidery to the other and back again. The process creates long, horizontal lengths of coloured threads stretching across the space between the two leaders, cynically hinting at complicity between them.

The works of these artists, like those of the previous sections, are pulling together some of the most exciting strands of contemporary visual culture today. Body empowerment, hybrid materials, radical new techniques and fresh interpretations of space suggest exciting new directions for both contemporary art and textile design.

Xiang Yang is a political activist and artist from Beijing who emigrated to the United States, where he continues to create art based on political themes. Here, Yang links images of Saddam Hussein and George Bush by embroidering their portraits onto plastic and pulling the threads back and forth between them.

As new forms unfold, with them come groundbreaking materials, new functions and new roles for the textile-based practices of the future.

## Feature Interview: Janet Echelman

Janet Echelman is an American artist who uses fibres to shape and define architectural space. Through her art, Echelman creates monumental public sculptures made of diaphanous, flexible nets that move and change shape. All of Echelman's commissions are site specific, and many of her sculptural installations are built outdoors, where they are designed to interact with natural forces such as wind and water. Because the nature of her work requires materials that allow air currents to move through her sculptures—a feature of her work that she describes as 'wind choreography'—Echelman discovered that strong fibres and lightweight fabrics are ideal materials for her art. Light also plays an important role in her work; rays of sunlight cast light and shadows over her sculptures by day, and by night, floodlights transform her work into glowing, luminous shapes. Echelman also considers how her sculptures project shadows onto adjoining surfaces, adding additional layers of movement and depth.

Janet Echelman's sculpture 'She Changes' is suspended from a massive ring of hollow steel hung between three steel poles of varying heights. It was crafted from Tenara, chosen for its resistance to strong winds and ability to retain its red pigment despite constant exposure to UV rays.

'She Changes' is a public artwork commissioned by the city of Porto in Portugal and situated near the port. The artist, Janet Echelman, designed its net-like structure to reference the region's seafaring and fishing history.

Janet Echelman uses fibres to shape and define architectural space. This public commission for the Richmond Olympic Oval in Richmond, British Columbia is crafted from industrial-strength Tenara.

Echelman designed and constructed one of the world's most extraordinary textile artworks in 2005. Titled 'She Changes', the sculpture was built on the waterfront in Porto, Portugal. Measuring forty-six metres in diameter and fourteen stories high, 'She Changes' is one of the biggest public sculptures in existence. The sculpture was created in collaboration with a textile manufacturer, an architect and a software developer. 'The artwork is actually a complex, multi-layered form created by twisting, braiding and knotting nearly one ton of Tenara fibres,' Echelman explains.[8] 'I got help from Phillip Speranza, a New York-based architect, to translate my drawings into 3-D computer models, then asked Peter Heppel, a sail software specialist based in Paris, to develop a software programme for the piece. The software showed me how the sculpture would move in the wind and revealed what engineering considerations there would be.' The textile structure was fabricated in Washington State by hand and by machine, then shipped to Portugal in pieces. Cranes were brought to the site to hang it, where it was suspended from a massive ring of hollow steel hung between three steel poles of varying heights. 'The sculpture is similar to a net', Echelman explains. 'It was created using a fibre that could withstand a windy environment with long periods of UV exposure. Tenara is light enough to respond to the wind and durable enough to retain its red pigment despite long periods of UV exposure. I had looked at plant fibres, silk and nylon, but none of them have the durability of Tenara.'[9]

Echelman used high tenacity multifilament polypropylene to create an indoor sculpture for a multistorey car park in Tampa, Florida. 'There's little natural light, so I included 36-degree ellipsoidal spotlights and dichroic glass filters in the work,' Echelman explains. 'There are two parts. The first part is a three-dimensional line drawing suspended from the ceiling. The second part has no physical presence at all, and is merely a projection of the other, creating a 400-foot-long shadow drawing. I began to see this as a contemporary interpretation of Plato's Allegory of the Cave, using urban infrastructure as a modern-day cave wall.'

Echelman uses fibres to relate the story of the tension between movement and stillness, between the tangible and the ephemeral. With fibres as her medium, Echelman's works show the extent to which textiles can be sculptural, tactile and architectural expressions. The scale of her work reveals that textiles have the potential to create large-scale installations, taking contemporary art to completely new heights.

# seven

# Interior Textiles

Interior architecture and contemporary textiles have an odd, somewhat unresolved relationship. Although fabrics hold the potential to structure space, dampen sound and emanate light, they are usually confined to a secondary role within the interior. Traditionally, interior textiles have been seen as soft furnishings and used as decorative accessories, but this is changing as materials such as glass filaments, carbon fibres, conductive wires and metal mesh begin to replace architectural substrates. Sensors and robotic membranes can be integrated into fabric more easily than they can be into conventional materials, paving the way for high performance textiles that line floors, walls and ceilings. And as they reveal their ability to emanate light, react to heat, dampen acoustics and interact with digital technology, the new textiles made for interior design are definitely making their presence felt.

For several decades, architects have been softening the built environment on many levels. Deconstructivist architects introduced a new porosity to the interior by bringing structural textiles indoors. Used to partition space, these materials were framed, stretched and pulled taut, yet continued to remain softer than conventional materials. To reinforce their architectural integrity, these textiles were seldom permitted to hang, drape or furl to express their inherent tactility. Things shifted in the 1990s when leading architects began to collaborate with textile designers rather than working directly with the fabrics themselves. Rem Koolhaas's collaborations with Petra Blaisse, for example, resulted in tactile interiors and soft membrane structures that redefined the role of textile design in architectural space.[1] They added tactile textures to sleek interiors, which enabled visitors to experience the whole building as a tactile form.

Although the new generation of interior fabrics are regarded as high tech devices, many can be described as beautiful too. Furnishing fabrics can be woven from fibre optic strands, and light-emitting diodes illuminate and sparkle, while thermochromatic

German architect Jürgen Mayer used pleated fabric to create these elliptical columns. The installation was designed for Nya Nordiska's exhibition at a design trade fair in Frankfurt.

surfaces project an ever-changing range of colour and motifs. Friction-free carpet, stain-resistant upholstery and wipe-clean surfaces were once considered to be desperately dull, but these days, they feature some of the richest textures and colourways found in the interior.

As interior textiles forge new relationships with the built environment, the projects that result are striking showcases of the unique textures and technologies that fibre-based forms can have. The sections that follow present these fabrics in completely new guises as they combine cutting-edge aesthetics with the amenities of contemporary interiors. The structures that result can be robust enough to replace architectural details yet beautiful enough to resemble contemporary art.

## Soft Walls

Throughout time, fabrics and soft furnishings have been considered to be an essential part of the interior, and now they are beginning to shape the way environments are designed and built. The use of interior textiles waned during the 1990s, when streamlined minimalism dominated interior architecture. Today they have resurfaced as tactile expressions of architectural forms, softening hard edges and soothing the rupture between the built environments of man and the textured landscapes of nature.

When it comes to interior fabrics, leading textile designers tend to think in terms of architectural space rather than two-dimensional planes. As textile designers work collaboratively with architects, preservationists and urban planners to create textiles that take shape in response to volume, function and spatial proportions, their input often shapes the whole project. Designers such as Hil Driessen and Anne Kyyrö Quinn specialize in site-specific work, and, as colour expert Ptolemy Mann explained in Chapter 4, her work usually begins even before the architects have broken ground. The sections that follow reveal how textile designers can shape and define space, moderate acoustics and temper lighting. As they do so, they enable textiles to transcend their decorative role yet continue to add elements of softness, colour and tactility.

## DRIESSEN + VAN DEIJNE

Textile designer Hil Driessen and interior architect Toon van Deyne are based in Amsterdam, where they work collaboratively as Driessen + van Deijne.[2] Their multi-faceted approach has landed a number of landmark interior design projects that have broadened the horizons of textile design. Like many other Dutch designers, their work is imbued with irony and irreverence and a drive to find new applications for traditional materials. But their style is unique, and so is their ability to bridge spatial extremes.

Driessen and van Deyne have designed exhibitions, created fabric motifs, launched ranges of fibre-based products and embarked on a project for DSM Dyneema to find new applications for one of the world's strongest fibres. Added to that, their portfolio includes an impressive number of high profile architectural commissions. 'From the beginning of my career, architects have used my work for acoustic applications, or just added them as decoration,' Driessen said.[3] 'When I was invited by Annette Marx from Marx & Steketee Architects in Eindhoven to work on a historical interior, it gave me the perfect chance to explore Baroque-style *trompe l'oeil,* which has long been a staple charm in the designer's bag of tricks.'

The City University of Utrecht had commissioned Driessen to produce wall-mounted textile panels for their nineteenth-century period rooms. The preservation architects had concluded that the original wallpaper had deteriorated too far to be restored yet decided to preserve the period paint finishes on the cornices and woodwork. 'It was important to preserve the paint work,' Driessen explained, 'but looking at them didn't quite transport you to another place. So I knew that the wall textiles would have to do that.'

Driessen started by folding and stitching a sheet of vinyl to create the silhouette of a spectral tree. The stitched vinyl was then photographed in the shadow of a real tree, and manipulated through digital software to give the image a ghostly appearance. The shadowy image that resulted was then printed onto Trevira CS fabric and mounted onto the walls where the original wallpaper had once hung. 'The digitally-printed fabric had visual depth and created a surprisingly tactile surface,' Driessen says. 'People wondered if it was a real landscape or a futuristic image. I saw people

Driessen + van Deijne folded and stitched a sheet of vinyl to create the silhouette of this two-dimensional tree. The stitched vinyl was then photographed in the shadow of a real tree and manipulated digitally before being printed onto Trevira CS fabric and mounted to the wall.

stretch out their hand to feel the texture of the knotted bark, then look again in wonder, realising they'd been duped.'

For a residential architectural project known as 'IJburg block 52a/b,' Driessen + van Deijne were commissioned by Jan Bakers Architects to design balcony railings for a waterside apartment complex. They created a print inspired by rippling water, turned it into a digital image and printed it onto 750 glass sheets, which they installed instead of balcony railings. By using an image of a textile they were able to relate the complex more closely to its surroundings and bring the illusion of the sun reflecting on water to apartments that did not have a waterside view.

The Dudok Wonen company commissioned Driessen + van Deijne to design an interior for a presentation room in their headquarters in Hilversum. They encircled the space with textiles hung from the ceiling, creating a flexible wall system that could screen the windows but also unify the space. Driessen was inspired by the work of the Britain-based American landscape architect Charles Jencks, the Dutch modernist architect Willem Marinus Dudok, who was actually the city architect for Hilversum, and historical panorama paintings. She also photographed layers of folded green velvet and organza, which resembled abstractions of the rolling hills and terraces seen in an undulating landscape. By combining this diverse range of inspirations and manipulating the imagery digitally, Driessen created a motif depicting rippling forms and shaded outlines, which they printed digitally onto lightweight Trevira CS.

Although Driessen is an expert when it comes to complex imagery, she also likes to create surface effects through simple means. 'Just by padding, stitching, cutting, folding or printing, I can reinvent cheap-looking materials such as imitation leather and rubber as sculptural textiles,' she says. 'But at the same time, it is important to me to stay in touch with technology and collaborate with the industry to develop new materials.'

By digitally manipulating photographs of folded green velvet, Driessen + van Deijne created a motif depicting an abstract landscape, which they transferred onto lightweight Trevira CS.

Driessen pioneered a new relationship between ceramics and textiles when she received a residency at the European Ceramic Work Centre in The Netherlands. 'As a textile designer, the challenge of working with ceramics was a lifetime experience,' she says. With the help of the technical staff, she was able to develop a process to create objects that were hybrids of porcelain and fibres. 'I dipped pieces of crocheted cotton into liquid porcelain and fired them in the kiln,' Driessen explains. 'The cotton burned away, but left its imprint behind. The objects that resulted were photographed and manipulated digitally using computer software, then printed onto cotton.'

A master of illusions, Driessen almost always anchors her work to the real world. As she marries textile forms to architectural substrates such as glass, metal and ceramics, she continues to create hybrid forms that dramatically reshape the environments they are made for.

## CAMILLA DIEDRICH

Swedish designer Camilla Diedrich was one of the first Europeans to structure textiles in terms of negative space. Diedrich likes cutting holes in fabric, and her early works seemed to relate more to deconstructivist architecture than it did to fabric design. From her base in Stockholm, Diedrich has produced an extensive range of

Swedish textile designer Camilla Diedrich uses lasers to create circular shapes and spiralling textures. Her A.H.I.T. design, shown here, was formed through computer-automated laser cuts.

wall hangings, room dividers and pendant lamps, manufactured in synthetic textiles and bulk materials.[4] Many of her designs, such as those produced by Kvadrat Sanden, are both printed and laser cut. The fabrics known as ASAP and EDT reinvent the traditional genre of floral fabric, giving it a high tech update.

Diedrich's first experiments with interior textiles explored a range of materials that, at the time, were usual in fabric design. 'I used rattan in some of my weavings and soaked them in a bath so that they would bend and expand,' she says.[5] 'I also wove with glass. When I was asked to make upholstery I created a double-weave technique that incorporated pieces of wool to give the surface a richer texture. I knitted and felted textiles to create unconventional surface textures, and made a sculptural, functional textile that looked like a footstool but unrolled flat to create an overnight mattress for a guest.'

Her penchant for empty spaces inspired her to experiment with laser cutting, which imbued her works with the transparency and texture more typical of a building façade than a length of fabric. Diedrich began using lasers to create circular shapes and spiralling patterns and to perforate fabrics with small holes to make them semi-transparent. Her work transforms flat surfaces into textured forms that challenge conventional ideas of how textiles can be used to divide space. Designs such as her AHIT, HIT, AHIT and EDT fabrics, designed for Kvadrat Sanden, are collages of laser cuts formed through computer-automated cut-outs, or laser shapes combined with printed motifs. Commissions from IKEA resulted in the Anno Fin, Anno Ljuv and Anno Skön series of textile panels. Italian manufacturer Rotaliana produce Diedrich's BPL pendant lamp, enabling her to combine her textile expertise and design skills in a single product.

Diedrich is currently exploring the potentials that photonic materials hold for interior textiles. 'I want to make fabrics that light up, but I want to develop a technique that makes it possible without using diodes,' she says. Diedrich's starting point was to print photonic pigments onto paper, which she mounted onto panels, ceilings and walls. It inspired Diedrich to create her Enlightened wallpaper range, which is printed and coated with materials that enable it to react to light.

## SOPHIE MALLEBRANCHE

The textiles produced by Paris-based designer Sophie Mallebranche are atmospheric and evocative without striving for effect. Her works are born out of understated sentiments, but they make strong statements. 'I'm a textile designer, but I'm also someone who is addicted to imagination, poetry and dreams,' Mallebranche says.[6] 'You could say that while I work, my mind is absorbed by a world of five square inches, but my intention is to lead the person who will touch my fabric to a dimension far beyond that.'[7]

Mallebranche takes textiles far beyond surface expressions as she uses them to create spatial forms. 'My challenge is to create three-dimensionally with a material that is often regarded as two-dimensional,' she says. 'I believe in extending the boundaries

French textile designer Sophie Mallebranche explores a wide range of unconventional materials in her work. She typically prefers rigid materials or substances that have volume, from which she can create structured textiles.

of textiles far beyond functionality. To do that, I search for sensitive materials, because it's essential to find the right way to integrate light, colour and texture.'

Mallebranche's experimentation with metal fibres has earned her a reputation as a material innovator. She transforms sleek metal fibres into gossamer meshes that come alive in the ambient light. 'I grew up with a fascination for metals,' Mallebranche said. 'As I child I played in the kitchen of my family's restaurant in Normandy, dashing between enamelled refrigerators, stainless steel workbenches and copper pans. Much later, when I was a student at the Duperré School of Applied Arts in Paris, I was still influenced by the kitchen environment. My thesis examined how one could bring sensitive awareness to the materials used in refrigerators merely by transforming them into something else. I thought it could be achieved by trying to weave these unusual materials, which were created in the second industrial revolution. So finding a sensitive expression for metals became my own artistic vocabulary.'

Metal fibres hold many potential applications for interior textiles, and Mallebranche has identified several that she would like to develop in the future. 'Because they can conduct energy, electromagnetic impulses and acoustic phonetics, they have the potential to give textiles these characteristics,' she says. 'Their capacity for transmitting solar energy is promising—I can imagine designing a curtain able to transform solar energy into light or heat. I may not be able to take these things forward when I work with fabrics today, but that's okay. I'm still focused on creating the textiles of tomorrow.' Although metal fibres do offer some sustainable solutions, Mallebranche points out that they may present environmental hazards also. 'I'm concerned about the quality, durability and environmental impact of metals,' she said, 'but they have positive properties too.'

Commissioned by luxury retailers such as Guerlain, leading hoteliers such the Hôtel Plaza Athénée and legendary restaurants such as Drugstore Publicis on the Champs-Elysées, Mallebranche's work is finding expression in some of the most renowned interiors in Paris. 'Most of the time I bring something theatrical to the space,' Mallebranche says. 'At that level, my creations can be considered to be architectural elements or interior textures. My starting point is to make an interesting response to the space. Then I concentrate on the joy of experimentation until I find solutions that may surprise myself.'

## GRETHE WITTROCK

Known for her distinctive style and individualistic textiles, artist and designer Grethe Wittrock is to Danish textiles what Arne Jacobsen was to furniture. Wittrock combined her studies at the Danish Design School with a scholarship to study fine art at Kyoto Seika University in Japan. Wittrock's work has been exhibited worldwide, in cultural capitals such as London, Paris, Munich, Sao Paolo and Kyoto. Wittrock lives and works in New York today, where her Nordic sensibilities shape her response to the values and lifestyles she encounters there.[8]

Wittrock says her approach is 'meditative', describing it as 'a process of repetition that allows me to create simple, strong, poetic works of art.'[9] While to some it may seem that Wittrock uses traditional techniques to create forward-thinking designs, she points out that the techniques she uses are actually ancient. 'I weave by hand, knotting and braiding strings of silk, gold and paper yarn.' Many of the materials Wittrock uses are custom dyed in Japan, often imbuing her Scandinavian élan with the understated elegance of traditional Japanese textiles.

Most of Wittrock's work has been anchored to sleek interior environments where her artworks, wall-hangings and fibre installations have been displayed. Large-scale

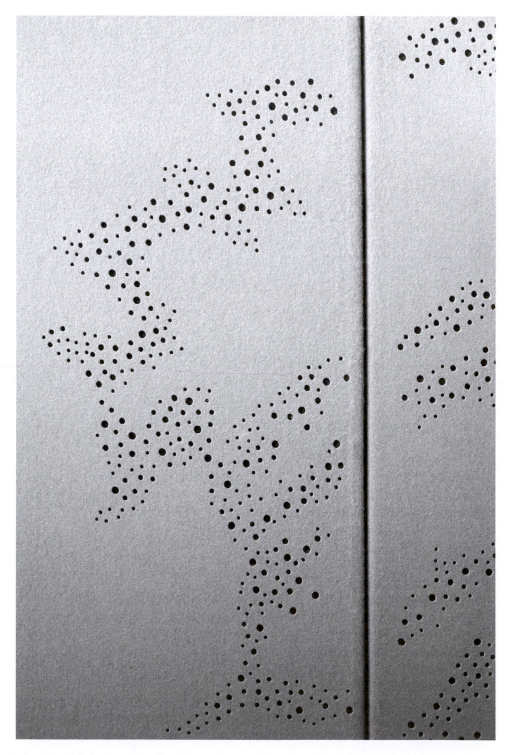

When Danish designer Grethe Wittrock was commissioned to help a bank resolve the acoustic problems they were experiencing, she designed sound–absorbing panels from wool fabric.

works such as 'The Cousin' (2004), 'Amulet' (2007) and 'Gold Reserve' (2009) have been installed in museums, galleries and a range of other public spaces. 'Gold Reserve' consists of thousands of knotted gold threads. The textile was crafted to tell the story of the Danish gold reserves shipped to New York before World War II for safekeeping. Wittrock used precious threads made from silk and strands of gold to represent the value of the cargo in textile form.

Wittrock's spectacular 'Aqua' wall-hanging was made to resemble a sea of shimmering light. Wittrock knotted each of the 73,000 threads by hand, using forty-two kilometres of translucent blue nylon to create the work. The blue-tinted fibres appear to capture the colour of the sea, as if they were seen through the water of an aquarium. The tips of the fibres emit an intense glow, sparkling as if tiny crystals have formed at the ends.

In 2004, a commission from the Danish Pension Bank in Copenhagen gave Wittrock an opportunity to explore the acoustic value of textiles. 'I was commissioned to help the bank resolve the acoustic problems that they were experiencing in their offices,' Wittrock explains, 'so I solved it by making sound-absorbing panels. For decorative, as well as acoustic reasons, I chose 100% wool fabric, which I perforated by hand.' Wittrock sought the advice of Anders Gade, an acoustic expert responsible for the acoustic quality of the auditoriums in Copenhagen's newly built concert hall. 'I had been working with him on several commissions to solve acoustic problems with textiles in new architecture constructed from steel and glass.' Gade recommended that Wittrock incorporate Rockfon, a sound-absorbing material, into the panels, so she used it as a substrate to mount the fabric on.[10] The perforations in the fabric enabled it to act as a filter, and any sound waves that passed beyond it were absorbed by the Rockfon. 'The combination of the materials completely solved the noise problem,' Wittrock says. 'The green and grey fabric I chose were colours from the bank's new colour scheme, which made the panels appear as if they were chosen to reinforce the bank's identity rather than soak up the noise made by their cheerful customers.'

## ANNE KYYRÖ QUINN

From her base in London, Finnish-born Anne Kyyrö Quinn is pioneering a sleek solution for the problem plaguing many contemporary interiors: noise. Recognizing the acoustic properties that 100 per cent felt wool can have, the designer developed a range of layered textiles engineered to dampen sound or absorb it altogether.[11] 'The surfaces of my fabrics are intricately structured,' Kyyrö Quinn explains, 'which makes them highly absorptive. Wool is too soft to reverberate, so the fabric diffuses the sound and reduces the decibel count by almost 75%. Loops and folds in the surface motif create tiny cavities that wick sound waves into the layer of fabric underneath. Like an acoustic sponge, the textile soaks up ambient noise.'[12]

Kyyrö Quinn discovered the acoustic properties of her designs by accident when she was on site to supervise the installation of her work. 'Three big textile panels were mounted onto a wall in a very busy, noisy space,' she says. 'They unwrapped them

Anne Kyyrö Quinn designed floor-to-ceiling felt panels for the conference rooms of Bovis Lend Lease's London headquarters to absorb background noises and make the sound quality of conference calls clearer.

and began mounting them on the wall, and I stepped back to take a look. Suddenly, I noticed that all the noise had disappeared, and I realised that the fabric had absorbed it.' Kyyrö Quinn took a selection of panels to the Sound Research Laboratory in Sudbury, Suffolk, where scientists concluded that, depending on the volume and density of the felt used in a particular design, the sound absorption coefficient varied from 0.55 to 1.00 (H). Kyyrö Quinn's textiles performed well, with signature designs, such as the classic Cable motif, rated class A (A being the highest on a scale of A–D). 'It is useful to have the report,' Kyyrö Quinn explains, 'because cinemas, theatres and auditoriums invest in acoustic materials, and now I have proof that my felt panels are one of them.'

Kyyrö Quinn's acoustic panels have been commissioned for showrooms and public spaces, famously at De Beers Diamonds' London showroom, where she created dramatic backdrops that echoed the facets of the cut gems. At Viva restaurant, Kyyrö Quinn's wall installations set the scene for fine dining while also transforming a noisy open-plan area into an oasis of calm. Floor-to-ceiling panels in the conference rooms of Bovis Lend Lease's London headquarters muffle background noises to make the sound quality of conference calls clearer. Kyyrö Quinn's acoustic designs were also

Kyyrö Quinn's wool acoustic panels were tested by the Sound Research Laboratory in Sudbury, Suffolk, where scientists concluded that they soak up ambient noise better than many man-made acoustic materials.

commissioned by the new National Tennis Centre near Wimbledon, but they were apparently chosen more for their resemblance to contemporary art than for their ability to dampen sound.

When renovations to a historic building situated at 80 Pall Mall in London were nearly completed, the art consultants involved in the project invited Kyyrö Quinn to view the space. 'They had seen my work in an exhibition at the Royal Academy and liked its decorative aesthetic, which they thought would suit the new interior,' Kyyrö Quinn says. 'I liked the idea of contributing to the project, and I could see that my work would suit it. The textiles I design are quite contemporary, as is the newly-refurbished interior they commissioned it for. Of course, the building itself was much older than the techniques used to renovate it, and felt, as a material and a technique, is so ancient that it predates any other fine art material used today. From that perspective, my work can be regarded as a synthesis of very old and very new, just like the interior at 80 Pall Mall is.'

Kyyrö Quinn designed and fabricated a floor-to-ceiling panel for the project, the largest single panel she has created to date. 'My clients wanted something on a particular wall that can be seen from the street,' Kyyrö Quinn says. 'In fact, it's a focal point for the ground floor of the building. Although the commission was to create something decorative, experience told me that the marble floors and walls would reverberate quite a bit from the noise of the street and the people working in the building. I knew it would take a huge felt surface to absorb the sound and dampen the noise levels, so I designed a panel six meters wide by three meters high. It did the trick.'

Like all of Kyyrö Quinn's work, the panel was cut, sewn and mounted by hand. The panel is made from a single colour, but slight differences in the fibres' densities and textures created subtle variations. The surface is embellished with strips of felt that twist across it diagonally, catching the light from some angles and casting shadows from others. 'You know, people look at my work and think it's really high tech,' Kyyrö Quinn says. 'They don't usually realise that I work with lo-tech materials and traditional hand-craftsmanship. My parents' generation used felt all the time, but today it is used so sparingly that people barely recognise it.'

In her book *Felt Furnishings,* Kyyrö Quinn describes felt as a simple material that has an impressive range of diverse functions.[13] 'As a child I used it to craft toys, and now, as an adult, I'm using felt as an acoustic textile, an art material and as fabric for interior furnishings,' she says. 'Felt is environmentally-friendly, tactile, soft, durable and easy to work with. It performs just like any other interior textile, sometimes even better. Thicker densities of felt possess unrivalled structure and strength, making them perfect for interior architecture. Felt can be fire-proofed like any other material, and because the fibres are so heavily compressed, it is as strong as it is beautiful.'

# Fibre Furniture

Although furniture fulfils a functional role, it is one of the most decorative forms found in the interior. Furniture has been a part of the human experience since mankind formed nomadic cultures, in the forms of hides, carpets, hammock-like slings and padded fabrics. Early furniture consisted of textile lengths bound to wooden frames, and fabric continues to play a strong role in furniture today.

Around the beginning of the twenty-first century, a trend to craft furniture from structural textiles and high performance fibres kicked off in Europe and spread to North America and Japan. Whereas furniture is traditionally constructed from a frame built from metal, plastic or wood and combined with textile parts, cutting-edge designers began using textile techniques to create seat, frame and surface in a single gesture. Furniture designers began exploring the potentials of memory materials, flexible supports, carbon filaments and aramid fibres in their work. As a result, techniques such as weaving, crocheting, braiding and felting were used to craft chairs, tables, chaise longues and room dividers. By finding new applications for traditional techniques, furniture designers opened up a new realm of potentials for textile design.

None of the designers featured in this section are textile practitioners, but each has produced work that makes a considerable contribution to the field. Their combinations of functionalism, artistic expression and skilful revival of textile techniques give

Marcel Wanders's acclaimed Knotted chair is fabricated from aramid fibres. Wanders used a macramé technique, knotting several hundred metres of aramid braid around a carbon-fibre core.

their works an unusual edge. Their designs are viewed as some of the most visionary examples of furniture made today and hold the potential to map out new directions for future textiles.

Award-winning designer Marcel Wanders has been at the centre of the Dutch design scene since graduating from the Hogeschool voor de Kunsten in Arnhem in 1988. Wanders was one of the first contemporary designers to explore techniques used in textile practice as a means of constructing furniture. As part of the Dry Tech series produced by Droog Design in 1996, Wanders designed the acclaimed Knotted Chair, a lightweight lounger completely fabricated from aramid fibres. By using a macramé technique, Wanders knotted several hundred metres of aramid braid around a carbon–fibre core. The chair was then impregnated with epoxy resin and hung in a frame to dry. The fibres hardened as they dried, creating a hard-wearing, lightweight structure that was flexible yet strong. The chair combines the tactility of a textile with the durability of quality furniture, while combining the low tech technique of mac-ramé with high tech epoxy resin. The Knotted Chair is considered to be iconic today and has been acquired by museums such as New York's Museum of Modern Art for the permanent design collection.

Following from his visionary use of macramé, Wanders found furniture applica-tions for another traditional textile technique: lace-making. Wanders used Swiss lace to create a low, cube-like side table characterized by a repeating floral pattern. Like the

Marcel Wanders's Fishnet chair is constructed from a rope of aramid twisted around a carbon-fibre core. The aramid is knotted into a chair shape, impregnated with epoxy and hung on a frame to harden.

Knotted Chair, the lace was impregnated with resin that formed a robust structure as it hardened. Wanders experimented with another textile technique in 2006, this time using crochet to fabricate an entire armchair. The armchair that resulted was a tour de force of traditional techniques, tactile fibres and impregnation processes that rigidified several square metres of crochet fabric. The Crochet Chair was produced in a limited edition of 20 for the Smart Deco project presented in Miami, jointly organized by Droog Design and the Barry Friedman Gallery.

In a collaboration with fellow Dutch designer Bertjan Pot, Wanders codesigned the Carbon Chair, a graphite-coloured side chair. The chair was completely fabricated by hand, made of carbon fibre without any other structural materials. The carbon-fibre

Marcel Wanders fabricated an entire armchair from crochet. Once the crocheted shape was completed, the armchair was impregnated to rigidify the crochet into a solid form.

rope was coiled to form the seat, backrest, rims and legs, then coated with epoxy to prevent the fibres from uncoiling. Although the mesh-like pattern appears to be random, it was carefully calculated to maximize the strength of the carbon fibre. Each point on the rim of the chair connects with each of the four points where the bolt anchors the seat to the legs. Pot used another fibrous material to design the glass–fibre pendant lamp Random. Although the shade is massive, its mesh-like construction breaks down the mass of its surface while still masking the light fixture inside.

Bertjan Pot has created a number of directional fibre-based furniture designs. His Molten Couch, designed in 2001, is formed by traditional upholstery stuffed with fibre filling.[14] A couch made without a frame or sub-frame, it is essentially a giant cushion. The couch has an organic shape that completely moulds itself to the shape of those seated in it. Perhaps the antithesis to the Molten Couch, Pot's Seamless Chair is made from a heavy metal frame upholstered using a felting technique. The chair was made for a project organized by the Dutch initiatives Stichting Sofa and De Ploeg, who invited Pot to invent a new means of upholstering furniture. By felting 100 per cent wool fibres directly around the frame, Pot used a traditional textile technique to create a new upholstery method.

A commission from the Audax Textile Museum in Tillburg resulted in Pot's Big String Sofa, a huge, high-backed seating arrangement designed to divide the space between the museum's entrance and the café. The sofa was crafted from a towering steel frame coiled with polypropylene string in a rainbow of different colours. Rather than design cushions for the seats, Pot used black sheepskin to introduce an unexpected colour and texture to the design.

Danish furniture designer Mathias Bengtsson is based in London, and like Wanders and Pot, he uses carbon fibre material. Bengtsson's commitment to research and experimentation with carbon fibres is unique and has led to innovations that revealed new aspects of the material to the rest of the design industry. Bengtsson's fascination with the material inspired him to embark on a quest for techniques that would enable him to craft furniture from it. Discovering that the material could be woven and braided, Bengtsson began spinning the fibres into a range of cylindrical shapes from which he crafted tube-like benches, sloping chaise longues and conical lounge chairs that cocoon those seated in a carbon fibre web.

Explaining his use of the material to create his 'Spun carbon-fibre chair', Bengtsson says: 'In making the chair I bridge two circles with a series of straight fibres rotated by a robot arm during manufacturing to form two cone shapes. As it does so, the top ring turns slowly on its own axis, spinning around 200 metres of carbon-fibre on the diagonal as it moves through the bottom ring and back again. Once completed, the fibres are impregnated with an epoxy solution that enhances their strength and durability. Despite its substantial strength, the finished chair weighs only 900 grams.'[15]

Bengtsson designed a carbon-fibre bench and a carbon-fibre chaise longue that are equally feather-light, and their semitransparent structure seems to disguise the extraordinary strength of the carbon. Bengtsson explains that he 'spins a single carbon fibre into a slender, mesh-like layer that weaves a cylindrical shape. The flexibility of the mesh moulds to the body as it cradles the sitter in the same comfort that would be afforded by a sprung base.'[16] Bengtsson's designs are unique in unilaterally merging surface, structure and suspension into a single form, eclipsing the need for additional supports or padding, and they could portend a new direction for outdoor furniture design.

Award-winning Danish designer Louise Campbell was one of the first furniture designers to find new applications for textiles. From her base in Copenhagen, Campbell works within a vast repertoire of materials, designing furniture and lighting. When she entered a competition to design a chair for Denmark's Crown Prince Frederik in 2001, she decided that the chair should express aspects of his personality in the design. Campbell says that the Crown Prince Frederik was 'bound by centuries of firm traditions, and yet a young man very much in touch with his generation who lives a life full of contrasts. These contrasts were the obvious inspiration in designing the chair.'

A commission from the Audax Textile Museum in Tillburg led Bertjan Pot to design the Big String Sofa, a high-backed seat that divides the museum's entrance from the café. The sofa was crafted from polypropylene string coiled into a rainbow of bright colours.

Campbell expressed the contrasts in her choice of materials, constructing the seat and backrest in a layered assemblage of powder-coated steel and rubber neoprene laminated with felt. She designed a lacy pattern for the seat and backrest, which she water cut right through the fabric and metal. Like a lace textile, the chair was solely structured by a intricate pattern that enabled the onlooker to see beyond its surface. 'There is a point to the transparency of the chair—it is hard for a prince to hide from the public eye,' Campbell says. 'On one level it illustrates a motif resembling fine old lace, on the other level the chair is produced using visibly high technology methods.'[17]

Danish designer Mathias Bengtsson created this carbon–fibre table by stringing a series of straight fibres between two circular shapes. The fibres were then impregnated with an epoxy solution to enhance their durability and strength.

The chair exemplifies how manufacturing processes developed to shape wood, metal and plastic can also be used to perforate textiles and create identical motifs in both. The process enabled Campbell to create an alternative to the bulky padding and cushioning typical of most lounge chairs. 'The steel creates the framework of this chair, the rubber gives it softness and comfort, a refreshing alternative to upholstery,' says Campbell.

Campbell had explored textiles in her work even before she designed the Prince Chair. She says: 'I wanted to fold a chair from a single piece of perfectly square felt, and I wanted to harden it with an equally natural material. I tested various solutions before I opted for gelatine. After dipping the felt in a huge basin of water and 750 sheets of dissolved domestic gelatine (an exercise which required timely precision, as the gelatine goes lumpy within about ten minutes) the wet material was suspended within a large wooden frame by hundreds of meticulously positioned strings. The felt was left to dry for two weeks before being dismantled. In all, a very low-tech way of achieving a rather complex and surprisingly strong construction. Why do all this? To see what would happen. Was it a waste of time? Certainly not. This chair has inspired many of my later works.'

A chair Campbell designed in 1998 was inspired by the spider's ability to spin silk as a means of trapping prey and building a place where it can retreat to. Known as the 'Lazy Greedy Chair', the funnel-like design resembles the intricate strands of a spider

Louise Campbell was one of the first furniture designers in Denmark to find new applications for textiles. This chair's seat and backrest are constructed from layers of rubber neoprene laminated with felt.

web. Campbell constructed the chair from a frame made of four-millimetre steel thread, which she wrapped with strands of white angora wool fibres that had a combined length of four kilometres. Four years later she designed the lattice-like 'Relief' chair, a low reclining lounger crafted from a single sheet of laser-cut aluminium that stretched open like mesh. Campbell wrapped the metal frame in nylon thread of different colours, creating a multicoloured chair that combined structure and surface in a single design.

Like Campbell, Japanese designer Tokujin Yoshioka began working with fabrics early on in his career. But because he came from a fashion background (Yoshioka studied design under Issey Miyake and worked for him from 1988 to 1992), textiles were an integral part of his training and trade.[18] But since establishing his design studio in 2000, the designer has used materials such as crystal, glass and resin to create furniture, lighting and electronics. As well as producing products under his own name, Yoshioka has designed furniture for manufacturers in Japan and Europe.

Yoshioka felt inspired to explore the potentials of fibres in product design after reading a *National Geographic* article about new types of textiles. Reading how some

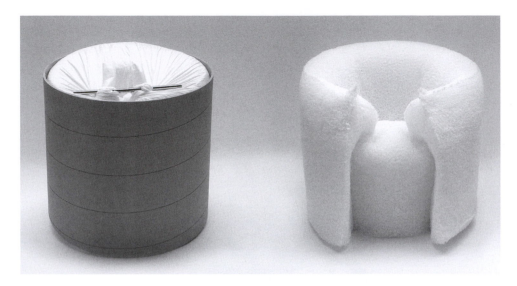

Tokujin Yoshioka crafted this chair from polyester elastomer fibres, using a cardboard tube to mould them into shape. The fibres were subjected to intense heat to fuse them together, enabling them to hold the shape after they were removed from the cardboard tube.

fibrous structures can be soft yet demonstrate great strength, Yoshioka realized that they may hold potentials for furniture design. He wanted to explore how they would react to force and to test their ability to absorb energy and disperse it throughout their forms.[19] Yoshioka's research led him to polyester elastomer fibres, which can be moulded into new shapes by heat. Yoshioka compressed several kilos of fibres into a thick semicircular wedge, which he curved into a circular shape. Pressure was applied to sculpt the wedge into a chair shape, which was bound in a fireproof sheet and then inserted into a cardboard tube. The chair was baked in a kiln at 104 degrees Celsius until the heat fused the fibres together, enabling them to hold the shape after they were removed from the cardboard mould.

Like oven-baked bread, the eponymous Pane Chair ('pane' means bread in Italian) was formed by a heat process rather being constructed through traditional processes. Yoshioka's approach mimics a felting technique, using pressure and energy to create a textile membrane. Yoshioka later used the principles behind the Pane Chair to design seating for Italian manufacturer Moroso in 2007, creating the Panna Chair. The chair is crafted from polyurethane foam attached to a metal skeleton with a textured upholstery woven from thick yarns. The Panna Chair's surface is crafted with stitching to reinforce its shape; an unbroken, continuous seam connects the base, back and sides, joined by seams that anchor the armrests in place. Moroso also manufactured Yoshioka's Bouquet design, a chair whose seat blooms atop a chrome stem. The chair's surface and structure are made from the same material, hand-folded fabric squares sewn into place one by one that represent the petals of a flower.

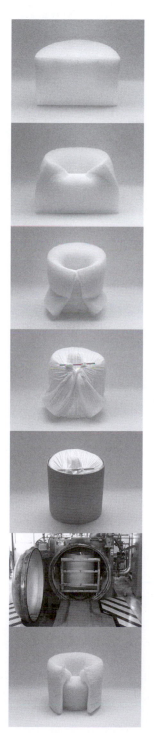

Tokujin Yoshioka begins forming the chair by compressing several kilos of fibres into a dense, semicircular wedge. The wedge is manipulated into a chair shape, then bound in a fireproof sheet before being inserted into a cardboard mould. The mould is placed in a kiln and baked at 104 degrees Celsius until the heat fuses the fibres together.

Tokujin Yoshioka used fibres to create a chair made from artificial crystals. Bundles of fibres were grouped into a chair shape, then immersed in liquid. Over time, particles in the fluid around the fibres created crystalline forms, which gradually expanded to form a rock–hard armchair.

In an interesting reversal, Yoshioka used fibres as a basis for creating a chair that does not contain a single other textile substrate. The Venus chair is constructed from natural crystals, which Yoshioka grows in an aquarium.[20] Bundles of fibres are grouped into a chair shape, forming arms, legs, seat and backrest, then immersed in liquid. Over time, particles in the fluid around the fibres create crystalline forms, which expand exponentially and form a dense, rock-like shape. Once the liquid is drained away, an assemblage of crystals comes into view, but not a single fibre can be seen. Yoshioka's furniture demonstrates how tiny fibres can create solid forms of considerable strength and weight.

Swedish designer Monica Förster is also known for material innovation. When Italian manufacturer Poltrona Frau commissioned her design of the Flow seating system for auditoriums and theatres, they probably expected that Förster's choice of material would be directional. Förster decided to explore shape-memory alloy materials, whose elasticity made them perfect for the project. Like conventional auditorium seating, Förster designed a cantilevering seat that would maintain an upright position against the backrest when unoccupied. She crafted the frame in steel and covered it in cold-pressed fireproof polyurethane foam padding, then fixed it to a pedestal base. Rather than using springs to return the seat to its upright position, the shape-memory materials used in the seat's construction merely morph back into their original form. As a result, the Flow system takes up less space and requires fewer parts than do most other auditorium seating.

Förster had designed textile structures earlier in her career when she used polyurethane balls and upholstery to create the bean bag-like Bob seating group in 2000. Three years later, when exploring ways to divide and partition space in open-plan environments, she looked at materials that could be used to create lightweight, portable screens and came across rip-stop nylon. Förster subsequently used the fabric to create inflatable rooms, designing big, billowing parachute-like structures she called 'Clouds'. Rather than using fabric merely to divide space, Förster sewed it into a tents that constructed interior spaces architecturally.

Hella Jongerius's designs have been made in a vast repertoire of materials, ranging from polyurethane, latex, foam and plastics to steel, felt, porcelain, glass, bronze and gold. But although she is a product designer rather than a textile practitioner, when she lends her hand to fabrics, she has the Midas touch. 'The basis of my work is often materials rather ideas,' Jongerius explains.[21] 'Once I have the materials in hand I start bending, gluing, sewing, or experimenting with other techniques,' she says.

Jongerius's regard for textile techniques enabled her to see ceramics in a whole new light. 'Ceramics are saturated with patterns and other kinds of embellishments,' she says. 'Many of the motifs resemble embroidery, which is a textile technique, but one that I discovered could also be applied to ceramics. Embroidery gave me a way of saying something about customs of eating and decorating, about being trapped in conventions and the role of etiquette. I decided to completely ignore the traditional use. When I embroidered the cups the punctures went right through the porcelain, so you couldn't drink tea out of them. But that wasn't actually so important, because the consumer could think up a different function for the cups.'

Swedish designer Monica Förster crafted a fabric bubble in rip-stop nylon to create an inflat-able room. The bubble is stored in a portable container, then unrolled and connected to an air compressor to inflate it. Once inflated, periodic blasts from the compressor enable it to maintain its shape.

The Bovist floor cushion Jongerius designed for Vitra in 2005 is a compact, rounded shape reminiscent of a mushroom's head. Rather than designing a conventional cushion, Jongerius structured Bovist by layering textiles and joining them with multiple seams on the sides. Rather than filling the cushion with conventional padding, Jongerius poured in a mixture of polypropylene balls and granulate. Bovist's most distinctive feature is its embroidered cover, which consists of two linen fabrics in contrasting colours. The cushion is embroidered with several abstract motifs sewn in various stitching styles and multicoloured threads. A motif called 'Homework' was inspired by a painting by the Dutch master Vermeer van Delft, showing a young girl engrossed in making an embroidery. The motif known as 'Porcelain' depicts an arrangement of antiquate pitchers with embroidered hearts hanging between them like bubbles floating through the air.

Also designed for Vitra in 2005, Jongerius's Polder sofa was embellished with tailoring techniques. The name 'Polder' refers to the tracts of land reclaimed from the sea in Holland by draining them and building dikes. Like the landmasses that share its name, the sofa is similarly low and flat, consisting of a wooden frame cushioned with four conspicuously voluminous, elongated cushions. The cushions and body are upholstered in five different fabrics in five coordinating colours decorated with large buttons made of natural materials like bone and mother of pearl, sewn to the cushions with bold, broad cross stitches. Through the selection of the threads, Jongerius creates a contrast of colours that further enhances the distinctiveness of this design feature.

When Italian furniture design company Paola Lenti opened in Milan, they practically created a whole new genre in furniture design. Francesco Rota, the company's chief designer, explores the potentials that textiles and fibres have to structure pieces of furniture, designing simple, uncomplicated shapes crafted from traditional weaving and time-honoured tailoring techniques. Rota's designs are contemporary yet also classic, crafted in materials that are durable enough to be left outdoors year round and still chic enough to be used inside. Ranges such as Float, Ami and Wabi, which include lounge chairs, sofas and poufs, feature woven supports and structures fabricated from textiles.[22]

Before Paola Lenti emerged on the scene, outdoor furniture was mostly produced using natural fibres, which limited their resistance to environmental conditions. Even when waterproof textiles, such as polypropylene and vinyl, were used to construct suspension webbing and rain-resistant cushions, they seldom enhanced the furniture. Paolo Lenti's point of departure was inventing an attractive waterproof fibre named Rope. As its name suggests, it is created from exactly that—rope. The company discovered the durability of high-modulus cables made from nylon and rubber and adapted this model to produce a sleekly woven textile.[23] Rope is waterproof, resistant to UV rays, chlorine and salt water, and also antibacterial, dirt resistant and easy to clean. This makes the furniture perfectly suited for contemporary interiors, poolside terraces and indoor/outdoor spaces, such as courtyards. Although Rope is synthetic and waterproof, the fabric it is woven into is soft enough to make it suitable for indoor upholstery, and the rugs produced from the fibre have the same performance both inside and outdoors.

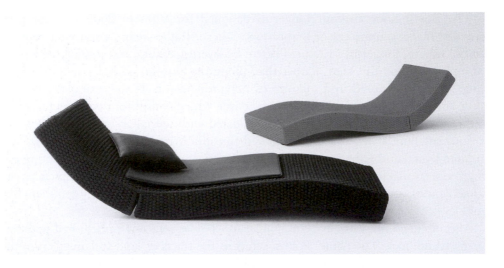

Italian furniture company Paola Lenti created Aquatech, a polyamide fibre that resembles natural straw. Because Aquatech is durable, weather resistant, easy to clean and quick to dry, it is an excellent choice for outdoor furniture.

Paola Lenti created another material called Aquatech, a polyamide fibre that resembles natural straw. Aquatech performs much like Rope: it is durable, weather resistant, easy to clean, quick to dry and can be woven into fabric. Whereas many furniture designers typically make good use of the materials on the market. Paola Lenti is moving forward by developing their own textiles.

Spanish designer Patricia Urquiola is also based in Milan, where she attended Milan Polytechnic and assisted Achille Castiglioni after graduating. Urquiola focuses on creating designs for the home, and her appreciation of woven forms and fabrics has resulted in textile-based surfaces that take furniture to a higher level. Urquiola first gained attention in textile circles in 2006 when her award-winning Antibodi lounge chair for Moroso introduced a richly textured, tactile aesthetic to contemporary furniture. Urquiola used a relief technique to add an element of padding to Antibodi's surface without quilting it, giving it an eye-catching, origami-like texture. The lounge chairs' covers are detachable, crafted in either leather or wool backed with felt. Each of the cover's sides has two distinct design identities. One side is carefully tailored, understated and subdued, while the other side is a riot of freeform texture, with two-tone, petal-like layers that react to movement.

Urquiola's interest in weaving can be seen in many of her seating designs. Her Flo chairs for Driade were designed with woven wicker seats and backrests in contrasting colourways, which were woven by hand in Indonesia. Urquiola's Tropicalia range of seating, produced by Moroso, is crafted with seats and backrest woven directly onto the furniture's steel frames. The Canasta collection Urquiola designed for B + B Italia is also based on traditional weaving but is given a contemporary edge by updating traditional caning technique for the twenty-first century. Bentwood furniture

Paola Lenti developed an attractive waterproof fibre named Rope from nylon and rubber. The fibre is used to produce sleek woven textiles with the resistance and durability of a high-modulus cable.

with caning in the seat and backrests was popular in the late nineteenth-century. The chair caning was woven in a narrow hexagonal pattern that was usually dense enough to create a screening effect. For Canasta, Urquiola used thick bands of polyethylene fibres rather than the traditional thin strips, recreating the pattern on a macro scale to give it a different effect altogether.

Although Urquiola believes in innovation, she seldom fabricates her designs from new materials or by using high tech processes. Perhaps this explains her preferences for textiles, fibres and woven forms. Textile techniques have been tried and tested over several millennia, whereas contemporary materials and modern processes may not, in the long run, withstand the test of time.

# Reactive Surfaces

Sensory surfaces are a source of inspiration in themselves. They imbue textiles with an intelligence that endows them with empathic characteristics, and they give them the potential to interact with humans and other objects. Preceding chapters described the emotive textiles, contaminate-aware fabrics and sensory surfaces designed with

Carole Collet's interactive Toile de Hackney fabrics were printed with thermochromatic pigments that changed appearance when people walked past them.

wearable applications in mind, and this part of the book reveals that they have potentials for interior textiles too.

Reactive surfaces, touch-sensitive pads and haptic interfaces can be found in many parts of the contemporary interior. Robotic membranes enable textile walls to move and change shape, while smart carpets embedded with microelectronic circuitry and proximity sensors respond to footsteps tracked across the surface. Photo-reactive coatings trigger responses in window shades and blinds, causing them to deflect sunlight or reflect it indoors. Light-reactive pigments enable patterns and motifs to change colours and return to their original design, and kinetic fabrics respond to a wide range of movements. Conductive fibres can respond to sunlight, wind, humidity and barometric pressure by changing colour, emitting light or varying in intensity.

German architect Jürgen Mayer designed thermochromatic bed linens with motifs shaped by the sleeper's body heat. Carole Collet's interactive Toile de Hackney fabrics were printed with thermochromatic pigments that responded to people walking past them. Teaming up with John Sawdon Smith to create an electronic interface, Collet set up a link between the fabric and a motion sensor, which enabled the device to relay signals directly to conductive fibres embedded in the lining of the toiles. Once activated, the lining emitted heat, and the temperature changes triggered

An electronic interface between the fabric and a motion sensor enabled the device to relay signals directly to conductive fibres embedded in the lining of the toile.

the thermochromatic patterns on the surface to respond by revealing new images. Clemens Winkler created a heat-sensitive tablecloth by weaving conductive threads and embedding the fabric with sensors that react to thermal contact. As the sensor detect heat, they change colour, temporarily embedding the shape of the object in the surface of the cloth.

## Sensory Membranes

Researchers in the emerging field of robotic membranes are pioneering sensory materials that can be programmed with the potential for movement and actuation. Practitioners in this area use the term 'textile' to reference both technology and material, aiming to create a membrane capable of sensing, reacting and moving in response to environmental triggers. A collaboration between Mette Ramsgard Thomsen and Karin Bech at the Centre for Interactive/Information Technology and Architecture (CITA) in Copenhagen, also supported by the University of Brighton's School of Architecture, brought robotic technologies and flexible materials together in a textile

The signals triggered the conductive fibres to emit heat, and the subsequent temperature changes caused the thermochromatic patterns on the surface to reveal new images.

Slow Furl is a responsive textile system that encourages individuals to interact with their surroundings. The project aims to dispel any sense of isolation associated with architecture, allowing the interior to interface with the occupant.

form capable of reacting and reshaping.[24] Ramsgard Thomsen and Bech call the membrane Slow Furl and describe it as a 'playful environment that engages the physical presence of its guests'.[25] As individuals interact with it, subtle recesses form in the surface, new cavities open and apertures and slits are revealed.

Slow Furl is constructed as a thirteen-metre-long textile installation that lines the wall in a soft and pliable skin. Still at prototype stage, Slow Furl's internal structure is currently a mechanized wooden skeleton. Its skin is a custom-made textile woven with conductive copper fibres. When two parts of the textile touch each other, the conductive fibres trigger the mechanical system, producing movements that change the structure's surface and shape. When individuals touch, stroke, sit on or lie within it, the surface reacts to their movements and cues the mechanized structure to reform.

Ramsgard Thomsen and Bech are pioneering a new approach to interior architecture, interpreting the space it in terms of 'flow, and responsive surfaces'. 'In architecture, the embedding of responsive systems influences how we imagine the experience and occupation of architect,' Ramsgard Thomsen explains. 'In classical and modernist

The Slow Furl project embeds information technology and digital systems into interior textiles to create architectural environments that interact with the occupants. The technology enables individuals to change the shape of the spaces they occupy.

architecture alike, the building is conceived as a structure created to be independent of the human body. Slow Furl achieves the opposite by engaging the inhabitant and guiding them through sequences of changing space. We use digital technologies to dispell the sense of isolation associated with architecture, allowing the building itself to be interfaced with by the user or inhabitant.'

The Slow Furl project highlights the potential for embedding information technology and digital systems into interior textiles, creating a reactive environment as a result. Through the agency of technical textiles and intelligent fabrics, interior architecture may become a reactive entity in itself.

## Smart Carpets

The surfaces beneath our feet may be the bottom layer of interior textiles, but when it comes to reactive technology, they are up at the very top. Carpets and fibre-based flooring provide thermal insulation, sound proofing and have acoustic properties, but when integrated with microelectronics and proximity sensors, they can track and record a wide range of movements and gaits and react accordingly.

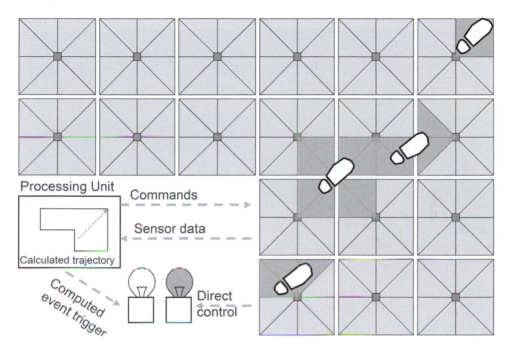

The SensFloor designed by Future-Shape reacts to footsteps by activating a sequence of location and time-specific sensors that relay data to a central control unit in real time.

A sensory, textile-based underlay that can be placed underneath virtually any type of floor covering has been developed by Future-Shape, a research organization founded by Christl Lauterbach, former project manager of Infineon's Smart Textile project.[26] Named SensFloor, the textile is embedded with a network of integrated sensors that detect movement on the surface above them. SensFloor is constructed in several layers, beginning with an insulating polyester fleece as base material with a sensory, smart membrane bonded on top. The smart membrane is a single-layer textile circuit board made with silver-plated copper wires. New developments are making it possible to integrate the two layers by interweaving the polyester fabric with conductive fibres, and even using an electroplating process to print a conductive pattern on the surface.

The SensFloor reacts to footsteps by activating a sequence of location and time-specific sensors that relay data to a central control unit in real time. Pattern recognition software analyses the data to determine a gait pattern, then matches it to those it has already recorded. The software is able to identify which one of the inhabitants (or pet) is moving through the space, and it can detect the presence of an intruder. In the case of a burglar, the carpet would record where they entered and track their movements throughout the space. The software could communicate with other systems, activating an alarm or alerting security personnel discreetly. Future-Shape claim that, unlike video surveillance, a SensFloor does not constitute an invasion of privacy but still records enough data to react to potential threats.

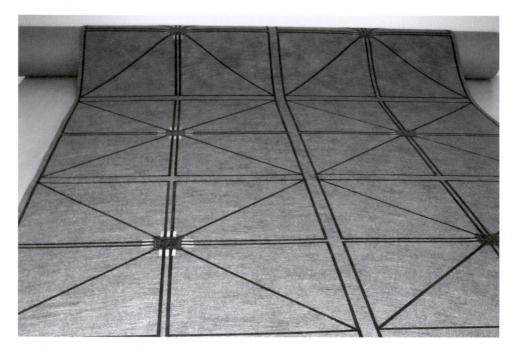

SensFloor is constructed in several layers. It has an insulating polyester fleece as a base material and a sensory, smart textile circuit board membrane on top. SensFloor is sensitive enough to function underneath virtually any type of floor covering.

Since SensFloor can monitor mobility, it has potential as a health care application for monitoring patients' movements. SensFloor would be able to identify a fall and replay the gait pattern that preceded it to determine the patient's identity. The system could also detect an unusually long period of inactivity and alert carers. SensFloor can also be programmed to react to behaviour and trigger environmental controls for patients with impaired mobility. Automatic doors, for example, could be opened and closed, and SensFloor could trigger lighting to come on as it senses a patient approaching a darkened room.

As Future-Shape continue to develop the system for public space, they plan to integrate LEDs to make it possible for SensFloor to provide an illuminated path to the nearest emergency exit. This would help make it possible for buildings to be evacuated much faster. In the case of rescue operations, SensFloor could potentially use the LEDs to guide rescuers directly to those who were injured.

## Reactive Rugs

While a graduate student at Virginia Tech, Meghan Quirk joined the e-textiles research group in the Bradley Department of Electrical and Computer Engineering.[27]

With funding granted by Intel, Quirk developed a reactive rug that can sense where an individual is walking or standing.[28] Stainless steel piezoelectric fibres and electroluminescent wires are woven into the textile so that the rug illuminates and is able to change light patterns as people walk on it.[29]

Quirk is part of a research unit developing software programmes and computer hardware for creating fully integrated e-textiles. The rug is based on the technology used to create other innovative textiles designed by the research group, such as the smart garments mentioned in Chapter 1 and the diagnostic Hokie Suit discussed in Chapter 4. As she continues to develop the rug, Quirk is creating methods of weaving the fabric to situate electronic elements at key points within the network of wires.

The advantage of using a reactive rug rather than a sensory carpet is its portability, which makes it suitable for military applications, trade shows, set designs and touring exhibitions. A reactive rug could potentially be used as a low-level light source in itself, lighting a path through the darkness when it senses footsteps approaching.

# Thermosensitive Materials

When design team Nuno Gonçalves Ferreira and Erin Hayne set up NunoErin in 2005, they updated the popular mood materials of the 1960s and 1970s for the twenty-first century. From their base in Jackson, Mississippi, Gonçalves Ferreira and Hayne were one of the first design studios to pioneer new applications for colour-changing materials.[30] With a determination to create interactive surfaces capable of bringing sensory experiences to everyday objects, the design duo began by injecting colour-changing inks into foam, which they moulded into interactive floor cushions. They also combined thermochromatic inks with rubber, which they applied to coat the moulded foam. As the body comes into contact with the material, an imprint is created, leaving a temporary mark that resembles a monochrome negative, such as those seen on film transparencies.

One of the first contributions that Gonçalves Ferreira and Hayne made to the field was to update the vernacular with terminology that reflected the material's sensory role. 'The word thermochromatic is typically used to describe colour-changing materials, but it is not one we were drawn to,' Hayne explains.[31] 'The word felt very clinical and didn't capture the intimate personal experience of using your body to interact with the world. Instead, we started using the word thermosensitive, which seems to capture the spirit of the experience in a more human way.'

NunoErin embarked on a collaboration with Sommers Plastics, a manufacturer of synthetic textiles, who use a similar type of colour-changing crystals. Sommers Plastics successfully incorporated the crystals into fabric, which enabled NunoErin to develop a textile suitable to use as an interior fabric. 'Our first application was upholstered seating,' Hayne says, 'which we chose so that people could experience the material with their entire body.' The series of stools and lounge chairs that resulted

The Sommers Plastic Products Company incorporates colour-changing crystals into fabric, enabling fashion accessories and interior textiles to change colour when exposed to heat.

were made with flat surface that could be used interactively to create temporary impressions in the fabric.

Some of NunoErin's high tech designs are based on organic forms, such as vegetation found in the bald cypress swamp, a microenvironment located near NunoErin's studio in Mississippi. 'The cypress swamp has an extremely sensorial atmosphere that abounds with texture, colour, light, scent and sound,' Hayne says. 'We were drawn to the tactile and sensorial pulse of this environment and wanted to bring its shapes and forms to our work. One of the first stools we designed was the "Cypress Stool", a stool with deep curves that we based on the trunk of the cypress tree. We were interested in how lines found in nature could serve as a kind of "sensorial ergonomics" in furniture. Bringing the deep contours of the cypress tree into our stool we created gentle grooves that people could comfortably sit in and adjust their body to. The effect of the curves creates different points of contact that give people new ways of experiencing the thermosensitive material.' Similar effects are created by their Touch Wall Panels, a series of vertical, wall-mounted pads, also made from thermochromatic fabric.

'Thermosensitive material has been a wonderful way for us to explore our broader interest in sensorial experiences and how people communicate with each other,' Gonçalves Ferreira says.[32]

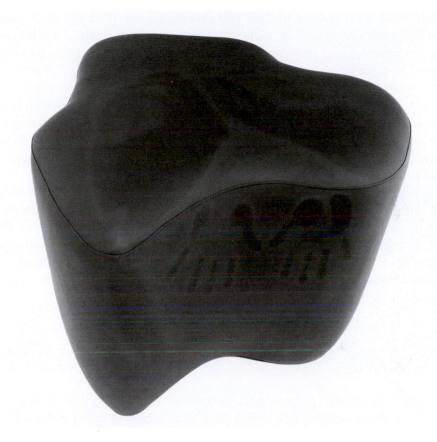

NunoErin upholstered a range of stools and lounge chairs with Sommers Plastic's colour-changing fabric. Temporary impressions are formed in the upholstery when the body heat of those seated reacts with the colour-changing crystals.

# Lighting

Light is to the interior what acoustics are for a concert hall. Carefully orchestrated, artificial lighting can function like a prism to reflect luminous colours along with the passing light. Natural light can strike a chord as poetic as music, creating a soothing atmosphere in the interior as it provides a visual symphony for the eyes. Textiles designers have always played a role in interior lighting, their main contributions being decorative lampshades made to conceal a light bulb or window treatments to temper the daylight streaming in. This is changing dramatically today as textiles designers take a hands-on approach to interior lighting. As fabric embedded with tiny LEDs can transform a textile into a light source, and materials such as Luminex can weave optic fibres into upholstery, curtains and table cloths, they portend a brighter future for interior textiles.

Arne Jacobsen is reputed to have said that light gives all things their presence, and when textiles emanate light, their surfaces change dramatically. They fill the gap between direct lighting projected by overhead light fixtures and the backlighting provided by hidden lamps. Luminous textiles can be atmospheric and evocative, creating a source of mood lighting, but they can also be programmed to gently pulsate or sparkle dynamically. Illuminated upholstery, textiles and carpets provided light yet minimize glare, giving them the effect of uplighting. Fixed to the ceiling, they revive the concept of the illuminated ceiling popularized in the 1960s and 1970s. Artworks crafted from optic fibres or neon filaments are not necessarily created to provide a primary light source, assigning them to the category of accent lighting.

Textiles' emerging relationship with interior lighting is bringing them into alignment with disciplines such as photometrics, architecture, energy conservation and electricity. As practitioners in these fields begin to appreciate the benefits of illuminated fibres, textiles can assume a whole new role in interior design. Luminous textiles can provide a sustainable light source; carefully planned, they can soothe the divide between environmental lighting and natural light. While lighting may be an ephemeral medium, its impact has long-lasting effects.

# Fibre Optics

Optic fibres are durable, programmable and even wearable, and their ability to provide light without emitting heat makes them comfortable to sit on and less likely to catch fire. Their commercial applications include curtains, wall panels and upholstery, but when used to create luminous artworks, they transcend their functional purpose altogether. One of the first to explore their applications in fine art, Finnish artist and designer Helena Hietanen fabricated eye-catching wall hangings and large-scale textile installations from strands of optic fibres.[33]

As an artist, Hietanen had previously explored fibrous materials such as rubber filaments and human hair. When she discovered fibre optics at a trade fair, Hietanen was curious to see if they could be used like yarn. Attempts to knit and crochet them didn't work, so Hietanen found other applications for them. 'One experiment led to another and I found a way to make the optic fibre illuminate along the whole length, not only just from the end point,' Hietanen explains.[34] 'Then I discovered how to adapt it to create traditional lace patterns by combining traditional hand craftsmanship with today's technology, which is what I had wanted to do all along.'

The spectacular wall-hangings that resulted are known as Technolace, a series of luminous creations that combine handicraft traditions with cutting-edge fibre-optic technology. As Hietanen became more adept at handling the material, she developed methods of combining the optic fibres with natural light and artificial light sources. Hietanen has created architectural structures, such as the light wall she designed for the Nobel Museum in Stockholm. Situated in the museum's reception area, the wall welcomes visitors with an eye-catching display of looped fibres encased behind a curving transparent wall.

Although much of Hietanen's work as an artist has centred around fibre optics, as a designer she uses other materials that react to light in a dramatic way. 'I'm attracted to surfaces that reflect natural light or technical materials that produces artificial light,' she says. 'The materials I like the most are silicon crystals, the tiny reflective beads used in the highway paints, LED lighting, metals with polished surfaces and pre-woven metal mesh. At one time my work revolved around fibres, but now my focus is on light itself.' Collaborations with architects led to a lighting commission for the façade of a seven-floor apartment building built in Helsinki. Hietanen felt that LEDs were a natural choice, as they could be discretely embedded into the building's handrails and architectural detailing installed along walkways.

'The LEDs are linked to sensors and to a computer interface that measures the movement of the occupants,' Hietanen explains. 'As people approach the building, LEDs in the walkways and handrails will begin to glow, then intensify in the areas where they detect movement. One of the things I like about LEDs is that their energy consumption is much lower than conventional lighting. Cold temperatures cause a reaction that makes them even brighter without using more electricity. So using LEDs in the cold, dark winter season in Finland means you can have brighter lighting yet consume less energy.'

# Electric Embroidery

Astrid Krogh works with light the way Jackson Pollock worked with paint; using fibre strands, she spreads it around, arcs it upwards or projects it over any area she likes. The bigger the illuminated surface, the more satisfied she is with the result. From her base in Copenhagen, Krogh weaves lengths of optic strands into site-specific iridescent tapestries that glow, illuminate and flare into a rainbow of brilliant colours.[35] 'My starting point, as a textile designer, is to identify how each place or individual room has it own atmosphere,' Krogh says.[36] 'I have to find out what makes the place special, or decide what I need to do to make it special. If my work is commissioned for an old building, I may take an aspect of its history and use it in contemporary context. If it is a new building, I try to understand the architecture and relate my work to it. For every project, I build models of the space to recreate the physical feeling of the design. I almost always try it out by creating a 1:1 scale to test how the light and materials will react in reality.'

Krogh has created spectacular fibre-optic wall panels for some extraordinary spaces. She humbly refers to these beautiful, light-emitting textiles as 'my weavings'. For Krogh, work with the fibre optics is not necessarily a textile methodology, but a process she describes as 'weaving with light itself'. 'Lightmail' (2000), one of Krogh's first fibre-optic installations, was an eight-metre-long wall hanging powered by devices

From her studio in Copenhagen, Astrid Krogh weaves lengths of optic fibres into site-specific tapestries. Once fitted in place and connected to a power source, they glow, light up and flare into rainbows of brilliant colours.

that streamed coloured light through the fibres. They were programmed to pulsate like a beating heart. 'Fibre optic textiles are the visual pulse of life,' Krogh says. 'They are a beautiful blend of light sources. My works incorporate artificial light but they are not artificial light sources in themselves.'

Krogh's 'Lightfall' (2007) installation was composed of two optic fibre weavings suspended from the top of a multilevel atrium-like space where it reacted to changes in ambient light as the sun moved through the sky. 'You could say that as my textiles become brighter, or less intense, they imitate the changes that occur in natural light throughout the day,' Krogh says. 'In fact, they are never the same from one day to the next, or even from one moment to the next. The way that light plays with shadows all the time makes small changes throughout the day.' With a length of fourteen metres, 'Lightfall' is one of the biggest woven fibre-optic panels ever made.

Although Krogh's fibre-optic weavings received much acclaim, she is probably best known today for the luminous tapestries she designs. Krogh uses LEDs to create colourful wall-mounted works that form new patterns continuously. 'Waltzing', for example, is a large-scale vertical tapestry measuring two meters wide and nearly seven meters in length. Its motifs were inspired by ikat fabrics, which the software driving the LED lighting reconfigures into new patterns constantly. Each pattern remains on view for four seconds, then, during an eight second sequence, morphs into a new pattern. The tapestry also has an interactive dimension when linked to a floor mat that enables viewers to control the patterns by the movement of their feet. Because LEDs use less energy than regular bulbs, 'Waltzing' conserves more electricity than Krogh's fibre-optic weavings.

Krogh was commissioned to design a tapestry for the Danish Parliament building, asked to bring light and colour to a long, dark subterranean corridor. She decided to create a large-scale neon wall hanging, aptly naming it 'Polytics'. Neon, a material often used in electric signage, may seem like an odd choice for a textile practitioner, but to Krogh, the long, slender glass filaments were more akin to colourful optic fibres then industrial lighting. She also used neon to craft 'Ornament', a large-scale artwork commissioned by a municipal art museum. Krogh was partly inspired by the kaleidoscope's ability to endlessly form and configure shifting patterns, and she set out to reproduce it in the commission. 'Ornament' was constructed from 186 neon tubes organized into ten illuminable units, each programmed to configure patterns randomly, capable of creating more than 1 million motifs. When the curators who commissioned it saw 'Ornament's production budget, they demanded to know why she wanted to produce such a costly artwork. Krogh's reply was priceless: 'Because dreams can't be measured in money'.

Although most of Krogh's projects are made for the interior, some are designed for the façade. Collaborations with urban developers and planning officials require her to think like an architect in order to make a response to pre-existing surfaces and built structures. Krogh designed her Flora motif in 2007 in response to a commission from the city council in Kolding, Denmark. She used neon tubes to embroider the façade of a historic building, where the tubes ornament the walls by day and create a spectacular light show at night. Whether viewed in the light of day or in the romantic dreamscapes of night, Krogh's luminous tapestries and fibre-optic weavings work in response to a transitional space between the interior and outside world. 'That is the reality of textiles today,' Krogh explains. 'They are a rich and diverse material that hold new possibilities for all aspects of contemporary architecture.'

## Feature Interview: Hsiao-Chi Tsai

Interior textiles have many associations: sensuous, functional, decorative and ritual. The ciphers and motifs stitched across them are rooted in a rich heritage of symbolism and storytelling. Although some experts claim that this historic practice is waning, a glance at the saga-like forms designed by Hsiao-Chi Tsai show that the tradition is alive and well in the present day. The London-based Taiwanese designer uses textiles to craft spaces for fantasy, imagination, fairy tales and dreamy reverie. Tsai does not weave, use embroidery techniques or appliqué, but she creates tapestries, nevertheless.[37]

Tsai probes her imagination for both the exotic and the everyday, and brings them to life in wavering, organic lines and fluid abstractions that seem to hover between dream and reality. She brings exotic vegetation to life, crafting yellow trees that flourish

Hsiao-Chi Tsai's designs are crafted from formable materials such as foam, plastic and metal mesh, which are typically combined with fabrics such as Lycra, polyester and felt.

Harvey Nichols department store commissioned Tsai to design and construct a continuous series of otherworldly shapes that were exhibited in the windows of the shop's forty-meter-long façade.

Tsai has a vast repertoire of shapes and materials. She has created interior textiles, lighting, outdoor installations and even fashion accessories, such as the hat shown here.

in purple forests, and variegated flowers with pod-like petals that blossom amid serpentine creepers. Tsai's textile designs are based on structure, and she relies on rigid materials that will allow her to create three-dimensional forms. Formable materials such as foam, plastic and metal mesh are combined with fabrics such as Lycra, felt and polyester. Tsai typically bonds hard and soft materials to create a single textile with a double-sided effect, which she cuts and moulds into three-dimensional forms.

While studying textile design at the Royal College of Art, Tsai discovered that she had a talent for creating large-scale installations. 'It was important to me to create work that was more than two-dimensional,' Tsai says, 'to create different aesthetics and appearances to be seen by viewers from every angle. The structure and texture of my work plays an essential role in giving volume, depth and space to forms that would otherwise remain two-dimensional. The role of structural form in my work enables the textile to become multi-layered by light and shadows and come to life in three-dimensional space.'[38]

Shortly after she graduated from the Royal College of Art, Harvey Nichols department store asked Tsai to design and construct a continuous chain of Christmas ornaments that would link the upper levels of their forty-metre-long display windows. 'It was a fantastic opportunity,' Tsai says, 'but after meeting me and seeing my portfolio, they offered me a bigger, better project. I created a single theme that ran through all of their windows for the spring of 2007, which was on display throughout February and March.' Tsai teamed up with Kimiya Yoshikawa, a sculptor, to contribute to the project with suggestions for creating three-dimensional forms. 'I combined Kimiya's knowledge of three-dimensional construction and his "Magical Balloon" theme with my 3-D foam cutting and together we created seven large-scale sculptures that we called "Futuristic Flowers".' The installations that resulted resembled a network of organic forms that meandered through the shop front and trailed across the ceilings and window surfaces. The installations created layered tableaux of three-dimensional textile motifs.

Tsai's talent for three-dimensional textile design has led to products such as lampshades, room dividers, hats and fashion items. 'I want to see how my installation-art method can be simplified yet continue to make use of elements such as form, light and shadow to create high-end interior products,' she says. 'I still see textile design as one of the most important ways to visually enhance almost everything in our everyday life, from what we wear to what we use and live with. I believe that eventually, all functional things will be made with a textile aesthetic. The future applications of textiles are enormous, because textile-based sensibilities will continue to grow and expand in product design, architecture and beyond.'

# eight

# Textiles for Architecture

Architecture constructed from textiles seems like a contradiction in terms. Architecture is built to last, whereas textiles seem to rip, pull apart and wear out. Buildings are equated with density and mass, while textiles can seem limited to lightweight decorative expressions. Although the two may appear to be poles apart, textiles and architecture share a long history. Early man once constructed habitats from hides, plant fibres and primitive fabrics, and textiles are still used to build nomadic dwellings in central Asia today. Fabrics disappeared from architecture as wood, stone, metal and glass became the materials of choice, but advances in textile technology have revealed their relevance to architecture today.

Contemporary architecture is characterized by metal mesh, woven skins, braided cables and tensile surfaces. Innovations such as carbon-fibre matrices, inflatable membranes and tri-axial meshes are popular alternatives to bricks and mortar, which they replace with carbon-neutral, sustainable structures. The pliancy and shock absorbency of fibres and textiles is revolutionizing the construction of earthquake-proof buildings, and landscape architects are literally taking fabric underground to sculpt and reshape the natural terrain. As soft materials change how architecture is designed and built, a new paradigm of lightweight, elastic architecture is beginning to take shape.

The sections that follow reveal that exchanges between architectural design and textile technology are blurring the boundaries between the two disciplines. When industrial cables and metal filaments are woven or braided, they form fibrous structures that create tension and compression more efficiently than masonry. An ever-widening variety of woven and nonwoven fabrics are being developed for architectural applications, and the integration of materials such as metal and glass into fabric is creating new areas of textile design. The textile-based paradigm emerging today is taking

Los Angeles-based architects Testa + Weiser are pioneering methods of weaving carbon fibres architecturally. They claim that carbon fibres can provide a quicker and more cost-effective means of constructing tall buildings than traditional materials can.

architecture to the cutting edge, and the potential to experience the urban landscape as a tactile arena could change our experience of architecture forever.

## Membrane Structures

Known variously as structural fabrics, architectural textiles or tensile membranes, supple surfaces have made their mark on modern architecture. From the turn of the twentieth century, when Russian engineer Vladimir Shukhov designed and built eight tensile structures for use as exhibition pavilions at the Nizhny Novgorod Fair in 1896, textiles have been a staple of temporary architecture. By the 1920s, American architect Buckminster Fuller also espoused the applications of textile panels in modular, prefabricated pods, subsequently inspiring avant-garde British architectural group Archigram to design supple, responsive structures with surfaces and skins in the 1960s. Also a pioneer of soft substrates, German architect Frei Otto gained acclaim for the textile roofs and membrane structures he built in Montreal at Expo 67 and the stadium he designed for the 1972 Summer Olympics in Munich.[1] Otto revealed that textiles could craft more than temporary tents, tepees, awnings and emergency shelters, paving the way for them to be used in permanent structures.

Ironically, Otto's own tensile designs were temporary structures built with a short life span in mind. But as the techniques required to build membrane structures became better understood, the use of textiles in permanent architectural projects became widespread by the end of the twentieth century. Tensile membranes seem to be a natural choice for use as roofs, as they can span large distances economically and attractively. Otto was also directional in his use of synthetic materials rather than organic fabrics. Because textile membranes are attached to cables and drawn taut in order to withstand impact, high performance materials with strengths that exceed those of plant-based fibres are required.

The genre of architectural textiles is wide and varied, but a feature common to all is a predictable warp and weft, whose tensile strength, modulus and breaking points have been tested and quantified. The most common fabrics are typically woven from electrical grade open-weave glass fibres or high modulus polyesters. They are usually bonded to other structural fabrics to create an insulative inner surface. Glass fibres can be coated with materials such as Tedlar, a polyvinylfluoride (PVF) film used to create a moisture barrier.[2] Materials such as Butacite, a transparent UV-resistant membrane engineered to be an interlayer, make it possible to incorporate UV-radiation-protection into architectural glazing.[3]

Award-winning British architect Ian Ritchie has designed and built a range of fabric structures in Britain and abroad.[4] Ritchie became known internationally for his innovative use of textiles from about 1986, when he incorporated an architectural textile into a striking roof design. Ritchie had been commissioned by the La Villette Museum for Science & Industry in Paris to reshape the appearance of the existing building's main structure. As a result, Ritchie designed an insulated double-skinned permanent roof from two layers of PTFE-coated spun fibreglass fabric. He sculpted the roof into two large dome shapes and constructed lightweight, wheel-like rotating mirrored devices at each of their apexes. The devices rotated automatically to follow the movement of the sun, and as they did so, their mirrors reflected the sunlight and channelled it into the entrance hall below.

The material Ritchie used for the roof membrane was translucent Fibair fabric, which he coated with Tedlar to create a moisture barrier. The layers were separated by a distance of approximately sixty centimetres to promote ventilation and circulation, yet they still channelled a great deal of light into the building. The Fibair has performed well over time, maintaining its insulative properties, shape memory and UV resistance.

In 1992 Ritchie was commissioned to build an extension to a primary school in Daours, a small town north of Paris near Amiens. He designed a textile roof to bridge the new structure to the existing one, creating a fabric-covered canopy that arced over the entrance to the school. Ritchie used the canopy to designate an intermediate zone between the building and the playground outside. As the children walk past the entrance on their way to their studies, the canopy overhead provides a subtle educational tool that teaches them that textiles and architecture can be one in the same.

Ritchie was one of the first British architects to use solar materials for a residential project. Fluy House, a project complete in 1976, was fitted with solar panels crafted

When architect Ian Ritchie was commissioned to reshape the appearance of the La Villette Museum in Paris, he designed a new roof constructed from two layers of PTFE-coated spun fibreglass fabric.

from an aluminium-coated woven polyester fabric. Originally developed by NASA, the material was highly reflective, yet semitransparent, making it ideal for external window blinds. The fabric disintegrated over time and was replaced in 1988 by Solar-Screen, a reflective woven fibreglass fabric made with UV-radiation inhibitors that deflect heat, glare and damaging rays.[5]

One of the most innovative examples of shading systems in urban architecture was designed by Japanese architect Shigeru Ban. The retractable external walls of Ban's Curtain Wall House created a novel dynamic in architecture. When the clients expressed their preference for indoor/outdoor terraces, light-filled living spaces and low tech systems, Ban decided to cut away two of the exterior walls and replace them with an aramid fabric coated with films that made it UV and pollution resistant. As a result, the two membrane walls on the east and south sides of the house open to the outdoors, revealing wide deck spaces on the second and third floors of the building. The walls' fabric construction enables them to fully retract, which channels more light and air into the core of the house as they increase the sense of volume and space. The textile membranes take the place of *shoji* and *sudare* screens and the *fusuma* doors that characterize the traditional Japanese house. In summer, the textiles deflect the sun and shade the interior, while in winter, sets of glazed doors slide into place alongside the curtain to completely enclose the house and insulate it against the cold.

The supple surfaces and pleated folds of the textile walls evoke the fluid construction of a garment more than they do architectural structures. Just as some garments are worn open or closed to reveal or conceal parts of the body, the walls of the house retract to expose the structure or close to conceal them from public view. Wind and weather conditions also cause the textiles to stir, giving the house a dynamic that challenges the notion that architecture should be an entirely fixed structure. Just as a garment can be rearranged on the wearer, kinetic structures such as the Curtain Wall House can be reconfigured, introducing an interactive dynamic in architecture.

Malaysian architect Ken Yeang is pioneering a system of bioclimatic architecture created by constructing buildings from layers of textiles.[6] Inspired by how clothing, as a micro-system, wraps the body in layers of apparel that are donned and shed as it moves in and out of the macro-systems designated by architecture, Yeang created a system that funnels ambient heat through a strata of fabric membranes. Yeang regards clothing as an armature that regulates body temperature as is separated or combined in different climatic conditions. As he interprets this procedure architecturally, Yeang describes it as a cybernetic enclosural system that responds automatically to climatic conditions. Like clothing, labile textile armatures could create temperate zones that regulate the temperatures within them. The energy harnessed by each textile layer can be circulated to create heating and cooling systems with minimal use of fuel.

Bioclimatic principles had been tested in the 1980s by Skidmore, Owings & Merrill, an international architectural consultancy, who used Teflon-coated fibreglass to construct the roof of the Haj Terminal at the King Abdulaziz International Airport near Jeddah, Saudi Arabia. Conical fabric forms were placed at angles that would draw heat upward and wick it outdoors, enabling environmental controls to function more efficiently.[7] Likewise, Yeang's bioclimatic system emphasizes energy conservation, promoting a uniquely sustainable model of architecture. In using textiles, Yeang is maximizing the functionality of the surface areas and minimizing the use of material. By structuring the built environment to conserve resources rather than expend them, Yeang is minimizing its ecological footprint and consumption of energy.

# Metal Textiles

Woven metals gained ground in architecture in the 1980s, when stainless steel became a popular construction material for architectural elements built into interior structures and façades.[8] Woven stainless steel was initially used in space dividers, ceiling liners, decorative panels, balustrades and grillwork, then became a popular material for solar shades, weather shields and landscape structures in the 1990s. Stainless steel continues to be the most popular material for woven architectural mesh, but filaments made from copper, brass, aluminium and phosphor bronze are also widely used.[9] Today, woven metals are used worldwide to construct building façades, suspended ceilings, external walls, exterior skins and mesh floors. The textiles are usually stretched over custom-made aluminium frames or attached to pre-existing structures with brackets and cables.

Metal textiles can be as beautiful as any other fabric. Metal itself has a unique lustre, and when strands of silvery metal are intertwined with brass, bronze, titanium and gold, they create spectacular colours and shimmering light effects. When woven metal is used to fashion a façade, they create a semitransparent skin that masks the building and screens it from the surrounding landscape. Architects use woven metal in renovation schemes to break down the imposing density of an existing façade or to soothe harsh angles and strong lines. Woven metal makes it possible to transform an otherwise conservative building into a radical new form. Metal textiles can create undulating surfaces, wavy forms, spirals, twists and tilted shapes, obscuring the structure behind them and the meanings they project. Although they can make a dramatic difference to the environment around them, metal fibres are sustainable enough to significantly reduce a building's ecological footprint.[10]

The concept of masking has been a central theme in architecture for more than half a century. Building a façade or a screen from textiles reinforces the analogy of the architectural surface as a form of dress and implies that the building is adopting the codes of revealing and concealing more common to the conventions of fashion than architecture. The use of metal textiles makes it possible to roll the façade away mechanically, opening and closing the surface as if it were a window blind, or unzipping it like a garment. Textiles enable the dualities of revealing and concealing to add an exciting dimension to new buildings, and they provide architects with the means to camouflage the shortcomings of a pre-existing facade.

Aesthetics aside, metal fabrics appeal to architects because they are practical, durable, nonflammable, resistant to corrosion and easy to handle. They are used to deflect sunshine and shade the building, creating so-called climate membranes that cool it.[11] Metal textiles can be made opaque to mask the building or transparent enough to reveal it, all the while providing an external barrier that protects he surface from wind and weathering. Most woven metal textiles can withstand gusts of wind up to 176 mph, enabling them to resist hurricane-force winds. Cambridge Architectural, an American manufacturer of metal fabrics, produce the super high performance Velocity textile, made to withstand extreme wind conditions. The textile is made to be attached with tension release hardware, anchoring it to a release mechanism that absorbs the impact and retensions automatically when the storm subsides.[12]

Metal textiles can be woven with a variety of textures. The metal filaments are often woven in a loose, or open, weave that resembles basketry or mesh. Tighter weaves can emulate chain mail or patterns such as herringbone, enabling the textile to drape in a manner similar to organic fibres. Many manufacturers, such as German-based GKD, describe their techniques as 'technical weaving'. GKD has developed methods of weaving textiles nearly nine meters wide and practically any

GKD, a German manufacturer of metal fabrics, describe their techniques as 'technical weaving'. Their industrial looms are capable of weaving textiles nearly nine meters wide and practically any length.

length. Ranging from large-scale, transparent open weaves to dense, opaque surfaces, many of their textiles are woven with lighting and digital media too. Fabrics such as Illumesh and Mediamesh integrate LEDs, surface-mounted devices (SMDs) and conductive fibres into the weave, enabling the textiles to illuminate, pulsate with colour and project images.

Metal textiles, in the hands of Dutch architect Lars Spuybroek, enable architecture, structure and texture to become one. Spuybroek's pioneering designs and influential publications have revealed the potentials that textiles hold for architecture at many levels.[13] Spuybroek became known internationally in the 1990s when he constructed a number of buildings that resembled waveforms and undulating shapes.[14] His work centres on the notion of soft architecture, advocating blob shapes and nonorthogonal woven structures as the basis for a nonrectilinear paradigm of architecture. Spuybroek uses textiles methodology to construct permanent structures, choosing soft materials that rigidify during the construction stages to become hard surfaces. Flexible aluminium panels, for example, become inflexible when fastened to supports, and woven metal meshes freeze into wave forms as they are riveted to metal frames. Spuybroek differentiates architecture from buildings, viewing architecture as an interactive system able to respond to its inhabitants. 'We should never mix up architecture and building,' Spuybroek says. 'Just because our buildings can't move, it doesn't mean our architecture can't. [Although] our buildings are hard and intransigent, our architecture could be active and liquid.'[15]

One of the best examples of Spuybroek's approach and methodology is his Maison Folie project, a cultural centre built in the French city of Lille in 2004.[16] The whole façade was conceived as an expression of labile form and constructed from Escale, a stainless metal textile produced by GKD in Germany. Maison Folie's dramatic textile exterior creates a distinctively fluid silhouette, mirroring many of the aesthetics typical of textile design. Although the building has a soft, wavy surface, its façade is rock hard. At night, light penetrates the textiles' surface, emanating light evenly across the exterior.

Well known for his use of glass-fibre fabrics in architecture, Ian Ritchie has also used a number of woven metal textiles in his work. Ritchie began to experiment with woven metal in 1986, when he decided to use an industrial textile known as Becobelt.[17] At the time, the material was an industrial product used for making conveyor belts (hence its name) and collapsible lift gates. Ritchie first used the material for a pharmacy he built in Boves, a town near Daours (where his primary school extension was built), to build aesthetic screens between two flanking walls. Ritchie used the fabric again at Bermondsey Underground Station in London in 1990, constructing panels from Becobelt to add additional reinforcement to the roof.

For the Theatre Royal in Plymouth, Ritchie used woven phosphor bronze to construct the external walls. The theatre is situated on a prominent waterfront site within the estuary valley of the river Plym, where the open space and light reflecting off the water create a shimmering landscape. The fabric forms a soft skin around the building that glistens as it reflects the ambient light around it. Although the fabric is drawn taut around the building, the surface tension is mild enough to yield slightly when prodded with a finger. The tactile effect is that of a dense building with a soft, fleshy, metallic skin.

In 2000, Ritchie built another shimmering structure, this time weaving bundles of fibre-optic filaments through industrial mesh to create a luminous structure. Ritchie won the Milan 2001 III Millennium Segno Luminoso competition to build a light monument in Milan, designing a unique, light-emitting structure made from optic fibres woven with stainless steel filaments. The fabric was stretched between two cantilevered metal tubes and supported by a network of stainless-steel cables. The porosity of the textile allows gusts of wind to pass through it, and the impact of extreme winds is dispersed through the network of cables. The optic fibres are encased in transparent plastic to prevent them from photo-degrading and to protect them from damage by insects or birds. The fabric can be cleaned quickly and easily with a water jet.

When French architect Dominique Perrault built the award-winning Bibliothèque nationale de France (BnF), he treated dense metal textiles as if they were lightweight fabrics, allowing them to drape and cascade throughout the space.[18] Perrault suspended GKD's Sambesi fabric from ceilings to create wave-like effects, and he constructed taut metals sheaths to divide the reading rooms from the main galleries. The

The Maison Folie cultural centre in the French city of Lille is constructed from stainless steel woven textiles attached to a metal framework.

Ian Ritchie used woven phosphor bronze fabric to construct the external walls of the addition to Plymouth's Theatre Royal. The fabric forms a tactile surface around the building that yields slightly when prodded with a finger, just like human skin.

floor lamps and ceiling-mounted lights were encased in braided metal sheaths, and their beams of light projected onto the textiles from angles that diffuse the beams across the textiles' surface. Perrault showcased the remarkable diversity and versatility of woven metal textiles in a single project, clashing and contrasting their textures while using them to provide visual links throughout the space.

Woven metal textiles have presented these and other architects with the means to create new style and fresh forms while still complying with structural regulations and stringent planning codes. As they endow architecture with a vocabulary of shapes similar to those found in fashion and textile design, they create tactile environments that are as pleasing to the eye as they are to the hand.

# Carbon Fibres

Carbon fibres underpin many aspects of architecture and design, often in surprising guises. We drive vehicles constructed from carbon-fibre parts, travel in aeroplanes made with carbon-fibre composites and sail boats propelled by carbon-fibre sailcloth. Could it be feasible, therefore, to assume that we may someday dwell in architecture built by carbon fibres? If you ask Peter Testa and Devyn Weiser, principals of the Los Angeles-based architectural firm Testa + Weiser, the answer to that question is a resounding 'yes'. They are proponents of fibre architecture, a system of constructing tall buildings through weaving and braiding techniques. The system they developed is based on building with carbon-fibre filaments, chosen because their high strength, flexibility and resilience gives them advantages over metal fibres of a similar weight and length.

Under tension, carbon fibres are five times stronger than steel, yet engineers are reluctant to use them in architectural applications. They are more expensive than metal cables, are not as fire resistant and have yet to have their performance satisfactorily quantified. Testa + Weiser are convinced that the potential to build with carbon fibres is strong, and they are pioneering methods of weaving them structurally to create skyscrapers. They maintain that carbon fibres provide a more streamlined method of constructing tall buildings, ultimately making the construction process quicker, more cost effective, less wasteful and more sustainable.[19]

Using computer modelling tools, Testa + Weiser have designed and built an architectural prototype of a carbon-fibre high-rise, a lightweight, streamlined structure crafted from carbon fibres, carbon-fibre composites and shatterproof glass. The prototype is the culmination of ongoing research in several other disciplines, such as material science and computer-aided engineering.[20] The prototype illustrates how a forty-storey skyscraper can be woven from bundles of carbon fibres rather than assembled from conventional construction materials. When built to scale, each carbon-fibre strand would be approximately four centimetres in diameter and nearly 200 metres long.

The structure is composed of forty helical bands that coil in two directions to create a cylindrical shape. These are situated around the building's perimeter, simultaneously forming the façade as they weave the structure. The building does not rely on a network of columns or an internal framework for support; the carbon fibres drawn from the base of the structure to the top carry the entire vertical compressive load and distribute it throughout the entire structure. Floor plates made from composite

Mathias Bengtsson's experimentation with carbon fibres has led to several woven and braided designs. Bengtsson also spun the fibres into a range of cylindrical shapes, from which this carbon-fibre footbridge evolved.

materials are anchored to the perimeter walls on each storey. Just as the floor plates are supported by the helix, the tension they create around the perimeter wall prevents the helix from collapsing.

Apart from the foundations, no concrete is used in the building. No steel is used either. This is unusual in skyscraper construction, which relies on the use of steel or concrete in compression to make the structure stable. Every major element in the building, including the walls and floors, is made of some kind of composite material. Rather than use conventional glass, Testa + Weiser, chose ETFE, a kind of transparent, blast-resistant plastic regarded to be an advanced glass substitute.[21] The synergy between the skyscraper's materials and techniques give the building the advantage of being earthquake proof. In the event of an earthquake, the fibres would absorb the seismic energy and disperse it throughout the entire structure, meaning that the building is more likely to flex and sway than crack and crumble.

## Inflatable Structures

Inflatable buildings are popping up practically everywhere, creating a uniquely light-weight system of pneumatic architecture that is simple to construct and virtually effortless to erect. Pneumatic structures are created from air-filled fabric membranes constructed from airtight textile substrates. Recent advances in material technology have made it possible to create air-filled voids from an ever-widening variety of woven and nonwoven fabrics. Inflatable architectural fabrics are made from high performance, reinforced fibres capable of withstanding extreme pressure and heavy-duty bonding techniques. Laminate films and PTFE coatings prevent air from leaking through the fabric wall, and advanced-strength adhesives and heat-seal coatings fuse their seams together.[22]

Archigram were one of the first to design portable pneumatic buildings. Constructed like clothing, these buildings were crafted from textile substrates and fused together by stitched seams and adhesives. As structures, they had more in common with fashion than architecture: they were portable, constructed from soft membranes and designed and assembled in accordance with tailoring techniques. Created as individual pods rather than whole structures, their modularity related more to the system of separates worn in fashion than to the architecture of the day.

Interest in pneumatic structures was revived by architects designing radomes, prefabricated buildings and portable architecture.[23] Because mobility is a key feature of temporary buildings such as exhibition pavilions, circus tents, trade show displays and structures designed for military campaigns, weight and transport are important considerations. Inflatable fabrics weigh considerably less then conventional building materials and can be packed into a container only a fraction of their inflated size. Like prefabs, they have the advantage of being constructed off-site, reducing the environmental impact that building sites create. Manufacturers of inflatable structures, such as Inflate and Architects of Air, are developing methods to make pneumatic buildings a carbon-neutral area of architecture.[24]

Designers and architects looked at the inflatable structures made for marine and aerospace applications to find strong, lightweight materials robust enough to be used in architecture.[25] PVC-coated synthetic mesh fabrics have good tensile strength and tear resistance, and many also offer flame-retardant properties, UV protection, and antibacterial films that prevent the growth of mould and mildew. Fibreglass and PTFE-coated fabrics perform well when subjected to air pressure, and the woven Vectran produced by Warwick Mills was developed with advanced adhesive technology that bonds urethane to Vectran indissolubly.

Fabrics developed for vehicle airbags and inflatable aerospace components are made with high tensile strength and energy absorption properties to enable them to withstand air pressure and substantial mechanical stress. Originally developed for airbags, textiles such as DuPont's Airbag Nylon 6.6-HT and Hytrel TEEE have proven to be two of the most reliable inflatable fabrics commercially available today. DuPont are pioneering a process of incorporating Kevlar fibres into the cell walls of a foam material they are developing for aerospace applications. Some day, the fabric may be used to create puncture-proof inflatable structures on earth.[26]

The Vienna-based Veech Media Architecture (VMA) is a leader in the field of pneumatic architecture. They have designed a number of inflatable structures in a response to commissions for lightweight portable architecture.[27] When commissioned to design Sprachpavillion a travelling exhibition centre, and Radionight, an elevated broadcasting stage, VMA investigated the potential that soft materials have to create structures that could be easily uninstalled and quickly reassembled. Like hot-air

The Vienna-based practice Veech Media Architecture designed a number of inflatable textile structures in a response to commissions for lightweight portable architecture.

balloons, life rafts and inflatable garments, VMA's structures relied on air contained within fabric membranes as a source of volume and strength. Both structures were lightweight, quick to disassemble and pack, and easy to transport. They could be recreated in different locations instantly, taking minutes to erect and later shrinking to one-tenth of their expanded size when deflated. The waterproof materials they were constructed from made them ideal for outdoor use.

Sprachpavillion was the central part of an exhibition that toured Austria as part of the European Year of Languages in 2001. VMA used the commission to explore flexibility, transparency, lightness and elasticity as a means of developing a portable structure. Sprachpavillion was designed to be a dome-like pneumatic structure whose volume was created as the fabric's membranes inflated and expanded. Supported by steel lintels, it held its ground as a portable outdoor building but could also be used as an indoor pavilion to house exhibitions or events. 'Inflatable structures work especially well in exhibition design', says Stuart Veech, who established VMA with Mascha Veech-Kosmatschof.[28] 'They can create a portable exhibition space that can be instantly recreated in the different venues the exhibition travels to. They make a potent response to the nomadic nature of twenty-first century life.'

The dome-like roof of Veech Media Architecture's portable textile pavilion was designed with ventricles in the roof to promote the circulation of cool air inside and enable hot air to escape.

Veech points out that, despite the advanced structural abilities that inflatable fabrics have, they are vulnerable to high winds and inclement weather, making them unviable as permanent outdoor structures. Even when supported by steel lintels and tension cables, strong winds could cause them to tear or blow them away completely.

VMA's inflatable Radionight structure was not a habitable environment like Sprachpavillion, but a voluminous membrane that could create the illusion of a floating form. Supported by lightweight aluminium supports, Radionight hovered seven meters above the ground as if it had suspended the laws of gravity and inexplicably transformed weight into lightness. Hydraulic lifts were installed to carry visitors up to its perimeter. The inflatable structures of Radionight and Sprachpavillion exemplify the strikingly weightless forms that inflatable materials can create.

## Fabric Formwork

Concrete is used more than any other manmade material on Earth, and its presence in structures around the world makes it nearly as ubiquitous as fibres. The textile industry is considered to be huge, but the production of concrete is massive by comparison. A total of seven cubic kilometres of concrete are manufactured each year, creating

Mark West, director of the Centre for Architectural Structures and Technology at the University of Manitoba, is developing a system of fabric formwork capable of creating refined details in the surface of cast concrete.

more than one cubic metre for every person on the planet.[29] This staggering figure includes many types of fibre-based concrete, which have been mixed with fibres to improve their performance.

Concrete and textiles are coming together in new and innovative ways, but the relationship between the two has existed for centuries. Historically, coarse wool and horsehair were added to mortar, and straw was used to fortify Roman cement. In France, hemp fibres have strengthened concrete for several centuries, with products such as Hempcrete used as a construction material for a broad range of applications today. Fibre-reinforced concrete contains filaments made from steel, glass, synthetic materials and natural fibres. The type and length of fibre used creates concrete with different characters, determining their geometries, orientation, distribution and densities. The addition of polypropylene fibres, for example, can improve the concrete's mix cohesion and impact resistance, and carbon-fibre reinforcements create thinner, lighter concrete panels than those made with steel rebars.[30] Almost every kind of formwork concrete can be cast and set in a fabric mould, and fibre-composite form liners can be used to create textured patterns on the surface.

Despite the exciting textures and shapes that can be created with concrete, the material is often perceived as a dull, flat, uninspiring substance. Perhaps inspired by imaginative artworks formed in concrete, architects, looking for methods of sculpting the material in nonlinear shapes, are pioneering ways of creating textile moulds. Fabric formwork has emerged as a technique for sculpting concrete into new shapes by pouring it into a textile sheath.[31] Architects have successfully created innovative soft interior landscapes and have used the technique outdoors to form retaining walls, columns, bridges and façades. The shapes and textures that result are integrating textiles and fibre technology into architectural aesthetics and fabrication methods.

One of the first to pioneer this field was the Japanese architect Kenzo Unno, whose methods of creating fabric-formed concrete walls have inspired architects around the world.[32] Unno discovered the possibilities of fabric-formed architecture in the 1980s, virtually by accident when he was pursuing a quest to simplify construction methods so that laymen could build houses for themselves.[33] At the time, he was also pioneering a zero-waste approach to architecture and was looking for alternatives to materials like plywood that are often discarded after just one use.

With both of these ambitions in mind, Unno began to explore the possibilities of using fabric moulds to shape wet concrete, and he developed several methods of using thin, flexible textile sheets to cast concrete walls. By constructing a simple steel frame and crafting fabric walls on each side, Unno created a reinforced structure into which liquid concreted could be poured. The back, or inner, wall is typically constructed from a rigid sheet of water-resistant insulation, while the front surface is formed by fabric alone. The sheet of insulation on the inner wall provides an energy-efficient layer that remains hidden from view after construction is complete. Tension applied to the outside surface compresses the wet concrete into the desired shape, creating rippling textures, bold relief or subtle contours. As the concrete dries, excess moisture is expelled, oozing through the surface of the textile. The expulsion of excess moisture enables the concrete to cure quickly, and the finished result resembles a high tech concrete panel, even though only low tech methods were used to produce it.[34]

Textiles such as woven polyethylene and polypropylene perform well when used in fabric formwork, but Unno's choice of fabric is typically the synthetic netting used to enclose construction scaffolding. Unno has found good use for a material that would otherwise be discarded. The netting presents a sustainable alternative to plywood, which is typically used to construct the heavy wooden moulds needed for standard concrete formwork. When casting is completed, plywood moulds are dismantled, often breaking in the process. They seldom last for more than a few castings before the concrete begins permeating the wood grain, peeling away the top layer of the wood. Although the fabric formwork panels are produced from inexpensive materials, they have the sculptural finishes typical of exclusive architectural detailing.

Another visionary in this field is Canadian architect Mark West, a professor at the University of Manitoba's Faculty of Architecture, and the director of the Centre for Architectural Structures and Technology (CAST). West's research with fabric moulds for concrete structures originated as a fine art practice but quickly progressed into techniques for developing architectural and structural concrete applications.

West's research connects with a handful of practitioners around the world who are exploring alternatives to the hard, heavy constructions used to form concrete structures. 'Concrete has been formed in rigid moulds since its invention in antiquity,' he says.[35] 'Rigid wood or steel formwork panels have been used since the mid-1800s, giving us a vocabulary of structural form that relies primarily on rectangular shapes. While traditional rectangular forms are simple to construct from rigid formwork panels, the structural members they produce will tend to use more material and carry more dead weight. By replacing rigid wood or steel forms with a flexible fabric membrane that is allowed to deflect under the weight of the concrete it contains, curved geometries become extremely easy to form.'

The sculpture-like forms West creates are formed through use of inexpensive polyolefin fabrics, known for their slick, nonadhesive surfaces, chemically inert properties, high strength and low cost. Initial trials revealed that concrete does not adhere to their surfaces, so unlike wood and steel formworks that need to be coated with release oils, polyolefin fabrics do not. The fabrics were durable enough to be reused many times, and flexible enough to create efficient, structurally defined curves. As West progressed the techniques, he created shapes that were more complex and more extreme, yet each time, the polyolefin formed them easily.

As West continued to advance the techniques, he watched a new language of architectural form emerge, providing a radically different understanding of the aesthetic potentials reinforced concrete architecture can have. 'The fabric formwork created a new and unprecedented level of refinement in the surface finish and texture of cast concrete,' West says, 'and provided an inexpensive, light weight, reusable and globally-available formwork material in place of wood.' West discovered that fabric has another advantage over wood in that it is permeable enough to allow air bubbles and excess water to seep out, yielding a stronger and more durable form of "case-hardened" concrete. When using the fabric formwork to form precast concrete panels, West created horizontal moulds for the wet concrete. The force of gravity drew the mould membrane down into a series of curved forms that were determined by the way the fabric was stretched and supported.

West's current method of forming funicular thin-shell structures utilizes the unique symmetry between fabric and concrete that results when they are curved as one. 'There is a natural synergy between fabric and concrete,' West explains. 'Concrete only resists compression forces (it loves to be squeezed, but cracks when it is pulled), so the most efficient use of this material is to form it into arched compression shapes. A pure compression arch is the mirror image of itself as a hanging string. Similarly, a pure compression vault is the mirror image of a hanging piece of fabric. By using hanging fabric sheets to produce moulds for thin-shell concrete compression vaults, we are using the inherent intelligence of textile (tension) structures to "calculate" and naturally produce the perfect shape for compression shell moulds. So, in structural terms, these two materials—the fabric mould in tension and the concrete in compression—they are made for each other. This is a marriage made in the deepest level of natural structural symmetry.'

One of West's most striking fabric formwork designs was a column created through the use of a sheath-like mould joined together with laces. West created the mould from two rectangular pieces of woven polyethylene fabric known by the trade name Propex 315ST, constraining the concrete exactly as a corset would cinch a waistline. 'By replacing rigid panels with a thin textile tension membrane, the vast majority of material normally required to restrain wet concrete was eliminated,' West explains. 'The only exterior support it required was scaffolding or bracing to hold the top of the form in position. No other restrains are needed to support the formwork.' When the mould was removed, a curvaceous silhouette was revealed. Its eye-catching shape and smooth surface stand as a one of many monuments to the integration of structural concrete and textile technology.

# Girli Concrete

Textiles can shape the appearance of concrete in a number of ways, dramatically embellishing its surface with soft textures, vibrant colours and striking motifs. New print and imprint techniques developed by Belfast-based practitioners Patricia Belford, senior research fellow in textiles at the University of Ulster, and Ruth Morrow, professor of architecture at Queen's University, are reinventing concrete as a soft surface material. The two are pioneering methods of embedding delicate fabrics deep within the harsh alkaline surfaces of concrete, creating a uniquely tactile material that architects love to get hold of.

Their venture is called Girli Concrete, a name chosen because it references the two young women who established the project and the response they receive from a public startled to see a soft, feminine texture applied to a material traditionally associated with masculinity.[36] Belford and Morrow experimented with the low tech methods of wet and dry concrete casting and a variety of high tech textile processes that include digital printing, laser cutting, etching and flocking. The combination of high tech and low tech methodologies enabled them to align fibre forms with architectural detailing, making the experience of architecture more accessible by cladding a cold, hard material with a warm and inviting texture.[37]

The high alkaline surface of the concrete proved to be incompatible with some fibres, which limited the fabrics that could be applied to the concrete.[38] Belford and Morrow experimented with many different types of concrete, varying their chemical consistencies to determine which combinations would yield the best results. Techniques such as lace-making and devore yielded lasting results, with the devore process eventually leading to the development of their Bubble concrete product. The Lava Lace motif, which seamlessly integrates the pattern and the concrete as it meshes them together, has emerged as Girli Concrete's signature design. A chemical reaction occurs when the fabric is immersed in the concrete, making it impossible to predict how the finish will dry. As a result, each Lava Lace piece creates a uniquely individual surface every time.

Belfast-based practitioners Patricia Belford and Ruth Morrow are pioneering methods of embedding delicate fabrics in concrete to give the material a soft, tactile surface.

Predictably, experiments with flocking resulted in a flocked concrete panel, but one that produced surprising results. Applying the fibres to the concrete softened the surface dramatically, enhancing the sound absorption and acoustic nature of the panels. Subsequently, Belford and Morrow collaborated with acoustic experts to determine the extent to which the technique could be developed to create acoustic panels. By varying the length and density of the fibres, the concrete can be endowed with a wide range of acoustic values.

Belford and Morrow have produced more than fifty varieties of concrete panels, of which they selected thirty for display at trade shows and exhibitions. As their research moves forward, they are aiming to develop a core range of fibres that are able to withstand the high alkaline consistency of the concrete while also lending themselves to customization. Future directions include designing and developing weaving techniques and technical processes that will fully integrate woven fabric and concrete.

# Geotextiles

Geotextiles take fabric underground, where they can sculpt, mould and shape the earth as a sculptor would form clay. Geotextiles are high performance permeable fabrics, engineered to be strong enough to hold boulders in place yet porous enough to allow water to pass through. When used to reinforce structures in the landscape, geotextiles filter, separate and drain yet prevent the soil from washing away. Geotextiles can create striking terraces in landscape architecture or be seamlessly integrated into topsoil to promote the growth of garden plants.

Advances in technical fibres have made geotextiles sleeker, stronger and more available than ever before. When used in environmental engineering, they are variously referred to as geosynthetics, geonets and geogrids—names inspired by their woven, mesh-like qualities. They are widely used in civil engineering applications, where they reinforce airfield landing strips, construct motorways and underpin agricultural sites. In the form of AstroTurf, they create smooth surfaces in sports arenas.[39] Used in conjunction with water management engineering, geotextiles line dams and canals, reinforce banks and are used to construct reservoirs and jetties.

Geotextiles are designed to be flexible but engineered to have low creep properties. Their malleability enables them to tolerate the contraction and expansion created by freeze-thaw environments, yet they are stable enough to withstand seismic pressure. They are invulnerable to corrosion from naturally occurring acids and alkalis in the soil, and they are resistant to the bacteria and mildew that cause other types of fibres to decompose.

Typically crafted from spun-bonded polypropylene or polyester, or woven from fibreglass yarns or nylon fibres, geotextiles can be produced in a variety of widths and weights. They can be made as a warp- or flat-knit polymeric fabric, industrial mesh or flexible tubes. Some types of geotextiles may resemble felt; constructed from needle-punch or heat-bonding techniques, they can have a dense structure or a gossamer, web-like appearance.

Some net-like geotextiles, such as Naltex, an extruded mesh that resembles an expanded net, are manufactured like apertured films rather than textiles.[40] Naltex is produced by embossing a thin polymer film with a perforated pattern and expanding the film to induce pores, thus creating a net or extruded mesh. Like all apertured

Geotextiles are among the strongest textiles produced today, engineered to reinforce cliff faces, sculpt smooth contours in the landscape or provide a stable base for a flat surface. Geogrids, such as the multidirectional Tensar tri-axial shown here, can bend and flex to accommodate for shifts in the ground around them.

films, Naltex is lightweight and thin, but it can be laminated onto a substrate to make it rigid or more absorbent. Also a nonwoven textile, Typar is composed of thermally bonded, continuous polypropylene filaments and is suited to a wide range of architectural and engineering applications. Typar has good filtration properties and high tensile strength in every direction. Made from 100 per cent polypropylene, Typar is also resistant to rot and bacteria.[41]

Comtrac and Fortrac are produced from high tenacity polyester filament yarns woven into an interlocking pattern. Both fabrics are flexible and have high strengths with proven track records in landscape architecture and civil engineering applications. Also made for soil reinforcement, Ringtrac is a continuous, round-weave tube fabric woven from high strength, low creep polymers such as polyvinyl alcohol (PVA).[42] Ringtrac may be embedded in a hillside and covered with soil, or used on the surface to dam mudslides or prevent erosion.

Geotextiles are forging new roles for textiles in the built environment. As architects and engineers use geotextiles to build surfaces underground, they use fabric to project architectural space far beyond the structure's outer walls. Just like other construction materials, geotextiles have the potential to create architectural conditions such as floors, walls and corners. Whereas built proportions are generally considered to be fixed distinctions, the invisible presence of geotextiles represents a continuum of structure and space.

## Feature Interview: Toshiko Mori

Toshiko Mori knows that the cutting edge of architecture is not streamlined and sharp, but sensuous and soft. Since establishing her practice in New York City two decades ago, Mori has explored the use of textile forms and traditional tailoring techniques, which she believes hold exciting new possibilities for both the experience and fabrication of architecture. 'In many architectural applications, high-strength fibres perform better than materials such as concrete and steel,' she explains.[43] 'Textile substrates can have unrivalled strength, capable of reacting to tectonic force and environmental stress by distributing the impact laterally across the surface. Used in architecture, this gives built structures the potential to be lighter, less dense and more durable.'

As well as managing her practice in New York, Mori is the Robert P. Hubbard Professor in the Practice of Architecture at Harvard University's Graduate School of Design, where she was also the chair of the Department of Architecture from 2002 to 2008.[44] When teaching, Mori has used textile metaphors to encourage students to see architecture in a new light. 'A skyscraper can be perceived as a system of individual spaces,' she explains, 'stacked one atop the other. The degree of separation between the spaces at the bottom and top can be considerable, and even isolate the inhabitants at each end. Imagine a massive fabric swatch woven from hollow fibres, each fibre conceived as an individual, habitable space. Weave the fibres together or braid them tri-axially and they intersect, shrinking the distance between individual spaces.'

Viewed from underneath, Toshiko Mori's proposed enclosure for the Smithsonian Museum in Washington, DC, resembles a tri-axial weave.

Mori's use of fibres has emerged as a hallmark of her work. Industrial-strength filaments have featured in Mori's commercial and residential projects, where cabling systems stretch systematically through space to suspend and support architectural details and whole structures. Mori designed the Issey Mikyake boutiques in Manhattan, where she used stainless steel cables to suspend and support clothing rails. When she designed a residential cliff-top house on a remote site in Taghkanic, New York, Mori placed it precipitously near the edge to maximize the views from the windows and terraces. She wound cables around the exterior, encircling the house in webs of sleek metal strands that formed a barrier between the open terraces and the vertiginous drop beneath them.

Mori has built homes in the Gulf of Mexico, where seasonal hurricanes challenged her to design buildings robust enough to withstand extreme weather conditions yet sleek enough to embody the lightness and transparency that characterize her work. Mori looked for lightweight, durable materials that could imbue the projects with a weightless character yet provide a viable alternative to concrete and steel. 'Materials

When commissioned to design a beachfront house in a hurricane zone, Toshiko Mori looked for lightweight, durable materials that could withstand the force of extreme winds and high pressure blasts of rain and salt water. Metal cables and fibreglass proved to be excellent choices.

used in hurricane zones must be able to withstand the force of extreme winds and high-pressure blasts of rain and salt water,' Mori explains. 'Yachts are made with fibreglass hulls that can withstand similar conditions, and high-performance racing sails are some of the strongest membranes made today. Fibreglass sails include strands of Kevlar and carbon fibres, and they withstand strong gusts of wind by channelling the impact in a particular pattern or dispersing it over the entire surface. Despite its strength, under certain conditions sailcloth can be very brittle, so architects must keep that in mind.'

For one of the Gulf of Mexico projects, Mori famously constructed an external staircase from a single length of a fibreglass textile. With the ease of unrolling a bolt of fabric, Mori created landings at the top and bottom of the staircase by smoothing each end of the textile into a flat surface and folding the tips of the fabric upward to form a banister for each level. The middle length was pleated like a fashion garment as Mori folded it thirty times to create the staircase's steps and treads. Mori's design was fabricated by a yacht manufacturer in New England, who stiffened it with the

Toshiko Mori used industrial-strength metal filaments to create a cabling system to suspend and support this fibreglass staircase.

resins used to strengthen the moulded fibreglass used in boat hulls. 'The staircase is structurally sound yet weighs less than 300 lbs,' Mori says, 'which is extremely light for a prefabricated staircase. The fabric performs perfectly as a staircase, and it can be maintained as easily as a boat deck. My only concern was that the material could photo-degrade due to the constant exposure to strong sunlight, so I coated it with a UV-resistant solvent to deflect the sun's rays.'

Mori foresees many other applications for textiles in architecture, including the potential to use it to construct whole structures. 'Fabric is essentially a thin, flexible material that can easily form a membrane for a built structure,' she says. 'It has many possibilities inside and out, but textile façades are especially interesting right now. While certain textiles are structurally strong, they are also porous enough to breathe without letting moisture leak through. This makes them perfect as an envelope around a built structure, where they can be used individually or layered. Like wearing an outfit, the layers that architectural textiles create promote ventilation, shade and insulation. Surface textiles could be pulled away to channel the heat of the sun inside, or rolled back in summer to deflect heat and cool the building. Fabrics made for these purposes could be encapsulated with phase change materials that store heat and release it later, or woven with fibres that expand when it's humid to make a breathable roof more rain-resistant. It seems that more can be done at a molecular level to heighten the performance of fibres than can be achieved with conventional architectural materials right now.'

Although Mori's clients are enthusiastic about the structural and aesthetic innovations textiles have to offer, they are seldom prepared to pay a premium to use them. 'Most hi-performance textiles were engineered for specialist applications, not as substitutes for building material,' she says. 'Many specialist materials are expensive to begin with, then become more cost effective as they trickle down into the mainstream. Textiles' first widespread use in architecture may occur in earthquake zones and areas prone to hurricanes and tsunamis. In those applications textiles could save lives, and that will showcase their potentials to architects in the rest of the world.'

# nine

## Extreme Interfaces

For most of their long history, textiles have been synonymous with energy. Their insulating properties create second skins capable of conserving body heat and responding to the kinetic energy generated by the wearer. The Phoenicians and ancient Greeks transformed fabric into sails, cast drag nets to reduce speed and utilized the compressive force of rope. The Persians crafted woven fabric into windmill arms that captured the power of the wind. The first kites were made from silk fabrics nearly 2,800 years ago, lifted into the sky by the wind and held up above by air pressure.[1]

Textiles continue to engage with the forces of nature to produce energy. They absorb the energy of the sun in reflective panels that store solar power. In space, graphite-fibre flywheels rotate at high speeds, generating kinetic energy that powers the satellites.[2] Compressor-like textile structures are being made wearable in order to transform the body's movements into a kinetic power source, and crystal-embedded fabrics have the capacity to capture electromagnetic energy. Phase-change fabrics can store energy and release it, and shock-absorbent fibres are engineered to transform the force they disperse into power.

Energy is all around us, occurring naturally and abundantly in forms that we rarely recognize. Energy is the result of natural phenomena quantified by the laws of physics. Textiles were among the earliest materials to work with these laws, transforming the forces of nature into energy expended by humans. Fabrics and fibres can harness many different forms of energy, including kinetic, thermal, gravitational, photonic, elastic, and electromagnetic energy. Although fossil fuels distracted humans from these renewable sources, awareness of them, and the role that textiles can play in harnessing their energy, is gaining currency today.

Textiles provide surfaces where energy can be harnessed and converted into another form. They can load batteries, energize generators, provide heat sources and

Lightweight, durable and able to absorb vibrations, hi-tech textiles are excellent materials for aeroplane engines. They can be crafted into joints, gaskets, connectors and rotary blades, as well as fasteners, seals and hardware components.

power electrical systems. They can attract electromagnetic radiation, such as microwaves, visible light, solar energy and gamma rays, which they convert into power. When engineered to create tension, such as in a stretched synthetic sheet, rubbery membrane or laminate film, they can generate surface energy.

In many cases, the ability to function as a power source has been made possible through fibre technology and high tech construction techniques. Sails, windmills, kites and other traditional methods have replaced organic fibres with synthetic fabrics and polymer coatings. Advances in conductive fabrics has led to photovoltaic (PV) textiles and woven energy cells. Through research conducted by physicists, scientists, chemists and nanotechnologists, textiles have been engineered to number among some of the most high performance materials on Earth. They are so sophisticated, in fact, that they are at the forefront of the cutting-edge materials made for space exploration.

The new breed of fabrics has emerged as the mega-material of our age, made to withstand environments so fierce that they virtually defy description. As they align with energy, perform in extreme applications and become instruments of biological warfare, textiles have the power to improve human life or become unwitting agents of its destruction.

# Surface Energy

Enough sunlight reaches the Earth's surface in one hour to power the planet for an entire year.[3] The energy in sunlight can be experienced on almost every surface: metal heats up, plastics change shape, ice melts and human skin releases melanin. In plants, photosynthesis occurs, converting carbon dioxide into organic compounds. PV fabrics perform similarly when their synthetic fibres react to light, transforming it into electricity. Just like the PV cells used in pocket calculators, the fabric's photonic abilities are derived from wiry fibres embedded in layers of noncrystalline amorphous silicon.[4] The fibres are sandwiched between a top surface doped with electron-rich materials, and a bottom layer of dopants that hardly contain any electrons at all. When light is absorbed by the surface, it causes the electrons to displace, channelling them through the middle layer to the bottom substrate. The process triggers a reaction in the fibres, causing them to send energy to conducting electrodes.

PV threads and flexible substrates such as steel foil are less expensive to produce than the bulk silicon and rigid solar cells developed for large-scale power grids.[5] Solar cells typically consist of a conductive film applied to glass, which requires a large surface area to function efficiently. PV threads operate with a much smaller surface area to produce the same amount of output power. Because they are lightweight, efficient and portable, they have the potential to provide power sources for wearable technologies.[6] The material can provide power for mobile phones, laptops, music players, cameras and virtually any other small-scale electronic device, which could create significant shifts in the consumer electronics industry.

Light-emitting optic fibres underpin many of the liquid crystal displays (LCDs) produced for keypads and control panels. Assembled layers woven from plastic optical fibres create durable, flexible light-emitting panels that do not generate heat or electromagnetic interference. The panels are made with a reflective layer attached to the underside to increase the light intensity and reflect it in a single direction, and a semitransparent diffuser layer on the top side to enhance uniformity. The optic fibres' light source can be a single LED (light-emitting diode), halogen lamps or low-current incandescent lights. The unique construction of the woven fibre-optic layers with computer-controlled micro-bends in the fibres makes possible the emission of the transmitted light from the sides of the fibres through the cladding.

From their base in Massachusetts, renewable energy developer Konarka has created a filament that seamlessly combines photovoltaic material and fibre technology. Known as Power Fiber, the filament is flexible and soft and can be woven into fabric effortlessly. Whereas most PV threads are layered onto a plastic substrate, Power Fiber is a complete PV unit in itself. Within the fibre, a primary electrode is positioned at the core and surrounded with a layer of active material. The transparent electrode takes the form of a thin membrane made to encircle and envelop the layer of active material. The electrode is surrounded by a transparent substrate that forms the fibre's outer surface.

By using nanotechnology, Konarka developed a PV film that can be printed on clothing, building materials and substrates that can be woven into fabric or used

Photovoltaic fibres and nonwoven components are replacing the bulk silicon and rigid solar cells previously developed for large-scale power grids. Photovoltaic threads are lightweight and efficient and also have the potential to provide power sources for wearable technologies.

to coat architectural components.[7] Known as Power Plastic, the inexpensive material promises to revolutionize the solar power industry by dramatically reducing the high cost of manufacturing photovoltaic cells out of silicon. Konarka describe Power Plastic as a nanomixture produced without silicon, made instead with organic substances that can be economically produced in large sheets. Power Plastic is manufactured in a roll-to-roll process that produces a continuous ribbon-like band of material. Compared to the multistep assembly of traditional solar cells, the process is significantly less labour intensive.

As Konarka's PV fibres find a market, they are likely to power battery-operated personal electronic devices before being developed for consumer electronics connected to an electric supply. Future applications for PV-fibres include surfaces such as sensing shelves, illuminated wallpaper and touch-sensitive tabletops, which could be energized by Power Fiber and Power Plastic, or by fibres and films with similar properties. Interior textiles could be radically reinvented as autonomous devices, such as self-propelled exterior awnings, or blinds and shades with integrated power sources that enable them to open and close by themselves.

## Crystal Energy

Many types of crystals emit positive and negative ions, enabling them to conduct electricity. Certain crystals contain a source of endothermic energy and are capable of

Konarka have developed Power Fiber, a filament that integrates photovoltaic material and fibre technology. Shown here on the production loom, the fibre is flexible and soft, and can be woven into fabric easily.

transferring electrostatic energy and heat to surrounding objects.[8] Both simple crystals and multicrystalline structures are present in bulk silicon to heighten the material's PV properties. The prismatic abilities that crystals have has given them strong associations with light and, subsequently, with light energy. Alhazen, the eleventh-century

British industrial designer Ross Lovegrove designed a solar-powered concept car powered by Swarovski crystals. Since their photovoltaic energy could be a viable power source for lightweight vehicles, they could also provide a portable power source for wearable devices.

physicist, regarded rays of light to be streams of minute energy particles and believed that the term 'energy' evolved from a word that described the phenomena of light.[9] Part of his research was based on light refracted through minerals such as crystals, indicating that their ability to harness light energy has been known for many years.[10]

Crystals are in fashion today more than ever before. Thanks to Swarovski's collaborations with practitioners such as Sébastien Barilleau, and designers such as Hussein Chalayan, whose crystal-laden garments are detailed in Chapter 3, and British industrial designer Ross Lovegrove, who set out to harness crystals' PV energy, have presented crystals in a whole new light. Lovegrove designed a solar-powered concept car using Swarovski crystals, and by working in collaboration with Sharp Solar Europe, and the automobile manufacturer Coggiola, he revealed that their PV energy could be a viable power source for lightweight vehicles. As Swarovski continue to showcase crystals as unique energy sources, their applications for textiles are being considered from a new perspective.

Swarovski has produced a crystal laminate film that can coat virtually any fabric surface. The film is a transparent hot fix foil covered in tiny round and faceted crystals. This film can be glued directly onto most fabrics or sewn on. The film is produced in

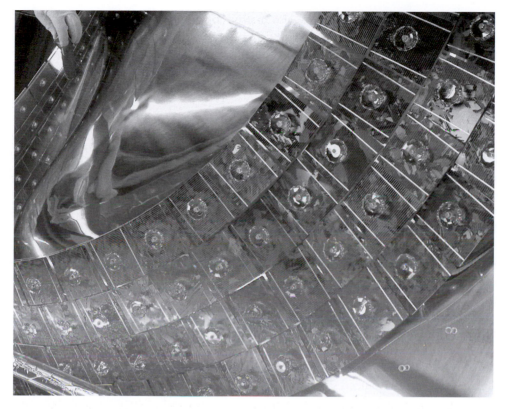

Ross Lovegrove proved the viability of using Swarovski crystals as a portable power source. Crystals such as these could be attached to textiles to create a unique power source for wearable electronics.

sheet form, available by the metre. Swarovski manufacture the material in a range of forty-six standard motifs, but custom-designed motifs can also be created by the process. Once the film has been transferred onto a textile, the translucency of the crystals enables the colours and textures in the fabric underneath to remain visible.

Liquid crystal emulsions are forming the basis of so-called mood materials that change colour as they detect temperature changes. Thermochromatic liquid crystal technology enables a textile substrate to sense the energy released by the body and transform the appearance of the surface. The emulsion is composed of polyurethane, ultraviolet radiation inhibitors, fixers and binders. Microencapsulated liquid crystals are contained within the polyurethane laminate, which is applied to a polyester-knit backing. The fabric is usable for interior applications, such as wall coverings, upholstery and rugs, and fashion applications include swimwear, footwear and accessories.[11]

Ceramics are crystalline in nature, giving ceramic-fibre fabrics the ability to conduct energy as efficiently as other types of conductive fibres. Ceramic fibres are used for sensors and actuators made for a wide range of mechanical, electrical, chemical and thermal applications. They are also crafted into composites made for use in energy harvesting applications.[12] Modern ceramic forging techniques are working with the materials' crystalline structure to produce conductive fibres capable of withstanding high temperatures.

## Flight

Sails have provided an efficient propulsion system for waterborne vessels for several millennia.[13] The potential that textiles held as an aerodynamic material was first discovered by Chinese scholars exploring the mechanics of flight, whose findings appear to have drawn upon the science of aeronautics originally developed by the ancient Egyptians. Sails continue to power a wide range of airborne vessels today: windsurfers, hang gliders, para gliders and even spacecraft use textile membranes to propel themselves. The textiles created for today's sails are designed according to principles of aerodynamics, factoring in the effects of lift and drag and any shock waves that may form around them.

Although some sailcloth continues to made from fibres such as flax, hemp and cotton canvas, when it comes to high performance applications, textiles such as carbon, aramid fibres and Mylar are the materials of choice. Vectran fibres are flexible but limit stretch, and can be woven in traditional bias directions and tri-axial techniques. One of the most advanced sailcloths made today is the Blue Water Weave produced by Warrington Mills.[14] The fabric is specially engineered to maintain off-axis stiffness and provide an efficient range of load transition to enable the sail to adapt to changes in the wind's velocity. The sailcloth's core fabric is made from Vectran, from fibres spun with a variety of core densities. The Vectran core is bonded with a bias cover fabric to heighten its off-axis stiffness and abrasion resistance. Unlike the glue-bonded laminate sails, whose surfaces are susceptible to film failure, and therefore to increased friction, Blue Water Weave provides inherent structural strength.[15]

Although sailcloth was originally designed for terrestrial environments, it is also used in air sports such as hang-gliding. A hang-glider is an unmotorized aircraft made from an aluminium or composite frame fitted with a fabric wing, which is steered through the air by a pilot. In the sport's early days, hang-gliders were limited to short runs at low altitudes, but new textile technology makes it possible for hang-gliders to glide longer and even soar higher. Hang-glider sails are typically made of either woven polyester textiles or composite laminate fabrics that include polyester film and polyester reinforced fibres. These fabrics are lightweight, flexible and have little creep, and offer a high level of performance.[16] They are also crafted with sufficient tension to reduce spanwise twist, a problem common to all types of sailcloth. Polyester film fabrics lose their tension over time, becoming less responsive. Expert hang-gliders generally prefer premium woven fabric, which has proven to last longer than even the best laminated materials. Fabrics such as Hydra-net, a trademark of Dimension-Polyant, and the layered Mylar PM and PX laminates, are among the most high performance sail materials currently produced.

Sailcloth made from Vectran is often crafted from a range of fibres spun with varying core densities. The Vectran layer is then bonded with a bias-cover fabric to heighten its off-axis stiffness and abrasion resistance.

STYLE: FLX13 PEN
FINISH: Optic 2
WEIGHT:

Dimension–Polyant's FLEX range of high-performance racing sailcloth is an acronym for Fill Laminate Extra. The FLEX styles are crosscut fabrics available with several fibre densities and a lock-tight fibre matrix that guarantees superior performance and durability.

High performance sailcloth is made from materials such as carbon, aramid and Mylar. Vectran fibres are flexible but limit stretch and can be woven in traditional bias directions and tri-axial weaves.

Paragliders, like hang-gliders, suspend the pilot in a harness attached to a textile membrane. The parafoil, a parachute-like fabric wing, is not fabricated from sailcloth, however. The parafoil is shaped by its suspension lines and the air pressure vented through it from front to back. It comprises two layers of fabric interconnected via a mesh-like net of fibres that form a row of cells. The force of air entering the cells keeps the parafoil inflated, creating its teardrop aerofoil shape.[17] Paragliders have been crafted from rip-stop nylon for more than half a century, enabling them to soar higher and fly faster than heavier textiles would. New types of fabric are being engineered especially for paragliders, structured by sandwiching high performance fibres between layers of lightweight polymer foil. The materials are fused together by heat and pressure processes, resulting in a lightweight, durable material.

Humans can soar through the sky at great speed using wing suits, wearable textile-based devices that shape the human body into an aerofoil capable of creating lift. Wing suits were first used in the 1930s by skydivers to enable them to move through the sky horizontally. Early wing suits were made of fabric such as canvas and silk attached to frames made from steel, wood or whalebone. They took a dramatic leap forward in the 1990s, when French skydiver Patrick de Gayardon developed a wing suit that enabled the wearer to fly laterally during his or her descent. They have evolved since then, typically resembling a jumpsuit crafted with fabric panels sewn between the legs and under the arms to create an aerofoil shape.[18] They are typically constructed from parafoil textiles made from Spectra fibres and a nonwoven polyethylene laminate. Atair Aerospace have designed a flexible wing suit constructed with advanced composite textiles. Known as the AeroSuit, the garment enables a skydiver to glide to a target far away from the drop point. The arms and legs of the AeroSuit are fitted with inflated webbed panels that give it wing-like properties. The webbed panels dramatically improve the skydiver's aerodynamics, transforming a freefall drop into a flight that covers considerable distances.

Atair Aerospace's EXO-X2 is a wing suit constructed from advanced aerospace composite materials. The suit is more rigidly structured than the AeroSuit, designed with more reinforcement in the body and wings. The suit is made for use with a twin micro-turbine-powered engine, so small and lightweight that it fits to the back like a backpack. Atair Aerospace describe EXO-X2 as 'the world's smallest human-piloted jet airplane'.[19]

In the form of sports such as skydiving and paragliding, flight is recreational, but in other contexts it can provide the means of emergency evacuation. In the last decade, personal parachutes have become regarded as a viable means of fleeing the upper floors of tall buildings, provided that they can be designed to open at low altitudes. To function fully, most parachutes should be deployed at a minimum height of fifty metres, and most high rise buildings are much lower. Some designers advocate combining the parachute with a wearable air compressor that would inflate at the beginning of the descent. Once made from silk, today's parachutes are constructed from woven nylon fabric, which is usually coated with silicone to enhance its drag. An inflatable parachute would have to include pressurized membranes capable of fully inflating in seconds. Designers at fashion and textile specialists Karada and Becagli are working collaboratively with engineers at SEVA Technologies to combine high performance fabric with vehicle airbag technology to create a low altitude parachute. The device is being developed as part of an emergency evacuation system created with urban environments in mind.

In space, the reflective membranes known as solar sails can harness enough energy to propel satellites through space.[20] Ordinary spacecraft may also use sails fitted with solar collectors and temperature-control panels to make minor attitude control corrections and orbit modifications without using fuel. Scientists at the Japan Aerospace Exploration Agency (JAXA) are developing a coilable extension mast and thin, flexible solar membranes for their space vessels. The sails may take the forms of

The landing airbags designed for NASA's Mars Pathfinder included several layers of woven Vectran made by Du Pont. Several of the layers were coated with silicone to improve their ability to withstand pressure when inflated.

immense, parachute-like membranes or spinning textile disks. Long, thin, overlapping membranes could spin like a propeller to generate energy for the craft.[21] The vessels will be equipped with parachutes made from fabrics such as nylon and polyester that will be deployed during the return journey to Earth to slow the craft's descent into the stratosphere.

Landing airbags are made of Vectran to cushion spacecrafts' contact with a planet's surface when landing.[22] The airbags designed for NASA's Mars Pathfinder included several layers of woven Vectran, some of which were coated with silicone to improve their ability to withstand pressure when inflated.[23] The explorer robot known as Tumbleweed Rover is designed to survey extraterrestrial terrain and is propelled by unexpected means. The robot is equipped with inflatable nylon airbags that will enable it to bounce dynamically over a planet's surface to carry out its mission.[24]

## *Kinetic Fabrics*

Kinetic energy is produced by motion, and, when harnessed, it can provide a power source.[25] Many types of textiles respond to the energy expended around them: in the form of insulation, fibres can retain heat or deflect it; as fashion fabric, they respond to the friction caused by the wearer's movements, hold heat close to the body or wick it away through the surface.[26] Shape memory alloys are used in the construction of kinetic electronic garments, where they respond directly to body heat and ambient temperature changes, morphing into new shapes and returning to their original form. Nitinol is a popular choice in textile substrates using resistive heating and control electronics.

Phase change materials, a type of substance originally developed for NASA, are capable of a high degree of heat fusion. They can melt and solidify at a certain temperature and are capable of storing large amounts of energy and releasing them later. Heat is absorbed or released when the material changes from solid to liquid and vice versa, and when they are bonded to fibres, they can transform the kinetic energy expended by muscles into a heat source. The use of temperature regulation materials in fashion ends the need for bulky layering. Phase change materials can be used in linings to equip coats with built-in thermometers that act as personal thermostats, keeping the body temperature constant while the wearer is journeying through transitional spaces. Phase change fabrics such as Outlast have tiny paraffin capsules embedded in the fibres.[27] When the body heats over forty degrees Celsius the paraffin molecules react and absorb the heat. When the temperature drops below 37 degrees Celsius they expand, releasing the heat they've stored. Outlast produces a comfort zone by maintaining a constant temperature for the wearer both inside and out, bringing the temperature under the control of the individual.

Researchers around the world are developing garments capable of changing colour and pattern depending on the activity of the wearer. Many of these garments currently remain at prototype stage as researchers develop methods of weaving the necessary sensors, connectors and circuit boards directly into the material. One of the most advanced examples is the KineticDress designed by CuteCircuit. The dress is embedded with sensors able to capture the wearer's movements. When the wearer moves, the sensors activate the electroluminescent embroidery tracing the surface of the dress. When the wearer is motionless, the surface looks black; when the wearer starts moving, the dress slowly illuminates and depicts circular patterns in iridescent blue.

Angel Chang was one of the first designers to use thermochromatic surfaces in high fashion applications. Chang's spring/summer 2008 collection featured motifs printed with thermochromatic dye. Her camouflage motif, for example, was printed on a pleated raglan sleeve dress and a georgette tunic, which made the garment slightly see-through when the motif disappears. The collection includes a white-on-white invisible grid motif printed on chiffon. The pattern only becomes visible when exposed to UV light. Another design features a Manhattan map motif that Chang developed in conjunction with Red Maps, a publisher of urban maps and guides.

The heat-sensitive dye used to print the motif only becomes legible when exposed to warmth; otherwise, the fabric appears to be completely opaque. Another heat-sensitive motif was transferred onto pleated georgette. 'The thermochromatic dye can react to body heat, sunlight and ambient heat, and as it intensifies the prints fade into a soft glow,' Chang explains.[28] 'I tease my clients that they have to be careful not to embarrass themselves, because their dresses may blush even if they don't.'

## Energy Absorption

Many fabrics have the ability to dissipate kinetic energy, effectively dampening the aftershock of strong vibrations by absorbing them in the fibres. Foam membranes, fibrous wadding and layers of padded textiles mimic the performance of coils, springs and torsion bars in their ability to absorb energy, and they provide sustained suspension with less friction than that which is normally created by rigid materials. Suspension structures, such as cable bridges, transfer weight and pressure to other supports, dispersing the stress created by additional loads.

Almost every fibre has a degree of elasticity that enables it to disperse energy along its length and return to its normal shape once the shock has dissipated. Whereas medium-strength filaments such as Spandex can absorb impact energy and quickly bounce back into shape, a high strength material such as carbon fibre will shatter under the same stress. Over time, spider silk has evolved into a compound capable of dispersing energy efficiently throughout the entire filament, which is what makes it virtually unbreakable.

Technologically advanced fabrics have enabled textiles to emerge as mega-materials. Super-strong, ultra-durable, flexible, incredibly lightweight and high performance, they are an ideal material for machine parts, engine components and industrial equipment. Textiles are pliable and absorb vibrations and have an excellent resistance to heat when coated with polymers. They can be water proofed and wind proofed, and coated to resist corrosion. Textiles provide excellent material for expansion and control joints, gaskets, connectors, bladed rotary turbo discs and pressure rollers, and they can easily be fashioned into devices such as fasteners, seals and pieces of hardware.

Rope and cables are widely used in the marine industry as towlines, anchor rope and yacht riggings. They are engineered to have a Spandex-like ability to disperse energy yet have the strength of filaments such as carbon fibre. Their durability is described in terms of break strength, indicating how much energy they can absorb before they fracture and fall apart. Tests revealed that a knot can significantly reduce a rope's break strength, as it creates an area of resistance analogous to a weak link in a strong chain.

Polymer fibre ropes, such as high tenacity oriented polyethylene, were once the filament of choice for the haulage ropes made for use by tugboats and ocean liners. Their ability to absorb energy on impact has been surpassed by high modulus polymer fibre (HMPF), one of the strongest rope materials every produced.[29] HMPF

Kevlar is strong, durable, flexible and lightweight, making it an ideal material for sports equipment. This kayak is made from Kevlar, rendering it strong enough to withstand strong currents and forceful impacts, yet still light enough to be carried during short treks.

evolved from PRD49, an organic fibre produced by DuPont. HMPF has a high elastic modulus that almost matches steel, and a version of it was marketed as Kevlar 49.[30] HMPF ropes are lightweight and corrosion proof, providing the perfect material for yacht rigging.

This is a close-up of Loop.pH's 'Archilace', a responsive, light-emitting architectural textile produced for a private commission in Geneva.

Polyurethane-coated Dyneema yarn, when strand-braided and constructed from high tenacity oriented polyethylene, creates a high strength rope with excellent abrasion resistance. Its stretch is minimal, and it has an extremely high strength-to-length ratio and energy absorption per kilo of rope.

Vectran fibres were used to craft a cable tether made to suspend a floating wind turbine that generates electricity. From its 300-metre-high perch, the turbine provides an alternative energy source, powered by blades rotating along a horizontal axis. The Vectran fibres form the core of a braided cable tether coated with copper to make it conductive. While providing suspension, the Vectran cable also functions as a connector interlinking generators on each side to the ground below. As the cable transfers the electricity generated to the surface, it can be used immediately or stored in batteries.

Like Vectran, the metal-coated HMPF yarn known as Zylon is electrically conductive and super strong.[31] The fibre is lightweight and flexible, and typically coated by metals such as silver, copper and nickel to give it conductive abilities. Because Zylon performs well under stress, it is widely used in to produce cables for telecommunications masts and power lines. Zylon cables can withstand storms and natural disasters, holding together even when the structures that support them have fallen apart. Impact test results show that braided Zylon fibres have a greater resistance to ballistic impact than does Kevlar. Zylon is capable of absorbing approximately twice as much kinetic energy as Kevlar fibres crafted in comparable weights and braid styles.[32]

Textiles have been used to generate energy for several millennia. Although contemporary designs typically replace fabric arms with metal blades, textile components can be found in the windmill's motor, generator and transformer.

# Extremophiles

Fireproof fibres can tolerate extreme heat, functioning perfectly in temperatures as high as 3,000°C. Metal filaments can withstand corrosive acids, enabling them to be knitted into mesh and lowered into vats of radioactive waste and lethal toxins. Nitrogen gas is used to freeze rolls of metallic fabric; the filaments they contain are strongest at −150°C, giving the fabric heightened performance in subzero temperatures. The most advanced textiles seem to be subjected to the most severe environments on Earth, and when it comes to those made for space, the conditions get a lot worse. Few materials can take the radiation of outer space, the heavy vibrations of rocket lift-off and the crushing compression of re-entering the Earth's atmosphere, but technologized textiles perform perfectly every time.

Not only are textile membranes and fibrous forms deployed to the deepest regions of space, but they are routinely submerged in the lowest depths of the ocean. Even on dry land, they are made to endure the most extreme conditions imaginable. High performance textiles go far beyond the notion of durability, enriching the world of humans by performing in environments where humans could never survive. The roles that such fibres play transcend labels such as 'radical' or 'extreme', because their performances cannot be quantified in absolute terms. They have taken textiles to frontiers that, until now, have remained uncharted.

An analogy between this new breed of textiles and the genus of life forms known as extremophiles sheds new light on their performance.[33] Extremophiles are said to be as old as the earth itself, and they thrive in environments so extreme that few organisms can endure them. Ranging from single-celled Archaea and slow-moving amoeba to complex bacterium and multicellular animals, extremophiles can be single-celled organisms or sophisticated life forms. Extremophiles include worms, insects and tiny crustaceans, such as Antarctic krill, Pompeii worms, glacier-dwelling ice crawlers and tardigrades (also known as water bears). Although extremophiles are greatly varied, many share similar characteristics, enabling biologists to divide them into seventeen categories. Although no fibres have been deliberately designed to mimic the extremophiles' biological functions to date, several types of textiles have been engineered to withstand environments similar to the types they thrive in.

Radioresistant extremophiles, for example, are organisms resistant to high levels of ionizing radiation, including organisms capable of surviving nuclear fallout. Research conducted at uranium deposits in Brazil identified organisms that thrive in radioactive environments, and studies carried out in the aftermath of the Chernobyl disaster cited species that remained unaffected by high radioactivity. When remote-control robots measured radiation levels in the remains of Reactor 4, they identified extremophile fungi growing on the remains of the reactor's walls.

In the aftermath of Chernobyl, the workers who treated radioactive debris inside the reactor's remains wore metal-fibre protective suits so heavy that their appearance seemed more machine-like than human, earning them the nickname of 'bio-robots'. Specific details of the fabrics used to construct the suits are not available, but based on current antiradiation fabrics produced by Xinxiang Zhuocheng Special Textile Company in China, the garments would have had to have had a minimum shielding rate of ninety-nine. Xinxiang Zhuocheng's antiradiation fabric is made of metal fibres blended with polyester cotton.[34] The conductive metals would have emitted a frequency between 50Hz and 120Hz to prevent electromagnetic waves from penetrating the suits. Even though the bio-robots' garments were probably the most durable ever worn on Earth, the workers still could not remain on site for more than 40 seconds at a time due to the extremely high doses of radiation remaining in the debris.[35]

Many types of extremophiles can survive such devastations and can even flourish in worse conditions. Xerophiles, for example, survive in deserts and extremely dry, desiccating conditions. They live in the driest areas on Earth, where moisture is virtually nonexistent, and temperatures are usually extreme. Similarly, thermophile organisms flourish in high temperatures, often living in thermal conditions that reach 105°C. They are impervious to noxious gases and toxic fumes, and they thrive in sulphur springs, hydrothermal vents and volcanic landscapes. They can even survive volcanic eruptions and lava flows.

Cryophiles are the thermophiles' diametric opposites.[36] Not only are they able to tolerate low temperatures, they can only survive in cold temperatures, because they need low temperatures in order to reproduce. They typically live in permafrost, polar ice, frozen soil and on the frigid bottom of the ocean floor, where piezophile organisms are also found. Piezophiles can tolerate a range of temperature extremes, but can only survive in environments subjected to high hydrostatic pressure. In addition to thriving in the deepest oceanic trenches, they also flourish in compressed soil far beneath the terrestrial subsurface. Their ability to endure temperature extremes as well as hydrostatic pressure makes them cryophiles and thermophiles too. Extremophiles often have the ability to endure two or more extremes, placing them in the category of polyextremophile.

The conditions of space are as extreme as any on Earth, yet the weight restrictions of rocket launch require that materials be as lightweight as they are durable. Textiles are present in almost every aspect of rocket, satellite and spacecraft design. Now that braided carbon-fibre epoxy matrices can create nozzles that are stronger and lighter than steel, metal nozzle cones are a thing of the past. The challenge for designers and technologists alike has been to find a material that, like the thermophile organism, will not change its shape in high temperatures or incinerate. Textile parts made for the crafts' engines have proven to withstand extreme heat, and they absorb vibrations enough to significantly reduce friction. Temperatures are high outside the spacecraft, too, where thermal blankets made from layers of Dacron, copper mesh, Mylar, Kevlar and ceramic fibres are used to protect the engine from the intense heat of the rocket's flames. The spacecraft's surface is cooled by shades and shields that deflect solar radiation as the spacecraft orbits the sun, and a heat-reflective sunshade constructed from Nextel shields it from the most intense solar rays.[37]

The Nextel Woven Ceramic Fabric contains ceramic fibres, and the textile was used to construct a strong, lightweight space shield for use on the Space Station Laboratory Habitation and other manned modules constructed in the United States.[38] Shields are necessary to protect spacecraft against collisions with space debris, meteorites and small asteroids. The textile outperforms other textiles resistant to high temperatures such as carbon, glass or quartz.[39] The textile has numerous applications here on Earth, where it is installed in industrial furnaces to provide thermal barriers that separate different temperature zones.[40]

Scientists at JAXA are developing new materials to make spacecraft lighter and more durable.[41] New materials for the M-V rocket include carbon-fibre-reinforced plastic, and the Mars Orbiter NOZOMI features an antenna made from carbon-fibre-reinforced polymers. JAXA are designing satellites as deployable structures, fitted with parts that fold inside the rocket's core during launch and extend into solar arrays when they reach orbit.

Yasser Gowayed, an associate professor in Auburn University's textile engineering program, is collaborating with NASA to transform graphite-fibre fabric into a new energy source for satellites.[42] The fabric would be used to create flywheels that function as solar-powered generators. Solar power would turn the flywheels at high speeds to create kinetic energy, which would in turn be converted into electrical energy. Satellites are currently powered by batteries that extract solar energy from the sun, which recharge when exposed to the sun's rays. The batteries are heavy and expensive to produce, whereas flywheels made of graphite fibre composites are lightweight and can be fabricated inexpensively. Not only will the flywheels provide an efficient energy source, they will also help the satellite orientate itself towards the sun as it travels through space.

Because the vacuum of space is virtually free of friction, the flywheels are able to turn effortlessly. Artificial vacuums are built to create low-friction conditions on Earth, providing manufacturers with chemically inert environments where textile fibres can be efficiently impregnated, encapsulated and sealed. Industrial-strength felt can be used to make cogs, rollers and pulleys self-lubricating, making it an ideal material for such environments. Processes such as vacuum-assisted resin transfer moulding (VARTM) produce composites by inserting woven or braided preforms into a vacuum where they are injected with polymeric resins.[43] This technique can quickly create complex shapes that would take considerable time to fabricate using conventional moulding processes. Vacuums also create environment where sensitive textile substrates can be efficiently distilled to remove solvents without damaging or chemically altering the fibres.

The aptly named fireproof textile Flamebreak was initially developed by Société Ariégeoise de Bonneterie for use on the Ariane 5 rocket launched by the European Space Agency.[44] The woven fabric is the fibre equivalent of the thermophiles that flourish at high temperatures. Flamebreak was engineered to be flame resistant and heat shielding in order to protect the rocket's equipment from the engine's flames. Société Ariégeoise de Bonneterie used a special knitting technique to combine Kevlar and Preox fibres in order to create a textile capable of blocking out 90 per cent of infrared radiation in extreme temperatures. The fabric is constructed in layers that reduce the transmission of heat. Flamebreak's flame resistance is heightened when impregnated with an aerospace silicon, which gives it a laminate surface. Flamebreak has been used by workers operating in the cooling systems surrounding nuclear reactor cores at the Commissariat à l'Energie Atomiques in France. Workers wore the fabric to shield them against temperatures ranging from 2100 to 2500°C and protect them from dripping molten metal. Transparent screens made from Flamebreak provided the workers with additional protection, enabling them to remain near the reactor core long enough to carry out tests.

Alphaweld is a fabric made from silicon dioxide quartz fibres, which, like Flamebreak, have been developed to perform at high temperatures.[45] It is incombustible and has a fire-retardant Neoprene coating on one side, making the fabric resistant to sparks, slag and flame from cutting torches. The fibres are made from pure quartz crystals produced in different diameters depending on the intended use. Alphaweld in

High tech textiles can save lives by protecting humans from danger. Here, nonflammable Nomex was used for this firefighter outfit, which provides protection against burns.

engineered to withstand temperatures up to 1,070°C, and when heated beyond that, the fibres devitrify into a crystallized form that stiffens the fabric without losing its insulating properties or changing its physical form. Alphaweld is typically used to make welding curtains, flash barriers and heat shields, or made into protective aprons, gloves, spats and gauntlets that shield the wearer from extreme heat.

Nomex is a flame-resistant meta-aramid material developed by DuPont and sold commercially since 1967. It is an aromatic nylon and regarded to be the meta variant of Kevlar, also an aramid. Nomex fibres are available in sheet form or in bulk for manufacture of composite structures. Like many flameproof fibres it is used for protective garments, but Nomex is also used as a material for crafting aeroplane parts.

Lightweight, durable and flame resistant, Nomex is ideal for producing composite structures such as tail fins, engine nacelles, propeller parts and helicopter blades. Nomex-based parts have unrivalled strength-to-weight ratios, which enables the aircraft to save fuel and reduces carbon emissions, therefore playing a role in making air travel more ecologically sound.[46]

As well as performing in extreme heat, textiles can also be engineered to perform in extreme cold. The field of cryogenics studies the behaviour of materials at the lowest temperatures known to humans. Cryogenic processing is a method of strengthening metals and alloys and other materials such as carbon fibre, Kevlar, polymers and some plastics. The materials are placed in a processor where they are cooled with nitrogen gas to a temperature of −150°C. After the cooling cycle has been completed, the material is heat treated before being slowly returned to room temperature. The process tightens the material's molecular structure, creating a denser microstructure while increasing surface area. This increases the fibres' stress relief and stability, enabling the textile to last longer and perform better. Cryogenic processes have revealed which textiles would perform best in cold regions of deep space and which would be suitable for use in Arctic and Antarctic applications. Unlike the cryophile organisms that thrive only in frigid temperatures, cryogenic textiles perform as well in the heat as they do in the cold.

# Textiles as Biological Agents

Textiles were among the earliest implements of biological warfare. In medieval Europe, catapults were used to hurl bales of plague-infected fabric over the walls of besieged cities.[47] Eighteenth-century British officers at Fort Pitt, Pennsylvania, attempted to decimate the local native Indian population by giving them blankets infected with smallpox. During the 1785 siege of the Algerian city La Calle, the invading Tunisian forces flung clothing worn by diseased men and women over the city's fortifications.

Living organisms continue to be used in warfare today, forming the basis of biological weapons intended to debilitate or kill the victims they infect. Because textiles can host a wide range of deadly pathogens, toxins and disease cultures, they can be used in biological warfare. Sometimes called 'defence fabrics', they are impregnated with chemical and biological agents.[48] Pathogens such as viruses, bacteria and fungi are able to survive when embedded in fabric, from where they can contaminate their hosts and reproduce inside them. Toxins do not even need to reproduce within the victim to be fatal. They only need a short incubation period. They can kill their victims within hours, sometimes even within minutes.

Many modern surveillance regimes include systems that can detect the presence of radiation particles and biological agents. While sensors are used to detect airborne threats, textiles also play an important role in protecting against them. Contaminate-aware fabrics, such as those mentioned in Chapter 2, are often included in bio-defence applications to identify chemical and biological agents.

American technical textile manufacturer Warwick Mills develop and produce a wide range of material resistant to chemical and biological warfare agents.[49] Their textiles are engineered to be chemically and biologically active yet also durable, light-weight and flexible. Warwick Mills developed a so-called active chemistry system that incorporates decontamination agents into fabric laminate in order to prevent biological contaminants from penetrating the textile's surface. The textiles are used to produce structures Warwick Mills refer to as chemical warfare tents for military camps and battlefields. The fabric can be made into tents that attach to metal, composite or folding frames, or it can be made into inflatable membrane structures sustained by air pressure.

When such systems are being engineered for wearable textiles, combinations of semipermeable and nonpermeable fabrics are necessary to balance performance, comfort and protection. Materials with nonporous, ultraporous and microporous abilities work in tandem to permit air to circulate next to the wearer's skin while creating a protective shield against biological and chemical agents. This type of protective garment is typically made with tiers of nylon tricot and polyurethane foam impregnated with activated charcoal.[50] As a system of layers, the arrangement of fabrics permits perspiration to evaporate without allowing contaminates to penetrate the textile's laminated surface.

Our bodies, vehicles, industrial compounds and manufacturing sites benefit enormously from these highly engineered textiles. Their extremophile characteristics endow them with capabilities shared by few other materials, giving them the potential to radically reinvent many aspects of our world. Their performance may be high tech, but their extremophile abilities also exist among organic life forms. Their ability to mimic nature gives them as much resonance with the natural world as with the human world, perhaps indicating that they may not actually be as extreme as we think.

# Feature Interview: Loop.pH

The London-based design duo of British-born textile designer Rachel Wingfield and Austrian artist Mathias Gmachl are designing the fabrics of the future. Their practice is known as Loop.pH. They believe that textiles hold the potential to harness energy, and they are developing prototypes that can do just that. Loop.pH are pioneering a new way of thinking about textiles; as they bridge the gap between the built environments of humans and the leafy structures of nature, they create boldly interactive designs that grow, glow, respond and even biodegrade.

'Our starting point is often a growing form, usually a plant, but other types of biological structures are also interesting to us,' Wingfield explains.[51] 'Plants fascinate us because they establish stable networks and use energy efficiently.' Wingfield cites Cambridge scientist John Walker—a recent Nobel Laureate—as a source of

Loop.pH are using houseplants to bridge the gap between the built environments of humans and the leafy structures of nature. Living designs, such as this Biowall, grow quickly, improve air quality and eventually biodegrade.

inspiration. Walker describes living cells as 'molecular machines' because of the energy released by individual cells. 'The relationship between energy and structure that John Walker researches scientifically is something that we explore in both textiles and wider design practices,' Wingfield explains. 'If Mathias and I can recreate a molecular structure in a dynamic textile and scale it up to architectural proportions, we can create a sustainable environment.'

Loop.pH are pioneering a textile that would harness ambient energy and feed it into a power source. 'Imagine a textile lampshade that can store the energy released by the bulb, then funnel it back into the bulb's power source,' Wingfield said. 'It could continually recharge itself.' Loop.pH's experiments with harnessing natural and artificial light energy led them to electroluminescent printing, a process that integrates the superfine electronic phosphor-coated circuits developed by NASA into fabrics. 'Our "Light Sleeper" bedding is a programmable duvet and pillowcase that functions as an alarm clock,' Wingfield explains, 'that wakes the sleeper by slowly lighting up, just like dawn breaking in the darkness.' Although Light Sleeper is still in development, a prototype reveals how viable the design is. 'Conventional bedding manufacturers are

Loop.pH's Light Sleeper bedding is a programmable duvet and pillowcase that functions as an alarm clock. It wakes the sleeper as it slowly illuminates, mimicking the break of dawn.

concerned that there may be some health and safety problems with electronic textiles, so we want to make sure that they're as safe as ordinary bedding before we move forward.' Kinetic textiles or phase-change materials capable of converting movement of into energy could conceivably provide an organic power source for Loop.pH's design if they were developed for domestic use.

Light effects and textile technology merge beautifully in Loop.pH's History table-cloth, which illuminates in response to the pressure of objects placed on it. As china and glassware are moved around the table, the impressions they make in the fabric create a visual record of where they have been placed and how long they have sat there. Another illuminating textile, Digital Dawn, is a wall hanging that glows brighter as

Loop.pH's Digital Dawn design is a self-illuminating textile that glows brighter as ambient light levels fall.

ambient light levels fall. 'New photovoltaics are forging fresh directions for textiles,' Wingfield says. 'We're focusing on translating some of the electronics created for material science into new textile forms. When decorative textiles store light energy and automatically release it when light levels fade, they become as functional as they are beautiful.'

# Notes

## Chapter 1: Body Technology

1. Haptic technology refers to systems operated by touch. This emerging technology has wide-reaching applications in many different fields.

2. The Luddites were an early nineteenth-century social movement of British textile artisans who demonstrated, sometimes violently, against the changes brought about by the Industrial Revolution. Mechanized looms led to less work, and artisans often mobilized and destroyed them.

3. See http://www.amberstrand.com for more information.

4. Peratech are leading developers of quantum tunnelling composite technology. See http://www.peratech.com for further information.

5. From an e-mail to the author.

6. Optical fibres are made from glass or plastic and transmit light along their entire length. They are widely used in fibre-optic communication because their bandwidth permits data transmission over longer distances and at higher data rates than many other forms of communications do.

7. For more information visit http://web.media.mit.edu/~awhiton.

8. CASPIAN (n.d.), 'Where Does CASPIAN Stand on Legislation?', http://www.spychips.com/about_us.html, retrieved January 2009.

9. Essinger, James (2004), *Jacquard's Web*, Oxford: Oxford University Press.

10. For more information on emotional signifiers see Frijda, Nico (1987), *The Emotions: Studies in Emotion and Social Interaction,* Cambridge: Cambridge University Press and Frijda, Nico (2006), *The Laws of Emotion,* Mahwah, NJ: Lawrence Erlbaum Associates Inc.

11. Quote taken from a press release issued by Phillips Design 23 September 2006.

12. Quote taken from Tillotson's Web site, http://www.smartsecondskin.com.

13. DeLancey, Craig (2002/2004), *Passionate Engines: What Emotions Reveal about Mind and Artificial Intelligence,* Oxford: Oxford University Press.

14. From an interview with Angel Change conducted by the author.

15. The X-Static fibre is coated in a layer of 99.9% pure silver, which is permanently bonded to the surface. It was developed as an industrial and medical product, made for high tech health care applications and smart military garments. In addition to being conductive, X-Static is antimicrobial and antistatic. See http://www.x-staticfiber.com for further information.

# Chapter 2: Synthesized Skins

1. See Stoller, Robert (1985), *Observing the Erotic Imagination,* New Haven, CT: Yale University Press.

2. Mouldable polymeric gels, for example, were originally designed for medical applications, but they are soft and comfortable enough to have the same direct contact with the skin that fashion textiles do.

3. Chalayan made the Remote Control Dress from a hard material so that wearable technology could appear to have been seamlessly incorporated into the garment. The fibreglass also made it possible to construct the dress with components that would mimic machine parts.

4. Schoeller-Keprotec was initially developed as a rub- and tear-resistant material for motorcyclists clothing. Through the use of reinforced aramid fibres, the fabric has become moisture permeable and more flexible. See http://www.schoeller-textiles.com for further information.

5. Twaron fibres were developed in the early 1970s by the Dutch company AKZO, later called Akzo Industrial Fibers. Twaron's research name was originally Fiber X, and it was also previously known as Arenka.

6. More information about Kevlar and Aracon can be found at http://www2.dupont.com.

7. The Aracon family of fibres was originally developed by DuPont. Micro-Coax announced the acquisition of ARACON brand fibres on 13 October 2006.

8. Superline is a trade name for rope made from Vectran. It is said to be one of the strongest textile filaments in existence today, even stronger than steel.

9. Other layers of the spacesuit include aluminized Mylar and Beta cloth to provide for lightweight insulation, and Teflon-coated fibreglass to increase the outer shell's flame-resistant properties.

10. For further information see http://www.vectranfiber.com.

11. Mechatronics is a research area comprising mechanics, electronics, control engineering, computing and molecular engineering. Researchers in these areas are sharing knowledge in order to create systems that are simpler, more economical, reliable and versatile. Mechatronics is sometimes referred to as 'electromechanical systems' or 'control and automation engineering'.

12. See Grunwald, Martin, (ed.) (2008), *Human Haptic Perception: Basics and Applications,* Basel, Switzerland: Birkhäuser.

13. See http://www.theyshallwalk.org.

14. Reed's prototype was inspired by the mobile infantry power suits detailed in Robert A Heinlein's military science fiction novel, *Starship Troopers*.

15. Nitinol, an acronym for Nickel Titanium Naval Ordinance Laboratory, is a family of intermetallic materials that contain a mixture of nickel and titanium. Other materials can be added to enhance or adjust the material's properties. Nitinol's unique properties are termed superelasticity and shape memory. Because the fabric's weave has five nylon fibres to every Nitinol fibre, the clothing made from it will be high performance, washable and comfortable. The orthogonally woven version of Nitinol is known as Oricalco.

16. The biannual Transat 6.5 regatta was first launched in 1977. Only boats of 6.5 metres in length are allowed, with only one person onboard and without GPS navigation or energy sources other than that provided by two solar panels.

17. See http://www.gtwm.gatech.edu for test specifics.

18. Nanotextiles initially became known for their stain-resistant qualities. Whereas normal textiles can be stained, fabrics coated with nanomolecules can't. The molecules attach themselves to one another, and then attach to the fabric to form a nanoshield against stains. Because nanotextiles are found in everything from car seats to clothing, they are having a huge impact on consumers' lives.

19. 'About ISN: History' (n.d.), http://web.mit.edu/isn/aboutisn/index.html, retrieved January 2009.

20. Quoted from Lurie, Karen, (October 2003), 'Instant Armor', http://www.sciencentral.com/articles/view.php3?article_id=218392121, retrieved 22 February 2009.

21. Rayon was invented in 1924, one of the first fibres to be derived from a liquid solution that solidified into a filament as it comes into contact with the air. Other liquid-based textiles have emerged since then, the most revolutionary of these being spray-on bandages and aerosol textiles such as Fabrican.

22. TechnoGel is a popular polyurethane gel used for footwear and fashion applications.

23. Elastomeric gel is technically an oil-extended tri-block copolymer. Gelastic and DuraGel are trade names of two popular types of elastomeric gel.

24. Grado Zero Espace is a part of the Karada Italia Group, a classic clothing manufacturer with an interest in producing added-value products. For more information about Grado Zero Espace's projects, visit http://www.gzespace.com.

25. Aerogel consists of 99.8% air and 0.2% of silica dioxide, making it one of the lightest solids in the world by volume.

26. The suit developed by Grado Zero Espace for the McLaren Formula 1 team was made with a cooling system produced by Canadian space research specialists Med-Eng.

27. Traditional knitting machines produce two-dimensional objects such as knitwear, hosiery, and so forth. Three-dimensional knit machines can produce thicker textures and a range of shapes, knitting objects that have dense surfaces and solid substance. They can also create cavities and openings within the structure.

28. Based in Italy, MTS is a self-styled 'small-to-medium-enterprise' manufacturer who specialize in processing and finishing technical fabrics with polymeric materials. Polymeric materials have a wide range of applications for fashion textiles. Polymeric coatings and photon-based imaging techniques are the most common.

29. In humans, sweating is primarily a means of thermoregulation, which is the process mimicked by this fabric.

30. Coatings provide protective treatment for textiles and leather by distributing a thin layer of protective polymers on the surface. Treatments such as Liquid Shell and Clariant, for example, enhance the surfaces to make them more resistant to abrasion, UV-A and UV-B rays, acid and alkaline moisture and contact with heat.

31. Stereolithography is one of the most common rapid-prototyping technologies. It provides highly accurate models and good surface finishes, and it can mimic techniques such as crocheting and knitting. The process traces a laser beam across the surface of a vat of liquid photopolymer to build plastic parts one layer at a time. Once a layer is completed it is lowered back into the liquid photopolymer and a subsequent layer is adhered to the previous one. Many layers are needed to create a complete three-dimensional textile.

32. See Tillotson, Jenny (2008), 'Fashion Fluidics', in R. Adams, S. Gibson and S. Müller Arisona (eds.), 'Transdisciplinary Digital Art: Sound, Vision & the New Screen', *Digital Art Weeks and Interactive Futures 2006/2007*, Berlin: Springer.

33. Short-lived scratch-and-sniff fabrics have been available for some time, but the fabric technology Tillotson proposes allows aroma-therapeutic scents such as mint, lavender, grapefruit, black pepper and tarragon to retain their true fragrance for an extended period.

34. Ballard, J. G. (1997). *A User's Guide to the Millennium: Essays and Reviews,* New York: Picador.

35. Wyart, Claire, et al. (February 2007), 'Smelling a Single Component of Male Sweat Alters Levels of Cortisol in Women', *The Journal of Neuroscience,* 7.

36. Androstadienone is a derivative of testosterone.

37. Visit http://www.kanebo.co.jp for further information.

38. For further information visit http://www.scentlok.com.

39. From an interview with Anne Toomey conducted by the author.

40. These fabrics also have applications for animals. For example, they could be made into collars that would show if the animals had been in contact with any environmental pathogens.

41. Visit http://www.cs.ucl.ac.uk/research/vr/Projects/envesci for more information.

42. 'Environmental toxins' refers to gases such as toxic fumes, industrial pollutants, car exhaust emissions and so forth.

43. For more information, visit http://w1.siemens.com/innovation.

44. From an interview with Vexed Generation conducted by the author.

45. For more information, see http://www.kevlar.com.

# Chapter 3: Surfaces

1. Martin Jay introduced the concept of 'scopic regimes', alternative ways of seeing and representing the world in both art and science. Jay, Martin (1988), 'Scopic Regimes of Modernity', in Hal Foster, ed., *Vision and Visuality,* Seattle, WA: Bay Press.

2. See Gibson, James (1983), *The Senses Considered as Perceptual Systems,* Boston: Greenwood Press.

3. The concept of the perceptual surface was introduced to me by Mohsen Mostafavi, dean of the Harvard Graduate School of Design. Thanks to his encouragement, I began pursuing this line of research and extrapolating it to textiles.

4. Moritz Waldemeyer is a German designer and engineer based in London. He has designed the technological interfaces for many of the world's top architects and fashion designers. Waldemeyer is pioneering a unique a fusion of technology, art, fashion and design.

5. A hyperlink, in this context, refers to the dynamic organization of data through links and connections that access other systems. A hyperlink can, therefore, represent a range of complex and dynamic systems of linking and cross-referencing.

6. Bachelard, Gaston (1994), *The Poetics of Space,* Boston: The Beacon Press, p. 107.

7. In German fairy tales, magical caps called *tarnkappes* are worn by dwarfs. The caps can make an entire village of dwarfs invisible.

8. A metamaterial is a substance structured by its architecture rather than its composition. Metamaterials behave differently than composite materials and are typically capable of making several responses to a single stimuli.

9. Zhang's research projects are chronicled at http://xlab.me.berkeley.edu/.

10. The net was created by stacking silver and metal dielectric layers on top of each other and then punching holes through them. The researchers created the structure by positioning silver nanowires in porous aluminium oxide at tiny distances smaller than the wavelength of visible light. The structure refracts visible light.

11. See http://www.imperial.ac.uk/P7837.htm for further information.

12. An MRI scanner, also known as nuclear magnetic resonance imaging (NMRI), is primarily a medical imaging technique used in radiology to analyse the structure and function of the body.

13. See Kouznetsov, Dmitri (1992), *Near-IR Spectrophotometric Technique for Fast Identification of Carboxycellulose in Linen Fibers—A Preliminary Report,* Moscow: Sedov Biopolymer Research Laboratories. The English-language version of Kouznetsov's paper was published in the *Textile Research Journal,* 65/4(1995): 236–240.

14. Polyethersulphone (PES) is a sulphur-containing polymer that has a high degree of durability and heightened electrical insulation. Derivatives such as Ultrason have ductile properties that make them excellent materials for membranes, filters and films.

15. For detailed accounts of stealth aircraft, see Sweetman, Bill (1999), *Inside the Stealth Bomber,* Osceol, WI: Zenith Press.

16. Italian textile manufacturer Industria Bergamasca Rifrangenti produce a Flashlight range of transparent, embossed and printed retro-reflective fabrics. See http://www.ibr.it for further details.

17. Collins, Dan (2003), 'The Amazing "Invisible" Coat', CBSNews.com, http://www.cbs news.com/stories/2003/03/30/tech/main546865.shtml, retrieved February 2009.

18. Robert Langer is MIT's Germeshausen Professor of Chemical and Biomedical Engineering.

19. The research Langer and his colleagues Joerg Lahann and Thahn-Nga Tran carried out was published in conjunction with other authors such as Hiroki Kaido, Insung S. Choi, Samir Mitragotri and Jagannathan Sundaram of the University of California at Santa Barbara, and Saskia Hoffer and Gabor A. Somorjai of the University of California at Berkeley. For further

information see Thomson, Elizabeth A. (2003), 'MIT's Smart Surface Reverses Properties', *MIT News,* http://web.mit.edu/newsoffice/2003/smartsurface-0129.html.

20.  Langer's work can be viewed at http://techtv.mit.edu/videos/547-switchable-surfaces.

21.  The research team's collaborative counterparts at the University of California at Berkeley had established a sensitive surface analysis technique called sum-frequency generation (SFG) spectroscopy that was used to manipulate the surface.

22.  Perfect, in this context refers to the distance determined by the researcher's earlier calculations.

23.  Raffle, Hayes, Ishi, Hiroshi, and Tichenor, James (2004), 'Super Cilia Skin: A Textural Interface', *Textile,* 2/3: 5.

24.  It is interesting to note that woven textiles played an important role in computer history, through Joseph-Marie Jacquard's automated patterned textile weaving machine in 1804, which led to punch cards in computing devices.

25.  Barbagli, Federico, Prattichizzo, Domenico, and Salisbury, Kenneth (2005), *Multi-Point Interaction with Real and Virtual Objects,* Vienna: Springer.

26.  With algorithms, the transition from one state to another is not necessarily deterministic; some algorithms, such as probabilistic algorithms, are intended to be random. Grundler, Darko, and Rolich, Tomislav (2003), 'Evolutionary Algorithms-aided Textile Design', *International Journal of Clothing Science and Technology,* 15/(3/4): 295–304.

27.  Sahr, Kevin, White, Denis, and Kimerling, Jon (2003), 'Geodesic Discrete Global Grid Systems', *Cartography and Geographic Information Science,* 30/2: 121–34.

28.  Visit http://www.gehringtextiles.com for information on D3 fabrics.

29.  See http://www.3tex.com for more information on 3Weave.

30.  See http://www.dna11.com for more information.

31.  Visit Proske's Web site for more information on his voiceprint fabrics: http://www.digitalstar.net.

32.  Second Life and the virtual world platform Second Life Grid were founded by Linden Lab, a privately held American Internet company. Entropia Universe is a multiplayer online virtual world designed by Swedish software company MindArk.

33.  Second Life has an internal currency, the L$ Linden dollar, used for commercial transactions.

34.  Tessellation can be described as a tiling of the plane, in which the surface is a collection of plane figures that fills it without overlaps or gaps.

35.  Examples of virtual textiles made on Second Life can be found on sites such as http://fashionplanet.worldofsl.com/, http://www.fashionfeedofsl.com/ and http://slfashion.metavirtual.us/.

36.  Robles-De-La-Torre, Gabriel (2006), 'The Importance of the Sense of Touch in Virtual and Real Environments', *IEEE Multimedia,* 13/3: 24–30.

37.  Visit http://www.tfrg.org.uk for more information about Textile Futures Research Group.

38.  Motion capture is a technology developed to record movement and represent it in a digital environment. The technology is used in filmmaking to create animated three-dimensional digital characters. It is also used in video games, sport software and medical imaging applications such as gait analysis. Harris uses it to record the movement of the spectral body that animates the fabric.

39.  From an interview with Jane Harris conducted by the author.

40.  Jane Harris is a textile designer, researcher and consultant. She is currently Professor of Digital Design Imaging at Kingston University having previously served as director of the University of the Arts, London Textile Futures Research & Consultantcy Initiative and held the post of Reader in Digital Textile Design and Media at Central Saint Martin's College of Art & Design. Harris is a National Endowment for Science Technology and the Arts (NESTA) Fellow.

41.  Motion capture's applications for health care include gait analysis, as referenced in Chapter 4, but in this case it is used in physiotherapy and medical rehabilitation for balance training.

42.  The Balloon top was designed for the Collection 7 collection, autumn/winter 1999.

43.  See http://www.ahrc.ac.uk for more information.

# Chapter 4: Vital Signs

1.  That is, intending to eliminate pathogenic microorganisms that transfer infectious diseases and cause lung-related disorders.

2.  Japanese textile manufacturer Fujibo claims that the presence of antibacterial ions in fabric has the added benefit of soothing and relaxing the wearer.

3.  Biosafe was developed by Japanese textile manufacturer Kanebo.

4.  Microcapsules made from ceramics, polymers or gelatine films. AgUARDIAN was one of the world's first polyurethane fabrics embedded with antimicrobial silver ions. It was first introduced by Sommers Plastic Products Co Inc. See http://www.sommers.com for more details.

5.  MIT researchers Alexander Klibanov, Jianzhu Chen and Jayanta Haldar have developed coatings of N-alkylated poly(4-vinylpyridines) and polyethylenimines (PEIs) that are highly microbicidal. The coatings they developed have been shown to kill bacteria such as staphylococcus and E. coli and fungi such as candida albicans on contact.

6.  The coated fabrics manufacturer CMI Enterprises applied nanotechnology to develop Nanocide, a groundbreaking biocide for the coated fabrics industry.

7.  X-Static is manufactured by biomaterial specialist Noble Biomaterials (formerly Noble Fibers). See http://noblebiomaterials.com for further details.

8.  Voriconazole is a triazole antifungal medication used to treat serious, invasive fungal infections.

9.  Visit the NanoHorizons Inc Web site for further information: http://www.nanohorizons.com.

10.  Chitopoly is a synonym for chitosan. Chitin is found in many organisms other than crustaceans. It is also present in certain types of fungi, insects, molluscs and cephalopods.

11.  The research team included Drs Thilagavathi, Rajendrakumar and Rajendran. Neem is a tree in the mahogany family native to tropical and semitropical regions such as India, Pakistan, Myanmar and Bangladesh.

12.  Antifungal treatments have been applied to textiles for many years to counter the mould and fungi growths that cause staining, discolouration and degradation of textile substrates. The application of prytheroid nanocapsules to a fabric gives it insecticidal properties that withstand successive washings and solar exposure.

13. See the manufacturer's Web site for more information: http://www.vestergaard-frandsen.com.

14. Visit http://www.rakuto-kasei.com for more information.

15. Cited in a report written by Gibson, Phil, and Schreuder-Gibson, Heidi (2004), *Patterned Electrospray Fiber Structures,* Natick, MA: U.S. Army's Natick Soldier Center.

16. Dyneema is also made as a standard fibre for marine applications, ballistic protection and netting, as well as for gloves and apparel.

17. Dacron, like Diolen, Tergal, Terylene and Trevira, is a polyethylene terephthalate fibre.

18. For further information about the Textro- range of products, visit http://www.textronicsinc.com/yarns.

19. For more information, see http://www.sensatex.com.

20. For further information, see http://www.verhaert.com.

21. Telemedicine is commonly confused with telehealth and e-health. Telemedicine refers to a type of remote clinical treatment and diagnostic services, while terms such as telehealth and e-health can refer to nonclinical services such as medical administration, education and research.

22. See http://www.numetrex.com for more information about their heart-sensing sportswear.

23. The SensFloor developed by FutureShape can also monitor patients' movements and detect falls. See Chapter 7.

24. Visit http://www.research.vt.edu/resmag/2007summer/textiles.html for more information.

25. Because the skin is a powerful barrier, pharmaceuticals must be specially engineered to make them suitable for transdermal delivery.

26. Lidocaine is used topically to relieve itching and pain caused by skin inflammations.

27. See http://www.fujibo.co.jp for more information about Fujibo's products.

28. See http://www.smartfiber.de for more information. Lyocell is a cellulose fibre made from wood pulp cellulose. It is created by an organic solvent spinning process.

29. Prurigo is a dermatological condition.

30. For more information, see http://www.rochester.edu/news/show.php?id=732.

31. Researchers at the University of California, San Diego, are developing similar substrates for food packaging, which would show a warning colour if bacteria is detected.

32. For more information, see http://www.conwedplastics.com.

33. For more information, visit http://www.corpura.com.

34. Colour therapy is also known as chromotherapy.

35. See http://www.carnegiefabrics.com for further information.

36. Louise Russell was interviewed by Currey, Mason (2007), 'Fresh Air Textiles', *Metropolis* (June).

37. Mann is a graduate in textile design, currently working in partnership with architects, art consultants and interior designers to produce hand-dyed and woven textile artworks to for domestic, corporate and public spaces. She also offers an architectural colour consultancy service.

38. From an interview with Ptolemy Mann conducted by the author.

39. Asked to explain the phenomenon of after-image, British colour theorist Garth Lewis, author of *2000 Colour Combinations: For Graphic, Textile, and Craft Designers,* sent an email to Mann stating: 'Staring at a colour for a minute or so, and then transferring your gaze to a white

surface results in seeing the after-image of the original colour, which will be its complementary colour or opposing colour.' Lewis explained that 'the eye automatically fatigues when staring at a colour and generates the opposing colour. This is not always the complementary colour as it appears in the conventional pigment-based colour wheel.'

40. For more information on the hospital project, see http://www.shca.com.

41. For more information, see http://www.ptolemymann.com.

# Chapter 5: Sustainability

1. Information on waste management can be obtained from the International Solid Waste Association (ISWA); visit http://www.iswa.org.

2. The global textile industry is said to be one of the most unsustainable. Cotton alone consumes 24% of the world's total pesticides, despite using only 2.2% of the world's cultivated area. Wool production is said to contribute to land degradation, and processing wool requires the use of solvents, chemicals and detergents. Most synthetic fibres rely on petrochemical sources, contributing to the depletion of fossil fuels. Fabric and fibre dye processes use toxic chemicals associated with harmful emissions. The textile industry is said to produce the largest amount of wastewater of any industry, which it typically discharges into the environment.

3. The fibres are synthesized from corn sugars, which are transformed into lactic acid and then polymerized into polylactic acid. This produces an alternative to oil-based polymer textiles that are grown as corn. The fibres are industrially compostable.

4. For more information about Alcryn and Duracryn, see http://www.apainfo.com.

5. For further information on NatureWorks activities, see http://www.natureworksllc.com. For further information on Cargill Dow Polymers, see http://www.cargill.com.

6. For more examples, see Owings Dewey, Jennifer (1991), *Animal Architecture,* London: Orchard Books.

7. For more information about Velcro brand products, see http://www.velcro.com.

8. For more examples like this, see De Brie Taylor, Benjamin (1974), *Design Lessons from Nature,* New York: Watson-Guphill Publications.

9. Together with biologist Dayna Baumeister, Benyus cofounded Biomimicry Guild in 1998, a research, education and consulting company. For further information, see http://www.biomimicry.net.

10. See Benyus, Janine (2002), *Biomimicry: Innovation Inspired by Nature,* New York: Harper Perennial.

11. For more examples of colour phenomena in nature, see Farrant, Penelope (1999), *Color in Nature,* New York: Sterling Publishing.

12. Morphotex was jointly developed by Nissan, engineering-design firm Teijin and Kawashima Textile Manufacturers.

13. For further information, see http://www.teijinfiber.com.

14. Descente is a worldwide manufacturer and designer of high performance apparel for athletes. See http://www.descente.com for more information about their textiles.

15. Not to be confused with centrifugal force, centripetal force is the external pressure required to make an entity follow a curved path.

16. Santoprene, a thermoplastic elastomer created by combining EPDM (ethylene propylene diene monomer) rubber and polypropylene, is typically chosen as a middle material for such applications. Santoprene performs well in extreme heat and sub-zero environments and is often preferred to rubber.

17. Bacteriophages are viruses that infect bacteria. They typically consist of an outer protein hull enclosing genetic material.

18. See http://www.gzespace.com for more information.

19. See http://www.speedo80.com for more information.

20. Parker's research is conducted under the auspices of the University Research Fellowships. See http://www.royalsociety.org for more information.

21. For further information, visit http://www.nees.uni-bonn.de.

22. More information about Lotusan can be found at http://www.lotusan.de.

23. See http://www.rdg.ac.uk/Biomim/projects.htm for further information.

24. Dawson, Colin, Vincent, Julian, and Rocca, Anne-Marie, 'How Pine Cones Open', *Nature* (18 Dec. 1997).

25. Stomatex is typically made from thermo-insulating closed-cell foam materials such as Neoprene. See http://www.stomatex.com for more information.

26. Suzanne Lee is a senior research fellow in fashion at Central Saint Martins College of Art & Design London and a creative consultant for fashion brands. Lee, Suzanne (2005), *Fashioning the Future: Tomorrow's Wardrobe,* London: Thames & Hudson.

27. Kombucha is the name of a fermented drink made from a culture containing acetic acid bacteria and yeast.

28. Suzanne Lee, from an e-mail to the author. For more information on BioCouture, see http://www.biocouture.co.uk.

29. In addition to the University of Wyoming, researchers at the University of the Pacific, the University of California at Riverside and Shinshu University were also exploring the potentials of spider silk at this time.

30. Researchers at MIT claim the hard and soft areas of the polymers can be partially aligned, giving the spider silk three different phases rather than two: hard, soft and intermediate. The hard segments are believed to anchor the partially aligned regions, holding them in place within a matrix of softer fibres.

31. To date, researchers in the United States and Japan have decoded silk-producing sequences for around thirty species of spider.

32. For more information, see http://www.nexiabiotech.com.

33. McDonough, William, and Braungart, Michael (2002), *Cradle to Cradle: Remaking the Way We Make Things,* Portland, OR: North Point Press.

34. Eco-fleece is a recycled textile, manufactured from polyethylene terephthalate (PET) soft-drink bottles. On average, it takes 25 plastic bottles to produce a jumper, and for every 3,700 bottles recycled, one barrel of oil is saved and half a tonne of toxic emissions are eliminated.

35. Swap-shops are organized events where participants bring items of clothing to exchange. They range from informal groups organized by friends to large-scale, flea-market type events.

36. From an interview with Becky Early conducted by the author.

37. For more information, see http://www.beckyearley.com.

38. For more information, see http://www.kategoldsworthy.co.uk.

39. From an interview with Kate Goldsworthy conducted by the author.

40. Further information about Guerra de la Paz can be found at http://www.daneyalmah mood.com.

41. For more information, see http://alabamachanin.com.

42. From an interview with Natalie Chanin conducted by the author.

43. See Chanin, Natalie, and Stukin, Stacie (2008), *Alabama Stitch Book: Projects and Stories Celebrating Hand-Sewing, Quilting and Embroidery for Contemporary Sustainable Style,* New York: STC Crafts.

44. For more information, see http://www.marciaganem.com.br.

45. From an interview with Márcia Ganem conducted by the author.

46. For more information, see http://www.conserveindia.org.

47. From an interview with Anita Ahuja conducted by the author.

48. Carole Collet is based at Central Saint Martins College of Art & Design in London, where she is director of the MA Design for Textile Futures course and an associate director of the University of the Arts, London Textile Futures Research Unit. She is also a consultant in the area of textile print, research and development, sustainable design and intelligent textiles.

49. From an interview with Carole Collet conducted by the author.

50. At the budding stage of the sunflower's development it exhibits heliotropism. At sunrise, the face turns toward the east. Over the course of the day, it follows the sun from east to west, and then returns to an eastward orientation at night.

51. Richard Bonser is a lecturer at the Centre for Biomimetics at the University of Reading and is a visiting lecturer at the MA Design for Textile Futures course.

52. The Nobel Textiles project is sponsored jointly by the Medical Research Council and Clinical Sciences Centre with the support of the ICA and Central Saint Martins College of Art & Design. The exhibition was held at the ICA 14–21 September 2008. For information about the Nobel Textiles initiative, visit http://www.nobeltextiles.co.uk.

53. Sulston was a joint recipient of the Nobel Prize in Physiology or Medicine 2002. He shares the prize with Sydney Brenner and H. Robert Horvitz. See http://nobelprize.org for further information.

54. For more information, see Sulston, John, and Ferry, Georgina (2002), *The Common Thread: A Story of Science, Politics, Ethics and the Human Genome,* Washington, DC: Joseph Henry Press.

# Chapter 6: Contemporary Art

1. From an interview with Dave Cole conducted by the author.

2. Cave, Nick (n.d.), 'Artist's Statement', http://www.jackshainman.com/dynamic/exhibit_ artist, retrieved January 2009.

3. Ibid.

4. Basualdo, Carlos (2002), *Hélio Oiticica: Quasi-Cinemas,* Ostfildern-Ruit, Germany: Hatje Cantz Publishers, p. 140.

5. From an interview with Pia Myrvold conducted by the author.

6. From an interview with Kahori Maki conducted by the author.

7. Gschwandtner created the installation at the Museum of Arts and Design in New York in an exhibition titled 'Radical Lace and Subversive Knitting'.

8. From an interview with Janet Echelman conducted by the author.

9. Tenara is made by expanding polytetrafluoroethylene (PTFE), a chemical found in Teflon, into a yarn coated with an expandable fluoropolymer. PTFE is the most inert polymer known. It is difficult to manipulate but can be coaxed into rod shapes that form fibres. Tenara has high tensile strength, doesn't creep and has excellent flex resistance.

# Chapter 7: Interior Textiles

1. For examples of their projects, see Blaisse's Web site: http://www.insideoutside.nl.

2. For more information on Driessen + van Deijne, see http:// http://www.hildriessen.com and www.toonvandeijne.com.

3. From an interview with Hil Dreissen conducted by the author.

4. See Diedrich's Web site for further information: http://www.diedrich.se.

5. From an interview with Camilla Diedrich conducted by the author.

6. From an interview with Sophie Mallebranche conducted by the author.

7. See Mallebranche's Web site for further information: http://sophiemallebranche.free.fr.

8. See Wittrock's Web site for further information: http://www.grethewittrock.com.

9. From an interview with Grete Wittrock conducted by the author.

10. Rockfon substrates are produced with a 100% pure stone wool core. The material is usually covered with a fleece textile bound to the fabric by a water-based adhesive.

11. For the full range of Kyyrö Quinn's designs, see http://www.annekyyroquinn.com.

12. From an interview with Anne Kyyrö Quinn conducted by the author.

13. See Kyyrö Quinn, Anne (2008), *Felt Furnishings,* London: Jacqui Small.

14. For more information on Pot's designs, see http://www.bertjanpot.nl.

15. From an interview with Mathias Bengtsson conducted by the author.

16. Bengtsson Design (2008), 'Spun Chaise Lounge', http://www.bengtssondesign.com/spun_ chaiselounge.html, retrieved March 2009.

17. Campbell, Louise (2006), 'Prince Chair', http://www.louisecampbell.com/#, retrieved February 2009.

18. For more information, see http://www.tokujin.com.

19. Fibre's ability to absorb impact energy is detailed in the section 'Surface Energy' in Chapter 9.

20. The Venus chair was designed and constructed as part of the Second Nature exhibition held at 21_21 Design Sight in Tokyo. For more information, see http://www.2121designsight.jp.

21. From an interview with Hella Jongerius conducted by the author.

22. The Wabi seating collection was designed by Francesco Rota.

23. For more information on high performance rope, see the section 'Energy Absorption' in Chapter 9.

24. CITA is a centre for researching the emergent intersections between digital technology and architecture. See http://cita.karch.dk for further information.

25. From an interview with Mette Ramsgard Thomsen conducted by the author.

26. For further information, see http://www.future-shape.com/sensfloor.html.

27. See http://www.research.vt.edu for more information.

28. Intel Corporation is a leader in silicon innovation and develops processor technologies. See http://www.intel.com for more information.

29. Piezoelectric fibres are able to generate an electrical pulse in response to mechanical stress or when they sense pressure or weight.

30. For more information, see http://www.nunoerin.com.

31. From an interview with Erin Hayne conducted by the author.

32. From an interview with Gonçalves Ferreira conducted by the author.

33. For more information on Hietanen's work, see http://www.anhava.com.

34. From an interview with Helena Hietanen conducted by the author.

35. For more information on Krogh's work, see http://www.astridkrogh.com.

36. From an interview with Astrid Krogh conducted by the author.

37. For more information, see http://www.hsiaochikimiya.com.

38. From an interview with Hsiao-Chi Tsai conducted by the author.

# Chapter 8: Textiles for Architecture

1. For more information see http://www.freiotto.com.

2. Tedlar is commonly used as a backing sheet to provide protection against the elements. See http://www2.dupont.com/Tedlar_PVF_Film/en_US for more information. The external surface of the textile is coated to make it waterproof and enhance its resistance to UV radiation. Transparent films and coating materials include Teflon (PTFE, or polytetrafluoroethylene) and ETFE (ethylene tetrafluoroethlene).

3. Butacite is derived from a polyvinyl butyral. Butacite is produced as sheeting and wound on a roll. It is flexible but tough and formulated to absorb UV radiation from sunlight rather than deflect it.

4. For more information, see http://www.ianritchiearchitects.co.uk.

5. For more information, see http://www.solar-screen.com.

6. Yeang is a principal of T. R. Hamzah & Yeang in Kuala Lumpur.

7. Grebe, Oswald W. (1984), *Skidmore, Owings & Merrill: Architecture and Urbanism 1973–1983*, New York: Van Nostrand Reinhold Publishers.

8. Reportedly, metal mesh was first used architecturally in the 1950s, when the Otis Elevator Co installed woven-metal panels in elevator units. The material was later used by American architects in the 1980s, spreading to Europe a decade later.

9. Phosphor bronze is an alloy of copper that contains tin and a significant phosphorus content.

10. Woven metal is 100% percent recyclable; architectural stainless steel contains 30% recycled material.

11. A superficial metal screen, or skin, built fifty to sixty centimetres in front of the surface can cast permanent shade on a building, dramatically lowering its temperature.

12. For further information on Cambridge Architectural, see http://www.cambridge archi techtural.com.

13. See Spuybroek, Lars (2004), *NOX: Machining Architecture,* London: Thames & Hudson.

14. Spuybroek is a professor and Ventulett Distinguished Chair in Architectural Design at the Georgia Institute of Technology in Atlanta.

15. Mulder, Arjen, and Post, Maaike (2000), *Book for the Electronic Arts,* Rotterdam: De Balie.

16. For more information, see http://www.noxarch.com.

17. The textiles typically used for conveyor belts today are Dyneema, Spectra and other ultra-high molecular weight polyethylene (UHMW PE) materials.

18. For more information, see http://www.perraultarchitecte.com.

19. A worldwide shortage of carbon in 2004 sparked initiatives to recycle all types of carbon waste and fabric construction materials from it. As a result, many sources of recycled carbon material are available for use.

20. For more information, see http://www.peter-testa.com.

21. ETFE is ethylene tetrafluoroethylene, a fluorocarbon-based polymer plastic engineered to have high corrosion resistance and strength over a wide temperature range. The material is known for its use in the Eden Projects biomes.

22. The area of adhesion chemistry engineers the calculated control of adhesion variables to create adhesives capable of forming a permanent bond between two materials.

23. A radome is a weatherproof enclosure built to protect antennas from weather conditions. Radomes are typically constructed from fibreglass or PTFE-coated fabric because they allow the signal transmitted or received by the antenna to pass through with minimal interference.

24. For more information see http://www.inflate.co.uk and http://www.architects-of-air. com.

25. Applications for inflatable marine fabrics include evacuation slides, emergency boats, pontoons, floatation devices and buoyancy systems.

26. From an interview with Stuart Veech conducted by the author.

27. See http://www2.dupont.com for more information.

28. For more information, see http://www.veech-vma.com.

29. See Lomborg, Bjørn (2001), *The Skeptical Environmentalist: Measuring the Real State of the World,* Cambridge: Cambridge University Press.

30. For more information on carbon-fibre grids, visit Chomarat's Web site: http://www. carbongrid.com.

31. 'Formwork' is the term that describes the moulding of concrete in moulds and casts.

32. For more information, see http://www.umi-aa.com.

33. This approach was later aligned with humanitarian aid efforts following the Kobe earthquake in January of 1995. Unno developed several simple building methods so that the people of Kobe could construct temporary shelters even though building resources were scarce.

34. Unno's methods are known collectively as Unno Reinforced Concrete (URC) and are followed by fabric formwork specialists around the world.

35. From an interview with Mark West conducted by the author.

36. The extent to which architecture can be considered gendered has been a subject of enquiry for architectural theorists, gender theorists and feminist for several decades. For more information, see Rendell, Jane (1999), *Gender Space Architecture,* London: Routledge.

37. For further information, see http://girliconcrete.blogspot.com.

38. Belford and Morrow are currently researching methods to counteract the high alkaline content.

39. AstroTurf is a carpet-like synthetic textile developed as a playing surface for sports. While commonly seen as an interior textile, its application as outdoor groundcover reveals that it is also a geotextile.

40. For more information, see http://www.delstarinc.com.

41. For more information, see http://www2.dupont.com/Typar.

42. For more information about Comtrac, Fortrac and Ringtrac see http://www.huesker.com.

43. From an interview with Toshiko Mori conducted by the author.

44. Toshiko Mori, FAIA, is the principal of Toshiko Mori Architect, which she established in 1981. Mori taught at the Cooper Union School of Architecture from 1983 until accepting a tenured professorship at the Harvard Graduate School of Design in 1995. Mori has been a visiting faculty member at Columbia University and Yale University, where she was the Eero Saarinen Visiting Professor in 1992. Mori edited *Immaterial/Ultramaterial* (2002), a book about material and fabrication research, and initiated *Toshiko Mori Architect,* a monograph on her practice. See McQuaid, Matilda (2007), *Toshiko Mori Architect: Works and Projects,* New York: Monacelli Press. Mori designed the exhibition architecture for the 'Surface and Structure' exhibition held at the Museum of Modern Art in New York in 1998. She also designed the exhibition architecture for the 'Extreme Textiles' (2005) and 'Fashioning Felt' (2009) exhibitions held at the Cooper-Hewitt Museum, also in New York.

# Chapter 9: Extreme Interfaces

1. See Hart, Clive (1999), *Kites: A Historical Survey,* Westport, CT: Praeger Publishers.

2. A flywheel is a device powered by inertia that creates rotational energy and stores it. Graphite is an allotrope of carbon. Is it reputed to be the most stable form of carbon and has the ability to conduct electricity.

3. For more information on sustainable solar energy, see the Prometheus Institute's Web site, http://www.prometheus.org.

4. Amorphous silicon is the noncrystalline allotropic form of silicon. The liquid crystal polymers used in liquid crystal displays are structurally similar to aramid fibres such as Vectran, which are spun from a liquid crystal polymer. When Vectran is combined with metals such as copper, its intrinsic conductive abilities are heightened considerably.

5. PV technologies have wide applications, and PV substrates occur in many forms, ranging from bulk silicon components to wafer-thin textile membranes.

6. Organizations such as the European Photovoltaic Industry Association (EPIA) promote PV power to government officials at regional, national and international levels to develop cost-

effective solutions that make it possible for a broader range of consumers to benefit from it. See http://www.epia.org for further information.

7. The PV film is manufactured in a process similar to that used by photographic film manufacturers. See http://www.konarka.com for further information.

8. Their heat-transferring properties is known as the 'lattice effect'.

9. As described in Alhazen's *Book of Optics,* written in 1021. See El-Bizri, Nader (2005), 'A Philosophical Perspective on Alhazen's Optics', *Arabic Sciences and Philosophy,* 15/2: 189–218.

10. Reportedly, the word 'energeia' ἐνέργεια first appeared in written form for the first time in Aristotles's *Nicomachean Ethics,* written in the fourth century BC. Alhazen may have been referencing Aristotle's explanation of the concept of energy.

11. For more examples of the applications of thermochromatic liquid crystal technology see http://www.sommers.com.

12. For more information about ceramic fibres made for energy harvesting, see http://www.advancedcerametrics.com.

13. The earliest known ships are believed to be papyrus boats built by the Egyptians around 4,000 BC.

14. For more information, see http://www.bluewaterweave.com.

15. Not only do materials such as carbon fibre and Kevlar feature in sailcloth, they are used throughout the hull of boats themselves. Lightweight boats designed for competitions are made from fabric impregnated with resin, or from carbon fibres and Kevlar interwoven with a range of other materials, such as wool or cotton. Unidirectional weaves are used to provide the highest strength, so that the textile can be layered and bonded into a plywood-like material. Yacht interiors can be constructed solely from advanced fibres, including built-in tables, beds, benches, storage compartments and basins.

16. Examples of hang-glider sailcloth that show applications of materials such as Dacron, Mylar, Spectra and polyester can be seen at http://www.willswing.com.

17. See Whittall, Noel (2002), *Paragliding: The Complete Guide,* Marlborough, Wilts: Airlife Publishers; and Pagen, Dennis (2001), *The Art of Paragliding,* Black Mountain, NC: Black Mountain Books.

18. An aerofoil is the shape of a wing, propeller blade or a sail as seen in cross-section.

19. Atair Aerospace (2010), 'Atair EXO-X2™ Twin Micro-Turbine-Powered Composite Wing Suit', http://www.atair.com/wingsuits, retrieved 11 March 2009.

20. Solar sails are also known as light sails or photon sails. They are able to use light sources other than the Sun.

21. These satellites occupy an area of space known as low Earth orbit, a region technically considered to be outer space, but close enough to the Karman Line to experience significant atmospheric drag. Most satellites in low Earth orbit fire their engines every few days to maintain position. The drag in low Earth orbit could be overcome by radiation energy absorbed by solar sails.

22. Vectran was chosen for its strength and puncture-resistant properties, but also because can withstand high temperatures.

23. For more information, see http://mpfwww.jpl.nasa.gov.

24. The Tumbleweed Rover is being developed at NASA's Jet Propulsion Laboratory (JPL) in Pasadena, CA. See http://mpfwww.jpl.nasa.gov for further information

25. According to physics, heat is only partly kinetic energy. It is also a form of potential energy.

26. Body heat is a form of kinetic energy. The body's internal organs and cardiovascular system are constantly in motion, generating a kinetic energy within themselves.

27. For more information, see http://www.outlast.com.

28. From an interview with Angel Chang conducted by the author.

29. For more information on mooring lines and marine cables, see http://www.cortlandcable.com.

30. Kevlar 49 was developed for aircraft composites, kayaks, canoes and small boats.

31. Zylon's technical name is polyphenylene bisoxazole. Zylon was developed commercially by Toyobo Co Ltd in Japan.

32. The tests were conducted at the NASA Glenn Research Center by J. Michael Pereira, Duane M. Revilock, and Dale A. Hopkins.

33. The noun 'extremophile' is formed from Latin 'extremus' and Greek 'philia'.

34. See http://xxzc.en.ecplaza.net for more information on antiradiation fabrics Xinxiang Zhuocheng Special Textile Company.

35. Other textiles were used to help contain the reactor's radioactivity. Jute bags containing 5,000 metric tonnes of sand, lead and boric acid were lowered by helicopter during the weeks following the accident.

36. Cryophiles are also known as psychrophiles.

37. More information on Nextel can be found at http://www.3M.com.

38. Although ceramic textiles are indisputably high tech, they are based on ancient sintering techniques. Fine-grained clay soil was combined with water to form a long filament, which was wound into a rounded shape to create a vessel. Similarly, ceramic fibres are made from dry binders, antiflocculants and ceramic powders, which are combined with water. The clay is then heated to fuse the ceramic particles into fibres. This exchange between ceramics and textiles could portend other congruencies between the two disciplines.

39. Nextel 312 Ceramic Fiber fabric performs well as a lightweight fire barrier that meets the Federal Aviation Administration's flame penetration standards.

40. Nextel Woven Ceramic Fabrics are engineered to perform at continuous temperatures of 1,093°C or higher.

41. More information can be found on the JAXA Web site: http://www.jaxa.jp.

42. Gowayed's research group includes George Flowers, an associate professor in the Department of Mechanical Engineering, and Faissal Hady, a visiting professor in the Department of Textile Engineering.

43. Several types of weaves and braid forms are used to construct composite fabrics. Weave varieties include plain weave, twill weave, satin weave and eight harness weave. Braids are typically sleeving or flat braids, with either bi-axial or tri-axial architectures.

44. Aérospatiale and the Société Européenne de Propulsion commissioned Flamebreak from Société Ariégeoise de Bonneterie in 1990.

45. For more information about Alphaweld, see http://www.alphainc.com.

46. For more information about Nomex, see http://www2.dupont.com/Nomex/.

47. That is, contaminated clothing, bedding and burial shrouds.

48. Many textiles developed for military applications can be referred to as 'defence fabric'. In most cases, the term refers to chemically resistant material.

49. For more information, see http://www.warwickmills.com.

50. See Adanur, Sabit (1995), *Wellington Sears Handbook of Industrial Textiles*, Boca Raton, FL: CRC Press.

51. From an interview with Loop.pH conducted by the author.

# Bibliography

'About ISN: History' (n.d.), http://web.mit.edu/isn/aboutisn/index.html, retrieved January 2009.

Adanur, Sabit (1995), *Wellington Sears Handbook of Industrial Textiles,* Boca Raton, FL: CRC Press.

Atair Aerospace (2010), 'Atair EXO-X2™ Twin Micro-Turbine-Powered Composite Wing Suit', http://www.atair.com/wingsuits, retrieved 11 March 2009.

Bachelard, Gaston (1994), *The Poetics of Space,* Boston: The Beacon Press.

Barbagli, Federico, Prattichizzo, Domenico, and Salisbury, Kenneth (2005), *Multi-point Interaction with Real and Virtual Objects,* Vienna: Springer.

Basualdo, Carlos (2002), *Hélio Oiticica: Quasi-Cinemas,* Ostfildern-Ruit, Germany: Hatje Cantz Publishers.

Bengtsson Design (2008), 'Spun Chaise Lounge', http://www.bengtssondesign.com/spun_chaiselounge.html, retrieved March 2009.

Benyus, Janine (2002), *Biomimicry: Innovation Inspired by Nature,* New York: Harper Perennial.

Blaisse, Petra (2007), *Inside Outside,* Rotterdam, The Netherlands: NAi Publishers.

Campbell, Louise (2006), 'Prince Chair', http://www.louisecampbell.com/#, retrieved February 2009.

CASPIAN (n.d.), 'Where Does CASPIAN Stand on Legislation?', http://www.spychips.com/about_us.html, retrieved January 2009.

Cave, Nick (n.d.), 'Artist's Statement', http://www.jackshainman.com/dynamic/exhibit_artist, retrieved January 2009.

Chanin, Natalie, and Stukin, Stacie (2008), *Alabama Stitch Book: Projects and Stories Celebrating Hand-Sewing, Quilting and Embroidery for Contemporary Sustainable Style,* New York: STC Crafts.

Colchester, Chloë (2007), *Textiles Today,* London: Thames & Hudson.

Collins, Dan (2003), 'The Amazing "Invisible" Coat', CBSNews.com, http://www.cbs news.com/stories/2003/03/30/tech/main546865.shtml, retrieved February 2009.

Currey, Mason (2007), 'Fresh Air Textiles', *Metropolis* (June).

Dawson, Colin, Vincent, Julian, and Rocca, Anne-Marie, 'How Pine Cones Open', *Nature* (18 Dec. 1997).

De Brie Taylor, Benjamin (1974), *Design Lessons from Nature,* New York: Watson-Guphill Publications.

DeLancey, Craig (2004), *Passionate Engines: What Emotions Reveal about Mind and Artificial Intelligence,* Oxford: Oxford University Press.

El-Bizri, Nader (2005), 'A Philosophical Perspective on Alhazen's Optics', *Arabic Sciences and Philosophy,* 15/2: 189–218.

Essinger, James (2004), *Jacquard's Web,* Oxford: Oxford University Press.

Farrant, Penelope (1999), *Color in Nature,* New York: Sterling Publishing.

Frijda, Nico (1987), *The Emotions: Studies in Emotion and Social Interaction,* Cambridge: Cambridge University Press

Frijda, Nico (2006), *The Laws of Emotion,* Mahwah, NJ: Lawrence Erlbaum Associates Inc.

Gibson, James (1983), *The Senses Considered as Perceptual Systems,* Boston: Greenwood Press.

Gibson, Phil, and Schreuder-Gibson, Heidi (2004), *Patterned Electrospray Fiber Structures,* Natick, MA: U.S. Army's Natick Soldier Center.

Grebe, Oswald (1984), *Skidmore, Owings & Merrill: Architecture and Urbanism 1973– 1983,* New York: Van Nostrand Reinhold Publishers.

Grundler, Darko, and Rolich, Tomislav (2003), 'Evolutionary Algorithms-aided Textile Design', in *International Journal of Clothing Science and Technology,* 15/3–4: 295–304.

Grunwald, Martin, ed. (2008), *Human Haptic Perception: Basics and Applications,* Basel, Switzerland: Birkhäuser.

Hart, Clive (1999), *Kites: A Historical Survey,* Westport, CT: Praeger Publishers.

Jay, Martin (1988), 'Scopic Regimes of Modernity', in Hal Foster, ed., *Vision and Visuality,* Seattle, WA: Bay Press.

Kouznetsov, Dmitri (1992), *Near-IR Spectrophotometric Technique for Fast Identification of Carboxycellulose in Linen Fibers—A Preliminary Report,* Moscow: Sedov Biopolymer Research Laboratories

Kyyrö Quinn, Anne (2008), *Felt Furnishings,* London: Jacqui Small.

Lee, Suzanne (2005), *Fashioning the Future: Tomorrow's Wardrobe,* London: Thames & Hudson.

Lomborg, Bjørn (2001) *The Skeptical Environmentalist: Measuring the Real State of the World,* Cambridge: Cambridge University Press.

Lurie, Karen (October 2003), 'Instant Armor', http://www.sciencentral.com/articles/ view.php3?article_id=218392121, retrieved 22 February 2009.

McDonough, William, and Braungart, Michael (2002), *Cradle to Cradle: Remaking the Way We Make Things,* Portland, OR: North Point Press.

McQuaid, Matilda, ed. (2005), *Extreme Textiles, Designing for High Performance,* New York: Princeton Architectural Press.

McQuaid, Matilda (2007), *Toshiko Mori Architect: Works and Projects,* New York: Monacelli Press.

Mori, Toshiko (ed) (2002) *Immaterial/Ultramaterial,* New York: George Braziller Inc.

Mulder, Arjen, and Post, Maaike (2000), *Book for the Electronic Art,* Rotterdam: De Balie.

O'Mahony, Marie, and Braddock, Sarah (2002), *Sports Tech,* London: Thames & Hudson.

O'Mahony, Marie, and Braddock, Sarah (2005), *Techno Textiles 2,* London: Thames & Hudson.

Owings Dewey, Jennifer (1991), *Animal Architecture,* London: Orchard Books.

Pagen, Dennis (2001), *The Art of Paragliding,* Black Mountain, NC: Black Mountain Books.

Quinn, Bradley (2002), *Techno Fashion,* Oxford: Berg Publishers.

Quinn, Bradley (2003), *The Fashion of Architecture,* Oxford: Berg Publishers.

Quinn, Bradley, ed. (2007), *UltraMaterials,* London: Thames & Hudson.

Quinn, Bradley (2008), 'Textiles at the Cutting Edge', in N. Monem, ed., *Contemporary Textiles,* London: Black Dog Publishing.

Raffle, Hayes, Ishi, Hiroshi, and Tichenor, James (2004), 'Super Cilia Skin: A Textural Interface', *Textile,* 2/3: 5.

Reiff Anawalt, Patricia (2007), *The Worldwide History of Dress,* London: Thames & Hudson.

Rendell, Jane (1999), *Gender Space Architecture,* London: Routledge.

Robles-De-La-Torre, Gabriel (2006), 'The Importance of the Sense of Touch in Virtual and Real Environments', *IEEE Multimedia,* 13/3: 24–30.

Sahr, Kevin, White, Denis, and Kimerling, Jon (2003), 'Geodesic Discrete Global Grid Systems', *Cartography and Geographic Information Science,* 30/2: 121–34.

Slade, L., Wilson, P., et al. (2003), 'Mechanical Testing of Electrotexile Cables and Connectors', in *Electronics on Unconventional Substrates—Electrotextiles and Giant-Area Flexible Circuits,* Warrendale, PA: Materials Research Society.

Spuybroek, Lars (2004), *NOX: Machining Architecture,* London: Thames & Hudson.

Stoller, Robert (1985), *Observing the Erotic Imagination,* New Haven, CT: Yale University Press.

Sulston, John, and Ferry, Georgina (2002), *The Common Thread: A Story of Science, Politics, Ethics and the Human Genome,* Washington, DC: Joseph Henry Press.

Sweetman, Bill (1999), *Inside the Stealth Bomber,* Osceol, WI: Zenith Press.

Thomson, Elizabeth A. (2003), 'MIT's Smart Surface Reverses Properties', *MIT News,* http://web.mit.edu/newsoffice/2003/smartsurface-0129.html.

Tillotson, Jenny (2008), 'Fashion Fluidics', in R. Adams, S. Gibson and S. Müller Arisona, eds., 'Transdisciplinary Digital Art: Sound, Vision & the New Screen', *Digital Art Weeks and Interactive Futures 2006/2007,* Berlin: Springer.

Van Langenhove, L., ed. (2007), *Smart Textiles for Medicine and Healthcare,* Cambridge: Woodhead Publishing Limited and CRC Press LLC.

Vollers, Karel (2001), *Twist & Build Creating Non-orthogonal Architecture,* Rotterdam, The Netherlands: 010 Publishers.

Whittall, Noel (2002), *Paragliding: The Complete Guide,* Marlborough, Wiltshire, UK: Airlife Publishers.

Wyart, Claire, et al. (2007), 'Smelling a Single Component of Male Sweat Alters Levels of Cortisol in Women', *The Journal of Neuroscience* (7 February 2007).

# List of Credits

## General Introduction

## Chapter 1

Page 27    Printed with permission from Philips Design. © Philips Design.

Page 31    Printed with permission from Angel Chang. © Dan Lecca; © Lee Clower.

Page 32    Printed with permission from Angel Chang. © Dan Lecca; © Lee Clower.

# Chapter 2

Page 36    Printed with permission from Fabrican. © Fabrican.

Page 42    Printed courtesy of DuPont. © DuPont.

Page 43    Printed courtesy of DuPont. © DuPont.

Page 44    Printed courtesy of DuPont. © DuPont.

Page 45    Printed courtesy of DuPont. © DuPont.

Page 49    Printed with permission from Freedom of Creation. © Freedom of Creation.

Page 50    Printed with permission from Freedom of Creation. © Freedom of Creation.

Page 51    Printed with permission from Freedom of Creation. © Freedom of Creation.

Page 53    Printed with permission from Jenny Tillotson. © Jenny Tillotson.

Page 58    Printed with permission from Vexed Generation. © Jonny Thompson; © Hannes.

Page 58    Printed with permission from Vexed Generation. © Jonny Thompson; © Hannes.

Page 58    Printed with permission from Vexed Generation. © Jonny Thompson; © Hannes.

# Chapter 3

Page 62    Printed with permission from Moritz Waldemeyer. © Moritz Waldemeyer.

Page 64    Printed with permission from Moritz Waldemeyer. © Moritz Waldemeyer.

Page 65    Printed with permission from Moritz Waldemeyer. © Moritz Waldemeyer.

Page 66    Printed with permission from Moritz Waldemeyer. © Moritz Waldemeyer.

Page 76   Photography: Kate Goldsworthy. Multisheer 3D sculpture created by Kate Goldsworthy and animated by Andrew Sides and exhibited at 'Textile Futures Island' in Second Life (2008) curated by Caryn Simonson & Jane Harris, Textile Futures Research & Consultancy (University of the Arts, London).

Page 77   Photography: Kate Goldsworthy. Multisheer 3D sculpture created by Kate Goldsworthy and animated by Andrew Sides and exhibited at 'Textile Futures Island' in Second Life (2008) curated by Caryn Simonson & Jane Harris, Textile Futures Research & Consultancy (University of the Arts, London).

Page 78   Photography: Kate Goldsworthy. Multisheer 3D sculpture created by Kate Goldsworthy and animated by Andrew Sides and exhibited at 'Textile Futures Island' in Second Life (2008) curated by Caryn Simonson & Jane Harris, Textile Futures Research & Consultancy (University of the Arts, London).

Page 81   'Bubble Top', by Jane Harris (2003). Fashion Design by Shelley Fox. 3D CG by Mike Dawson. Supported by Arts and Humanities Research Council.

Page 82   Empress's New Clothes by Jane Harris (2003). 3D CG by Mike Dawson. Performer/Choreography by Ruth Gibson. Supported by Arts and Humanities Research Council.

Page 82   Wireframe (2006). 3D CG by Mike Dawson. Performer/Choreography by Elli Garnett.

# Chapter 4

Page 86    Photographer Margaret Pate. © CSIRO.

Page 88    Printed courtesy of DuPont. © DuPont.

Page 89    Printed courtesy of DuPont. © DuPont.

Page 90    Printed courtesy of DuPont. © DuPont.

Page 92    © Össur for Textile Futures.

Page 93    © Össur for Textile Futures.

Page 94    © Össur for Textile Futures.

Page 95    Printed with permission from www.maximounds.com. © Maxi Mounds.

Page 96    Printed with permission from www.maximounds.com. © Maxi Mounds.

Page 105  'Interlocking Violet Lime' (2008). Hand-dyed and -woven mercerized cotton stretched over wood, various depths (50 ×50 cm). Photography by Ptolemy Mann. © Ptolemy Mann.

Page 106 'Parrot Check' detail (2008). Hand-dyed and -woven mercerized cotton stretched over wood (40 ×50 cm). Photography by Ptolemy Mann. © Ptolemy Mann.

Page 107 'King's Mill Hospital Façade' (2006). Colour specification: Ptolemy Mann. Project architects: Swanke Hayden Connell. Rendering by GMJ.

# Chapter 5

Page 110 Printed with permission from Becky Earley. © Becky Earley.

Page 116 Printed with permission from Suzanne Lee/Biocouture. © Gary Wallis, photographer.

Page 117 Printed with permission from Suzanne Lee/Biocouture. © Gary Wallis, photographer.

Page 121 Printed with permission from Becky Earley. © Becky Earley.

Page 122 Printed with permission from Becky Earley. © Becky Earley.

Page 123 Printed with permission from Becky Earley. © Becky Earley.

Page 124 Printed with permission from Becky Earley. © Becky Earley.

Page 125 Printed with permission from Becky Earley. © Becky Earley.

Page 127 Courtesy Kate Goldsworthy. Photo credit Full Focus.

Page 128 Courtesy Kate Goldsworthy. Photo credit Full Focus.

Page 129 Printed with permission from Guerra de la Paz. © Guerra de la Paz.

Page 130 Printed with permission from Guerra de la Paz. © Guerra de la Paz.

Page 132 Printed with permission Alabama Chanin. © Alabama Chanin.

Page 133 Printed with permission from Alabama Chanin. © Alabama Chanin.

Page 134 Printed with permission from Alabama Chanin. © Alabama Chanin.

Page 136 Printed with permission from Márcia Ganem. © Ricardo Fernandes.

Page 137 Printed with permission from Márcia Ganem. © Ricardo Fernandes.

Page 139 Printed with permission Anita Ahuja/Conserve India. © Anita Ahuja.

Page 140 Printed with permission Anita Ahuja/Conserve India. © Anita Ahuja.

Page 141 Title: Suicidal Pouf Series. Printed with permission Carole Collet. © Simon Denton.

Page 142 Title: Suicidal Pouf Series. Printed with permission Carole Collet. © Carole Collet.

Page 143 Title: Suicidal Pouf Series. Printed with permission Carole Collet. © Carole Collet.

# Chapter 6

Page 146 Printed with permission Galerie Grässlin. Photo © Wolfgang Günzel, Offenbach.

Page 147 Photo Credit: Jason Mandella. Image Courtesy of Greene Naftali Gallery, New York.

Page 148 Photo Credit: Jason Mandella. Image Courtesy of Greene Naftali Gallery, New York.

Page 149 Printed with permission from www.theknittingmachine.com and Judi Rotenberg Gallery. © www.theknittingmachine.com and Judi Rotenberg Gallery.

Page 150 Printed with permission from www.theknittingmachine.com and Judi Rotenberg Gallery. © www.theknittingmachine.com and Judi Rotenberg Gallery.

Page 151 Printed with permission from GV Art. © Bayard.

Page 152 Printed with permission from Piper Shepard 2005. © Dan Meyer, photographer.

Page 155 Printed with permission from Pia Myrvold. © JW Berge, photographer.

Page 157 Printed with permission from Kahori Maki. © Kahori Maki.

Page 158 Printed with permission from Kahori Maki. © Kahori Maki.

Page 160 Printed with permission from Benji Whalen. © Benji Whalen.

Page 161 Printed with permission from Benji Whalen. © Benji Whalen.

Page 163 Printed with permission Annet Couwenberg. © Dan Meyers, photographer.

Page 164 Photo courtesy Anila Rubiku and Gallery Alessandro Bagnai, Florence, Italy. © Anila Rubiku.

Page 165 Printed with permission from Dean Projects. © Dean Projects.

Page 165 Printed with permission from Dean Projects. © Dean Projects.

Page 166 Courtesy www.echelman.com. © Joao Ferrand.

Page 167  Courtesy www.echelman.com. © Joao Ferrand.

Page 168  Printed courtesy www.echelman.com. © Peter Vanderwalker.

# Chapter 7

Page 172  Printed with permission Anne Kyyrö Quinn. © Anne Kyyrö Quinn.

Page 174  Printed with permission from Constantin Meyer. © Constantin Meyer, Cologne.

Page 175  Project: Drift 23, University of Utrecht. Printed with permission from Driessen + Van Deijne. © René de Wit. Courtesy Marx & Steketee Architects, Eindhoven.

Page 176  Printed with permission from Driessen + Van Deijne. © Jannes Linders, photographer. Courtesy Kunst en Bedrijf, Amsterdam.

Page 178  Printed with permission Camilla Diedrich. © Camilla Diedrich.

Page 180  Printed with permission from Sophie Mallebranche. © Sophie Mallebranche.

Page 182  Printed with permission from Grethe Wittrock. © Sven Berggreen, photographer.

Page 183  Printed with permission Anne Kyyrö Quinn. © Anne Kyyrö Quinn.

Page 185  Printed with permission from Marcel Wanders Studio. © Marcel Wanders Studio.

Page 186  Printed with permission from Marcel Wanders Studio. © Marcel Wanders Studio.

Page 187  Printed with permission from Marcel Wanders Studio. © Marcel Wanders Studio.

Page 189  Printed with permission from Bertjan Pot. © Bertjan Pot.

Page 190  Printed with permission from Bengtsson Design. © Bengtsson Design.

Page 191  Printed with permission from Louise Campbell. © Erik Brahl.

Page 192  Printed with permission from Tokujin Yoshioka Design. © Tokujin Yoshioka Design.

Page 193  Printed with permission from Tokujin Yoshioka Design. © Tokujin Yoshioka Design.

Page 194  Chair created for the 'Second Nature' exhibition held at 21_21 Design Sight in Japan. Printed with permission from Tokujin Yoshioka Design. Courtesy Tokujin Yoshioka Design.

Page 196 Printed with permission from Offecct. © Offecct.

Page 198 Printed with permission from Paola Lenti Srl. © Paola Lenti Srl.

Page 199 Printed with permission from Paola Lenti Srl. © Paola Lenti Srl.

Page 200 Title: Toile de Hackney. Printed with permission Carole Collet. © Carole Collet.

Page 201 Title: Toile de Hackney. Printed with permission Carole Collet. © Carole Collet.

Page 202 Title: Toile de Hackney. Printed with permission Carole Collet. © Carole Collet.

Page 203 Printed with permission from Mette Ramsgard Thomsen. © Mette Ramsgard Thomsen.

Page 204 Printed with permission from Mette Ramsgard Thomsen. © Mette Ramsgard Thomsen.

Page 205 Printed with permission from Future Shape. © Future Shape.

Page 206 Printed with permission from Future Shape. © Future Shape.

Page 208 Printed with permission from Sommers Plastic Products Co Inc. © Fred Schecter.

Page 209 Printed with permission from NunoErin. © NunoErin.

Page 212 Printed with permission from Astrid Krogh. © Ole Hein Pedersen

Page 214 Printed with permission from Hsiao-Chi Tsai. © Hsiao-Chi Tsai.

Page 214 Printed with permission from Hsiao-Chi Tsai. © Photography by Hee Seung Chung, Ryosuke Kawana and Kimiya Yoskikawa.

Page 215 Printed with permission from Hsiao-Chi Tsai. © Ryosuke Kawana, photographer. Make-up by Lisa Prentis.

# Chapter 8

Page 218 Printed with permission from Testa & Weiser. © 2004 Testa & Weiser, Los Angeles.

Page 220 Designed by Rice, Francis & Ritchie (RFR). Printed with permission from Ian Ritchie Architects. © Jocelyne van den Bossche, photographer.

Page 223 Printed with permission GKD/ag4. © GKD/ag4

Page 225 Printed with permission from Nox Architecture. © Nox Architecture.

Page 226  Printed with permission from Ian Ritchie Architects. © Jocelyne van den Bossche, photographer.

Page 228  Printed with permission from Bengtsson Design. © Bengtsson Design.

Page 230  Printed with permission from Veech Media Architecture. © 2000–2001 Sabine Gruber.

Page 231  Printed with permission from Veech Media Architecture. © 2000–2001 Sabine Gruber.

Page 232  Printed with permission from Mark West. © Mark West.

Page 236  Girli Concrete ™. © Girli Concrete.

Page 238  Printed with permission from Tensar ®. © Tensar ®.

Page 238  Printed with permission from Tensar ®. © Tensar ®.

Page 240  Printed with permission Toshiko Mori Architect. © Toshiko Mori Architect.

Page 241  Printed with permission Toshiko Mori Architect. © Paul Warchol.

Page 242  Printed with permission Toshiko Mori Architect. © Paul Warchol.

# Chapter 9

Page 246  Printed courtesy of DuPont. © DuPont.

Page 248  Printed courtesy of DuPont. © DuPont.

Page 249  Printed with permission David White and Kathy Geraghty, Konarka Technologies Inc. © Konarka

Page 250  Printed with permission Pierre Jusselme. © Pierre Jusselme.

Page 251  Printed with permission Pierre Jusselme. © Pierre Jusselme.

Page 253  Printed with permission from DIMENSION-POLYANT. © DIMENSION-POLYANT.

Page 254  Printed with permission from DIMENSION-POLYANT. © DIMENSION-POLYANT.

Page 255  Printed with permission from DIMENSION-POLYANT. © DIMENSION-POLYANT.

Page 257  Printed courtesy of DuPont. © DuPont.

Page 260  Printed courtesy of DuPont. © DuPont.

Page 261  Printed with permission from Loop.pH Limited. © Loop.pH Limited.

Page 262  Printed courtesy of DuPont. © DuPont.

Page 266  Printed courtesy of DuPont. © DuPont.

Page 269  Printed with permission from Loop.pH Limited. © Loop.pH Limited.

Page 270  Printed with permission from Loop.pH Limited. © Loop.pH Limited.

Page 271  Printed with permission from Loop.pH Limited. © Loop.pH Limited.

# Colour Plates

Plate 1    Printed with permission from Mark West. © Mark West.

Plate 2    Printed with permission GKD/ag4. © GKD/ag4

Plate 3    Printed with permission GKD/ag4. © GKD/ag4

Plate 4    Printed with permission GKD/ag4. © GKD/ag4

Plate 5    Printed with permission from Demakersvan. © Joost van Brug.

Plate 6    Printed with permission from Demakersvan. © Joost van Brug.

Plate 7    Printed with permission from DIMENSION-POLYANT. © DIMENSION-POLYANT.

Plate 8    Printed with permission from CuteCircuit. © CuteCircuit.

Plate 9    Printed with permission Anne Kyyrö Quinn. © Anne Kyyrö Quinn.

Plate 10  Printed with permission Anne Kyyrö Quinn. © Anne Kyyrö Quinn.

Plate 11  Printed with permission from Driessen + Van Deijne. © Cornbread Works / Jannes Linders. Courtesy Kunst en Bedrijf, Amsterdam.

Plate 12  Printed with permission from Sophie Mallebranche. © Sophie Mallebranche.

Plate 13  Printed with permission from Sophie Mallebranche. © Sophie Mallebranche.

Plate 14  Printed with permission from Veech Media Architecture. © 2000–2001 Sabine Gruber.

Plate 15  Printed with permission from Mark West. © Mark West.

Plate 16  Printed with permission from Márcia Ganem. © Ricardo Fernandes.

Plate 17  Printed with permission from Grethe Wittrock. © Anders Sune Berg, photographer.

Plate 18  Printed with permission from Astrid Krogh. © Ole Hein Pedersen.

Plate 19  Printed with permission from Astrid Krogh. © Ole Hein Pedersen.

Plate 20  Printed with permission J Mayer H Architects. Courtesy Galerie Magnus Müeller, Berlin. © Christina Dimitriadis, photographer.

Plate 21  This image of LUMINEX® fabric is printed with permission Luminex S.p.A. © Luminex S.p.A.

Plate 22  Printed with permission from Poltrona Frau. © Poltrona Frau.

Plate 23  Printed with permission from Poltrona Frau. © Poltrona Frau.

Plate 24  Courtesy www.echelman.com. © Joao Ferrand.

Plate 25  Courtesy www.echelman.com. © Joao Ferrand.

Plate 26  Printed with permission Alabama Chanin. © Alabama Chanin.

Plate 27  Printed with permission Alabama Chanin. © Alabama Chanin.

Plate 28  Printed with permission from Guerra de la Paz. © Guerra de la Paz.

Plate 29  Printed with permission from Guerra de la Paz. © Guerra de la Paz.

Plate 30  Printed with permission from Mette Ramsgard Thomsen. © Mette Ramsgard Thomsen.

Plate 31  Printed with permission from Mette Ramsgard Thomsen. © Mette Ramsgard Thomsen.

Plate 32  Printed with permission from Future Shape. © Future Shape.

Plate 33  Printed with permission from Testa & Weiser. © 2004 Testa & Weiser, Los Angeles.

Plate 34  Printed with permission from Testa & Weiser. © 2004 Testa & Weiser, Los Angeles.

# Index